TURBOCHARGERS

by Hugh MacInnes

Mechanical Engineer; Member, Society of Automotive Engineers,
Society of American Military Engineers,
American Society of Mechanical Engineers.

TABLE OF CONTENTS

NOTICE: The information contained in this book is true and complete to the best of our knowledge. All of the recommendations on turbocharger sizing, matching, installation and use are made without any guarantees on the part of the author or H.P. Books. Because design matters, engineering changes and methods of application are beyond our control, the author and publisher disclaim any liability incurred in connection with the use of this data or specific details.

This is an independent publication—not associated with AiResearch Industrial Division of Garrett Corporation, Rajay Industries, Inc., Schwitzer Corporation, Roto-Master Division of Echiln, or any other turbocharger manufacturer or installer, or kit builder.

Publisher & Editor: Bill Fisher; Editor-In-Chief: Carl Shipman; Art Director: Josh Young; Book Design & Assembly: Nancy Fisher, Laura Hardock; Typography: Lou Duerr, Marcia Redding, Connie Brown, Cindy Coatsworth; Figures: William Pine, Erwin Acuntius; Cover Photo: Photomation; Photography: Hugh MacInnes, Bill Fisher, Howard Fisher.

Published by **H.P. Books**, P. O. Box 5367, Tucson, AZ 85703 602/888-2150
ISBN 0-912656-49-2
Library of Congress Catalog Card Number: 76-6002 © 1978 **H.P. Books**
Printed in U.S.A.

Cover Photo: 454 CID Chevrolet from Gale Banks Engineering. Engine details and a picture of the boat the engine powers are on page 9

INTRODUCTION

In the introduction to my book, *How to Select and Install Turbochargers,* I mentioned it started out as a 10-page pamphlet but kept growing. By the time it was published it had grown to a 144-page book. After three years, it was due for a revision. This book started out as that revision. It soon became apparent that enough new items were being added to make it far more than a simple revision. So, I decided to start at the beginning and rewrite each chapter besides adding about five more.

When the original book was published there were about a half-dozen turbocharger kits for passenger cars and light trucks. Today there are so many kits for passenger cars, trucks, motorcycles and boats that I have lost count.

In my first book I pointed out that only a few men had successfully applied turbochargers to high-performance engines in spite of the fact that their success should have sparked interest among many more. In the short time interval between then and now, turbocharger classes have been added to the drag-race circuits, been reinstated in offshore motorboat racing, and tractor pulling has become an extremely popular spectator sport in the midwest.

Because of this rise in interest in turbocharging engines, many performance-minded people who had not considered turbocharging in the past are now thinking about trying this method of getting added power instead of the old methods of boring, stroking, special cylinder heads, etc. Inflation has rapidly increased engine-component and labor costs. Now you can turbocharge an engine to get more usable horsepower for less cost than you'd spend blueprinting a racing engine.

One of the deterrents to turbocharging a stock engine in the past was the compression ratio of the engine, particularly high-performance V-8's, was so high that

Author Hugh MacInnes speaking on his favorite subject.

very little turbocharging could be done without using an anti-detonant—even with the highest octane gasoline available. As we all know, the advent of emission controls on passenger cars has caused a considerable drop in compression ratio to reduce combustion temperatures. This lowers oxides of nitrogen in the exhaust and also allows using low-octane gasoline. The lower compression ratio means it is possible to turbocharge these engines to at least 10 pounds boost pressure *without any major modifications.* The compression ratio is fine for turbocharging.

I hope this book will accomplish three things: First, enable the average automotive enthusiast to turbocharge his own engine with a reasonable chance of success. Second, allow the individuals or companies who manufacture turbocharger kits for the after-market to design, build and test kits without having to go through all the cut-and-try methods that were necessary several years ago because no one had any previous knowledge on which to lean. Third, I hope the information contained in this book will be helpful to engine manufacturers who may consider turbocharging a small engine to do the job of a large one without sacrificing fuel economy.

Because energy conservation has become a factor equally as important as air pollution, the turbocharger can help to create engines with *minimum* exhaust emissions and *maximum* fuel economy.

Most of the book is devoted to the conventional gasoline-fueled spark-ignition reciprocating engine because the vast majority of engines in this country are of that type. Anyone familiar with diesel engines knows turbochargers improve them from any viewpoint. This includes fuel consumption, smoke, noise, power output, engine life and exhaust emissions. Diesel engines have hardly made a dent in the passenger-car market—particularly in the United States—but they could become a major factor in the future because of their excellent fuel consumption and low emissions.

Other engines with a good chance of becoming more popular are those using the so-called stratified-charge system. There are many variations of this system but the type using the Texaco Controlled Combustion System lends itself very well to the use of a turbocharger and is a candidate for the "Engine of the Future."

The hardest thing about writing a book is sitting down and doing the work of putting it together. On the other hand, it has given me the opportunity to become acquainted with many interesting people whom I never would have met otherwise. In the 26 years I have been associated with turbochargers, I can truthfully say there has never been a dull day. I doubt if there are many other manufactured items that cover such a broad spectrum of mechanical engineering, including thermodynamics, metallurgy, lubrication, machine design, stress analysis, manufacturing techniques and internal-combustion engines.

1978 Buick V-6 uses AiResearch T-3 turbo with built-in wastegate to produce up to 165 HP from 231 CID. Small box at front (arrow) is the Electronic Spark Control. It works with a microphone-like sensor on the intake manifold to sense detonation and retard spark electronically until detonation ceases. The ESC allows use of optimum spark advance under all operating conditions. 1979 engines make about 180 HP with a four-barrel carburetor. 15-HP improvement is due to new cylinder-head porting, plus new intake and exhaust-manifold design.

1 SUPERCHARGING & TURBOCHARGING

Many times when discussing engines and turbocharging with hotrodders and auto enthusiasts it is assumed they are familiar with the principles involved and many things are left unsaid which should have been explained. For this reason, I will start this chapter with the basic principles of operation of a typical four-stroke cycle, internal-combustion engine showing how supercharging and, in particular, turbocharging affects its operation and output.

Standard automobile engines made in the United States are naturally aspirated four-stroke cycle, spark-ignition, with four, six or eight cylinders. The schematic cross section of one cylinder of this type engine is shown in Figure 1. This schematic, familiar to all persons who have worked with automobile engines, has the following sequence:

A. Intake Stroke—Fuel/air charge is drawn through open intake valve.
B. Compression Stroke—Charge compressed with both valves closed.
C. Power Stroke—Charge ignited by spark plug pushes piston down.
D. Exhaust Stroke—Burnt gases expelled through open exhaust.

In addition to the number of cylinders, an engine is classified by its cubic-inch displacement, usually abbreviated CID. This is the number of cubic inches of air which will theoretically flow through a four-stroke cycle engine during two complete revolutions. Because it is only a matter of time before the United States joins the rest of the world in using the metric system, engine displacement is frequently listed in cubic centimeters (cc) or liters (l). One liter is almost exactly 61 cubic inches but where both are listed on a chart in this book, I have used 60 cubic inches to the liter to make the chart a lot easier to read.

In practice, the engine does not flow an amount of air equal to the displacement because:

1. There is always a slight pressure drop through the carburetor.
2. Intake ports and valves offer some restriction.

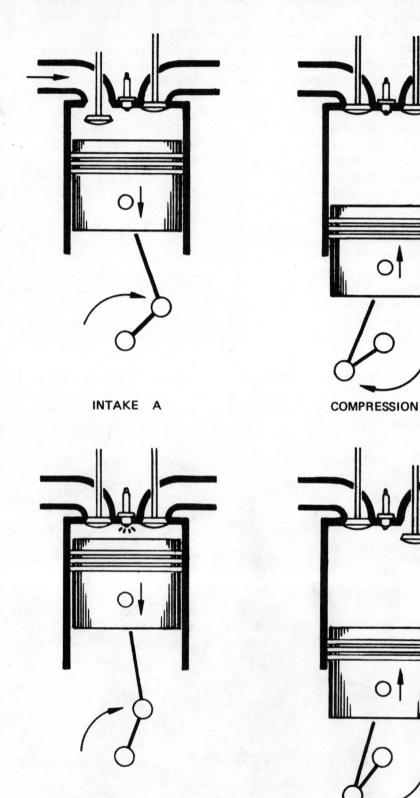

INTAKE   A

COMPRESSION   B

POWER   C

EXHAUST   D

Figure 1—Simple four-cycle engine

3. The exhaust stroke does not expel all burnt gases because of the clearance volume.
4. The exhaust valve and exhaust pipe offer some restriction.

A normal automobile engine flows only about 80% of the calculated amount of charge, called *80% volumetric efficiency* or η_{vol} = 80%. It is possible to tune an engine to get higher volumetric efficiency by using the correct length intake and exhaust pipes for a given engine speed. This, coupled with oversized valves and ports and carefully designed intake and exhaust passages, make it possible to have an engine with a volumetric efficiency exceeding 100% at a certain speed. This is frequently done with racing engines but it is not practical for street use where a broad speed range is required.

Figure 2 shows a compressor added to the basic engine. This may be done either before or after the carburetor. In either case, if compressor capacity is greater than that of the engine, it will force more air into the engine than it would consume naturally aspirated. The amount of additional air will be a function of the intake-manifold-charge density compared to the density of the surrounding atmosphere. *Density* as used in this book is the weight of air per unit of volume. There are two basic types of compressors: Positive-displacement and dynamic. Positive-displacement types, Figure 3, include reciprocating, lobe and vane compressors. There are lesser-known types in this category. These compressors are usually driven from the engine crankshaft through belts, gears or chains. The compressor pumps essentially the same amount of charge for each revolution of the engine regardless of speed, and because it is a positive-displacement device, all of this charge must pass through the engine. Assuming the compressor displacement is twice that of a normally-aspirated engine, the intake-manifold pressure must rise to enable the engine to flow the same weight of charge delivered by the compressor. This type of supercharger has the advantage of delivering approximately the same manifold pressure at all engine speeds but has the disadvantage of using crankshaft power to drive it. The Roots-type lobe compressor also has the disadvantage of inherent low efficiency—below 50%. This causes excessive charge heating

Al Lidert and Chase Knight of Ft. Lauderdale, Florida, run this Chrysler-powered dragster. Roots blower runs at 80% normal speed and puts out only 5-10 lbs. boost. Schwitzer turbos do the rest. Engine has been run at 6 to 1 compression ratio.

Figure 2—Engine with supercharger

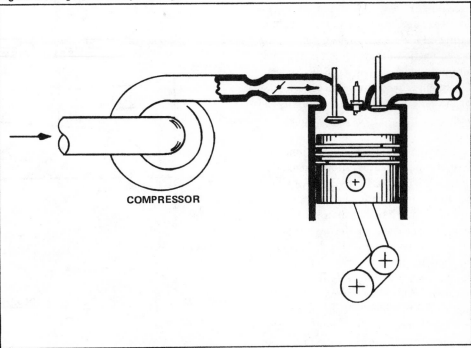

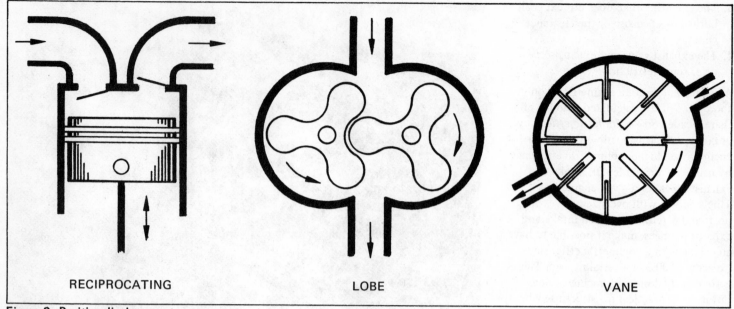

| RECIPROCATING | LOBE | VANE |

Figure 3—Positive-displacement compressors

and therefore higher thermal stress on the engine. The Lysholm-type lobe compressor has much higher efficiency—up to 90%—but is extremely expensive and not practical for automotive use.

The reciprocating type has been used for many years on large stationary engines. Because it usually is attached directly to the crankshaft, it runs at crankshaft speed. It is rather large and cumbersome for use in an automobile engine. The sliding-vane type is sealed internally by the vanes rubbing against the outer housing. Because of this, lubricating oil is usually mixed with the charge to prevent excessive wear on the sliding vanes. This lubricating oil lowers the fuel's octane rating. An eccentric-vane type such as the smog air pump used on many U.S. Passenger Car Engines does not require lubrication of the vanes but like the Lysholm-type is very expensive in sizes large enough for most U.S. cars.

Dynamic compressors also come in several types. Figure 4 shows an axial compressor which is basically a fan or propeller. Because it is difficult to obtain a compression ratio much higher than 1.1 in a single stage, it is necessary to have several stages when this type is used. The Latham supercharger fits this category. All dynamic compressors are inherently high-speed devices because they depend on accelerating the gas to a high velocity and then slowing it down by diffusion to obtain compression. Diffusion is the process of

Figure 4—Axial compressor

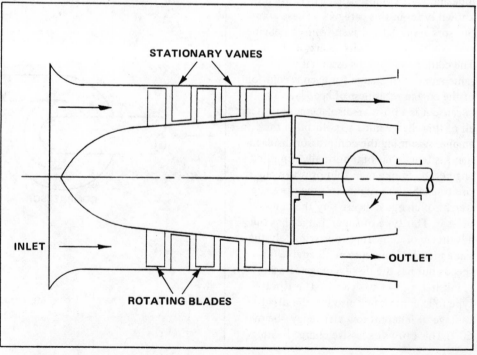

STATIONARY VANES

INLET

OUTLET

ROTATING BLADES

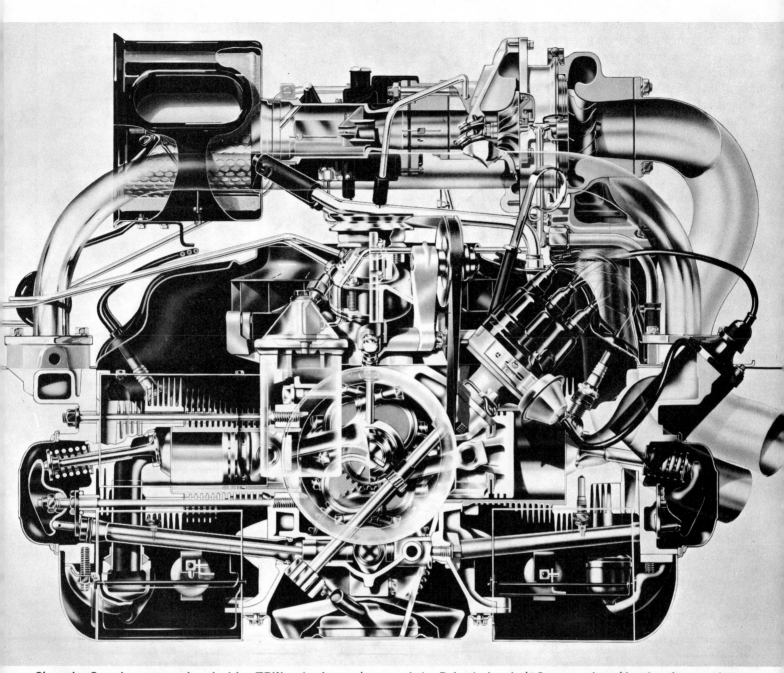

Chevrolet Corvairs were produced with a TRW turbocharger (now made by Rajay Industries). Cutaway photo/drawing shows turbo inlet and exhaust connections. The turbo raised the output of the 100 HP Corvair to 150 HP for 1962-64; to 180 HP in 1965-66. Until 1977, Corvairs represented the largest automotive use of turbochargers in history . . . about 50,000 units. In 1978, Buick introduced an AiResearch T-3 turbo on their V-6 engines, starting a Detroit stampede toward turbocharging small emission-controlled engines for performance. Illustrations courtesy Chevrolet Public Relations.

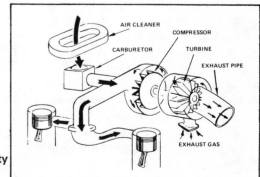

Line drawing shows ultimate simplicity of a turbocharger installation.

slowing down the gas without turbulence so velocity energy is converted into pressure energy. A centrifugal type is shown in Figure 5. This differs from the axial-flow in that the direction of the gas is changed approximately 90° and because the air is in contact with the blades of the compressor impeller for a longer period of time per stage than in an axial-flow compressor. It is possible to achieve considerably higher pressure ratio in a single stage of a centrifugal flow compressor. A 4:1 pressure ratio is not uncommon.

Although there are other types of dynamic compressors such as mixed-flow and drag-type, they are not ordinarily used for supercharging engines. I have not covered them in this book.

Because the centrifugal compressor must be driven at very high speed, it is difficult to drive from the crankshaft. As can be seen from the compressor map in Figure 6, a compressor capable of supplying a pressure ratio of 3:1 with a flow capacity large enough for a 350 CID engine, must run at around 115,000 RPM. It would require a step-up gear of higher than 20:1 on an engine running at 5,000 RPM. This is impractical, not only because of the cost of the transmission, but also because sudden changes in engine speed occurring during shifting would wipe out the supercharger gears unless a slip clutch were included in the system.

During the 1920's, gear-driven centrifugal superchargers were used with success on race cars turning out as high as 300 HP from 90 CID engines. That was 3.33 HP per cubic inch displacement. Because the gear-driven supercharger probably used about 60 HP from the crankshaft, the same engine equipped with a turbocharger would have produced about 360 HP—4 HP per cubic inch. The top race-car engines today are producing about 900 HP from 160 CID—about 5.6 HP per cubic inch or a 40% improvement in 45 years. Engine builders back in those days lacked the high-strength materials we have today, so they cooled the charge between the compressor and the engine, reducing both the thermal and mechanical load while increasing the output. Advantages of intercooling are discussed in Chapter 10.

The biggest disadvantage of the centrifugal compressor when used as a super-

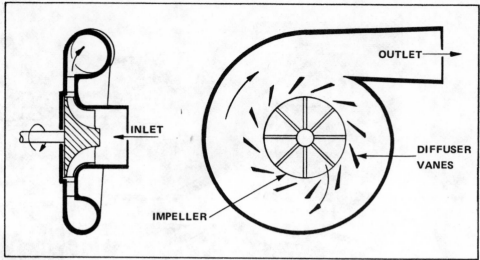

Figure 5—Centrifugal compressor

Figure 6—Typical centrifugal compressor map, Rajay 300E

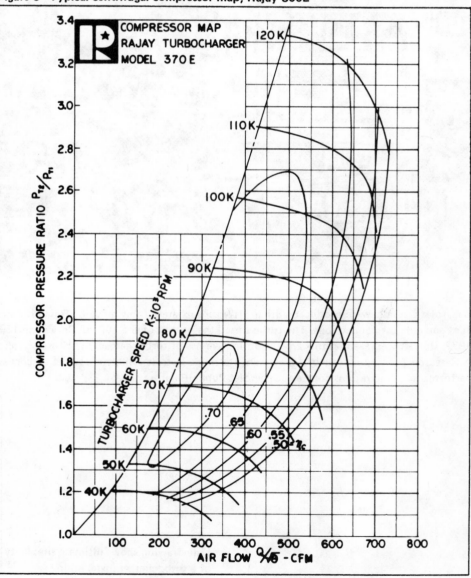

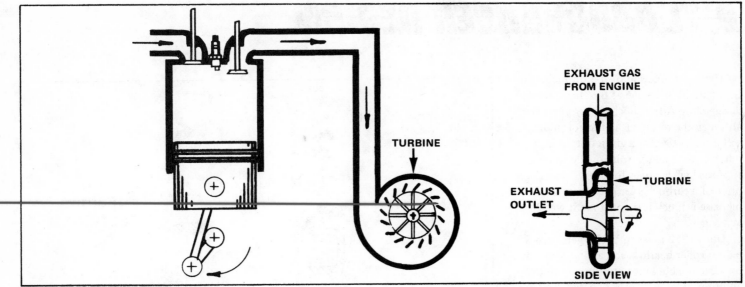

Figure 7—Engine driving gas turbine

charger is: Pressure output from the compressor varies considerably with compressor speed. Looking again at the typical map in Figure 6, we see this particular compressor puts out 1:2 pressure ratio at 40,000 RPM. This represents approximately 3 pounds boost pressure at sea level. This same compressor will produce 1:92 pressure ratio at 80,000 RPM, 13.8 pounds of boost pressure. In this particular case doubling the speed increased the boost pressure over four times. A rule of thumb is: Boost pressure increases as the square of the speed of the compressor. About the only way to overcome this problem with an engine-driven centrifugal compressor is to have a variable-speed drive. The Paxton supercharger which came out in the early '50's had a variable V-belt drive actuated by the accelerator pedal. When the accelerator was in normal driving position, the supercharger ran at a relatively low speed. When the driver pressed the accelerator to the floor, an actuator decreased the supercharger-pulley size and caused it to run much faster. This system worked well but was an added complication.

In addition to its higher overall efficiency—some centrifugal compressors operate at better than 80% efficiency—the centrifugal compressor has another advantage over the positive-displacement compressor. Because it is not a positive device, it can withstand a backfire through the intake system without

damage. A backfire on a turbocharged engine is no worse than on a naturally-aspirated engine. This is not so with a positive-displacement compressor. A small backfire can usually be handled by pop-off safety valves mounted somewhere between the supercharger and the engine. A large backfire may remove the supercharger completely from the engine.

Because of the inherent high speed of the centrifugal-type compressor, the size and weight of the unit are considerably less than the positive-displacement type. A complete turbocharger system capable of enabling an engine to produce over 1,000 HP weighs only about 25 pounds.

Driving a centrifugal compressor would always be a problem except that a turbine is also a high-speed device. For this reason, we can couple them directly together without the use of gears. The turbine is driven by the exhaust gases of the engine, utilizing energy usually dumped overboard in the form of heat and noise. The exhaust gases are directed to the turbine wheel through nozzle vanes as shown in Figure 7.

Many people feel this exhaust-gas energy is not free because the turbine wheel causes back pressure on the engine's exhaust system. This is true to a certain extent, but when the exhaust valve first opens, the flow through it is critical. Critical flow occurs when the cylinder pressure is more than twice the exhaust-manifold pressure. As long as this condi-

tion exists, back pressure will not affect flow through the valve. After cylinder pressure drops below the critical pressure, exhaust-manifold pressure will definitely affect the flow and the higher cylinder pressure of the turbocharged engine during the latter portion of the exhaust stroke will still require some crankshaft power. When an engine is running at wide-open throttle with a well-matched high-efficiency turbocharger, intake-manifold pressure will be considerably higher than exhaust-manifold pressure. This intake-manifold pressure will drive the piston down during the intake stroke, reversing the process of the engine driving the gases out during the exhaust stroke. During the overlap period when both valves are open, the higher intake manifold pressure forces residual gases out of the clearance volume, scavenging the cylinder. Intake-manifold pressures as much as 10 psi higher than exhaust-manifold pressures have been measured on engines running at about 900 HP. Good scavenging can account for as much as 15% more power than calculated from the increase in manifold pressure of the naturally-aspirated engine.

Exhaust-gas temperature will drop as much as 300°F. (133°C.) when passing through the turbine. This temperature drop represents fuel energy returned to the engine by the turbocharger. In summary, for a given type of fuel, more power can be obtained from an engine by turbocharging than by any other method.

2 TURBOCHARGER DESIGN

The basic function of the turbocharger is essentially the same as the first one designed by Alfred Büchi many years ago, although the mechanical design is more simple. The size for a given output is much smaller and in spite of the trend towards higher prices for everything, the price of a turbocharger per horsepower increase is much less now than it was 20 years ago.

Until 1952 most turbochargers used ball or roller bearings and an independent oil system including a built-in pump. In addition, they were water-cooled. Today's units use floating-sleeve bearings lubricated by the engine's oil and pump. They are cooled by a combination of oil and air. Turbocharger design varies from one manufacturer to another but basically all have a compressor on one end and a turbine on the other, supported by bearings in between. See Figure 8. There are seals between the bearings and the compressor and also between the bearings and the turbine. This prevents high-pressure gases from leaking into the oil drainage area of the bearing housing and eventually into the crankcase of the engine. Seals are much better known for keeping oil from leaking into the compressor or turbine housing. How well they do this job often depends on the installation.

COMPRESSOR DESIGN

The centrifugal compressor consists of three elements which must be matched to each other for optimum efficiency: The impeller, the diffuser and the housing. The compressor impeller rotates at very high speeds and accelerates the gas passing through it to a high velocity by centrifugal force. The diffuser acts as a nozzle in reverse, slowing the gas down without turbulence. This causes it to increase in pressure and, unfortunately, in temperature. The housing around the diffuser is used to collect this high-pressure gas and direct it to wherever it is used. In some cases, the housing itself is also a diffuser. Over the years, the design of compressor impellers used in superchargers has varied considerably due to "state of the art" in the thermodynamic design of compressors and in manufacturing tech-

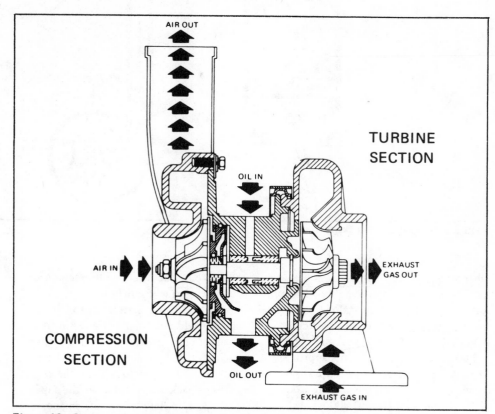

Figure 10—Cross-section drawing of typical turbocharger. Courtesy Schwitzer.

Rajay turbocharger internal configuration is shown in this display cutaway.

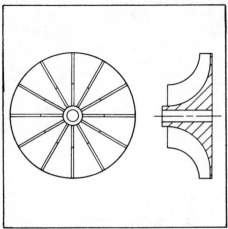

Figure 9—Simple compressor impeller

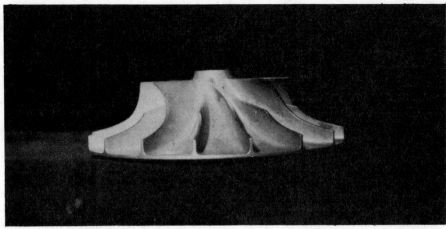

Figure 10—Impeller with curved inducer

niques. Figure 9 shows a simple straight-bladed impeller with no curved inducer section. This shape is relatively easy to produce by die casting, permanent-mold casting, plaster casting, or even milling. It has not become too popular because of its relatively low efficiency caused by shock losses at the inlet. Figure 10 shows a similar impeller, but with curved inducer blades. The angle of curvature at the inlet of the inducer blades is designed so the air entering the impeller will be at exactly the same angle as the blade, thereby reducing inlet losses to a minimum. Originally, this type of wheel was rather expensive to cast because it required a separate plaster core for each gas passage. These cores were then pasted together by hand to make the final mold. In more recent years this type of compressor impeller has been cast by the investment or lost-wax method. When a wheel is cast by this method, a die is made similar to that for die casting except that wax is cast into the die rather than metal. The wax is then covered with liquid plaster and after the plaster has hardened, it is heated to remove the wax by melting. The molten aluminum alloy is then poured into the cavity left after the wax is removed. This process makes smooth, high-strength impellers but is still expensive.

More recently foundries have been using a process called the *rubber-pattern process.* In this method, a die similar to the wax die is constructed but instead of being filled with molten wax, it is filled with a rubber compound which solidifies in the die. This rubber pattern is then covered with liquid plaster which is allowed to harden the same as with the

wax pattern. At this point, the process differs in that the flexible rubber pattern can be removed from the plaster after it hardens. After the rubber pattern is removed from the plaster, it returns to its original shape and may be used again. This method of casting has made possible the use of compressor impeller shapes which were not considered economical from a casting viewpoint a few years ago.

In Figure 11 we see what is known as a *backward-curved compressor impeller.* In this design, the blade elements are not radial but actually curved backward from the direction of rotation. Wheels of this type produce very high efficiency but do not have as high a pressure ratio for a given diameter and speed as the 90° radial wheels. Strength is inherently less than that of the 90° radial wheel because the centrifugal force at high speed tends to bend the blades at their roots. Because of the lower pressure ratio for a given speed and the inherently lower strength of this type wheel, it is not normally used at pressure ratios above 2:1.

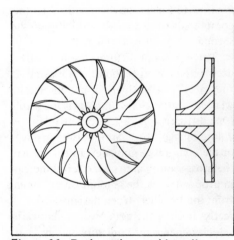

Figure 11—Backward-curved impeller

Figure 11A—Photo of backward-curved inducer

Figure 12 shows a shrouded impeller. This design is certainly the most expensive to manufacture and is the weakest of all the designs because the blades must carry the weight of the shroud as well as their own.

Maximum efficiency of a shrouded impeller is usually very high because there is minimal recirculation from the impeller discharge back to the inducer. The low strength, high cost and tendency for the shroud to collect dirt has just about eliminated the use of the shrouded impeller in automotive use.

In 1952, the turbocharged Cummins diesel-powered race car which ran in the Indianapolis 500 had to retire from the race due to dirt buildup on a shrouded impeller. In the late 1950's when shrouded impellers were used on construction equipment, the service manual included a preventive-maintenance procedure showing how to flush soapy water through the compressor to remove dirt buildup on the shroud.

Three types of diffusers are normally used with centrifugal compressors, and they may be used singly or in combination with each other. The simplest is the scroll-type diffuser, Figure 13. It consists of a volute or snail shape around the outside of the compressor impeller. In this design, the cross-section area of the scroll increases in proportion to the amount of air coming from the impeller. When designed correctly, it slows the gas down and converts velocity energy into pressure energy.

Figure 14 shows a parallel-wall diffuser which has an increase in area from the inside diameter of the diffuser to the outside diameter proportional to these two diameters, Figure 15. In other words if R_2 is twice as great as R_1 then A_2 is twice as great as A_1. Assuming the gas were flowing in a radial direction, the velocity at R_2 would be half that at R_1. The gas actually flows in a spiral rather than a purely radial direction but regardless of this, the gas velocity at the outer diameter of the diffuser is considerably less than at the inner diameter.

Figure 16 is a compressor with a vane-type diffuser. The vanes are designed so the leading edge will be in line with the direction of gas flow from the impeller. From this point, vane curvature will force the gas to flow and be slowed down to

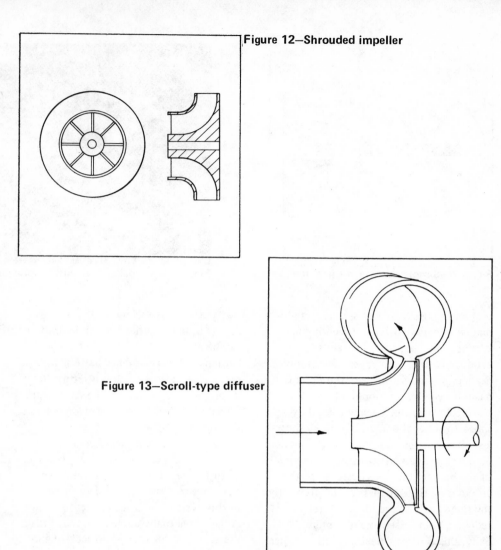

Figure 12—Shrouded impeller

Figure 13—Scroll-type diffuser

Figure 14A, B—Parallel-wall diffuser

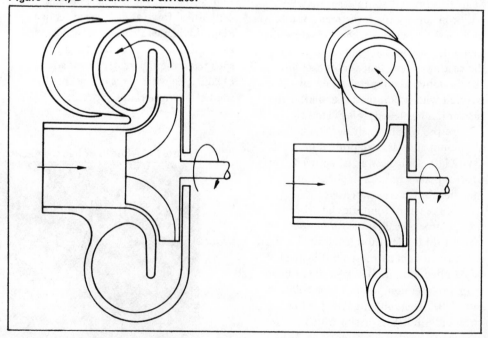

favor a specific condition. Compressors with vane-type diffusers normally have a very high peak efficiency but frequently a narrower range than a vaneless diffuser. Broadness of range is the number of different size engines on which a given compressor may be used. In each case, the diffuser increases the static pressure of the gas in the compressor. The difference between static and total pressures is shown schematically in Figure 17. A static-pressure probe is not affected by the velocity of the gas. A total-pressure probe measures the static pressure plus the velocity pressure of the gas.

Figure 15—Area increase of parallel-wall diffuser

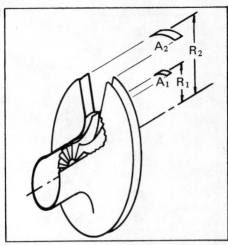

Figure 16—Vane-type diffuser

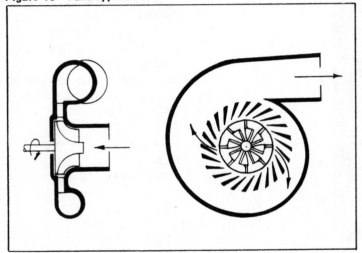

Figure 17—Static and total pressure

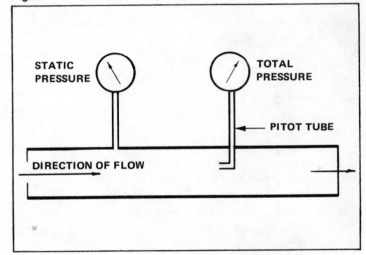

AiResearch TE0670 used on championship race cars. There is no mechanical seal on the compressor end. A seal is not required because the turbo supplies pressurized air to the engine. Fuel is injected after the turbo. Photo courtesy AiResearch.

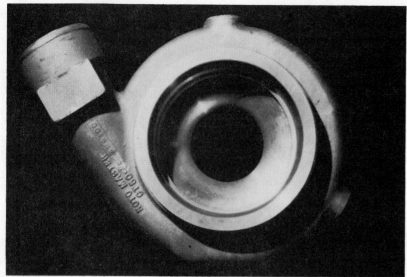

Figure 18A—Example of scroll diffuser

Figure 18B—Example of vane diffuser

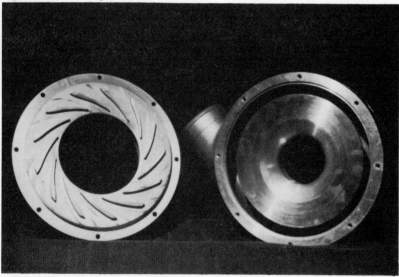

Figure 18C—Example of parellel-wall diffuser

The surface of the compressor impeller, the diffuser and the compressor housing are made as smooth as is economically practical. Any roughness on these surfaces may cause some of the gas to detach itself from the surface causing eddy currents which reduce the overall efficiency of the compressor. Figure 18 shows examples of various types of compressor housings and diffusers.

As mentioned earlier in this chapter, a centrifugal compressor, even a good one, will always raise the temperature of the gas when it raises the pressure. The formula for this temperature increase at 100% efficiency is:

$$T_2 = T_1 \left(\frac{P_2}{P_1}\right)^{.283}$$

Where

    T_1 = Inlet temperature °R
    T_2 = Outlet temperature °R
    °R = °F + 460
    P_1 = Inlet pressure absolute (ABS)
       = Usually barometric pressure
    P_2 = Outlet pressure ABS
       = Usually gage pressure + barometer

Example: Assume inlet temperature of
        70°F.

Then

    T_1 = 70 + 460
       = 530°R

Assume inlet pressure is 0 psig

Then

    P_1 = 0 + barometer
       = 0 + 14.7 psia
       = 14.7 psia

Assume outlet pressure is 17 psig

Then

    P_2 = 17 + barometer
       = 17 + 14.7 psia
       = 31.7 psia

The Theoretical outlet temperature T_2 will be

$$T_2 = (70 + 460) \times \left(\frac{17 + 14.7}{14.7}\right)^{.283}$$

    T_2 = 530 (2.16)$^{.283}$
    T_2 = 530 x 1.243
    T_2 = 659°R (or 199°F.— a temperature rise of 129°F.)

This calculation assumed 100% adiabatic efficiency—about as obtainable as perpetual motion. Compressors referred to in this book are capable of putting out around 70% efficiency. Although this is very commendable for compressor impellers of three-inches diameter, it tends to increase the temperature of the compressed air still further. At 70% adiabatic efficiency, the actual temperature rise is computed:

$$\frac{\text{Ideal Temp. Rise}}{\text{Adiabatic Eff.}} = \text{Actual Temp. Rise}$$

In this case, the $\frac{127^\circ}{.7} = 181^\circ F$. Adding this to the compressor inlet temperature, $70^\circ + 181^\circ = 251^\circ F$. In terms useful to the end user, a supercharger compressor producing 17 psi boost pressure at sea level on a 70° day will result in an intake-manifold temperature of 251°F.

This series of calculations may look like a lot of work but most of it can be eliminated by the use of Table I.

With the table you can calculate discharge temperature directly with simple addition and multiplication. Assume the following conditions:

Inlet Temp. = 80°F.
Pressure Ratio   r = 1.9
Compressor Efficiency
$$\eta_c = .65$$
From Table 1 where
$$r = 1.9$$
$$y = .199$$
Ideal temperature rise
$$\Delta T_{ideal} = T \times Y$$
$$= (460^\circ + 80^\circ) \times .199$$
$$= 107.5^\circ$$
Actual temperature rise
$$\Delta T_{actual} = \frac{\Delta T_{ideal}}{\eta_c}$$
$$= \frac{107.5}{.65}$$
$$= 165.4^\circ$$
Compressor Discharge Temperature
$$T_2 = T_1 + \Delta T_{actual}$$
$$= 80 + 165.4$$
$$= 245.4^\circ F.$$

This means if you start with 80°F. air, compress it to a pressure ratio of 1.9 with 65% efficiency, you will end up with air at 245.4°F. If this sounds bad, a roots-type blower with 45% efficiency will produce a temperature of 319°F.

The Y Chart in Table 1 is for demonstration purposes only. A more detailed table in the appendix has pressure ratios up to 10:1. A few years ago 3:1 pressure ratio was considered more than adequate but the farm-tractor boys now run manifold pressures of over 100 psig in the tractor-pulling contests. That is not a misprint. *It is actually over 100 psig intake-manifold pressure!*

TABLE 1

r	Y	r	Y	r	Y	r	Y
1.1	.027	1.6	.142	2.1	.234	2.6	.311
1.2	.053	1.7	.162	2.2	.250	2.7	.325
1.3	.077	1.8	.181	2.3	.266	2.8	.338
1.4	.100	1.9	.199	2.4	.281	2.9	.352
1.5	.121	2.0	.217	2.5	.296	3.0	.365

r = pressure ratio

$$Y = r^{.238} - 1$$

Figure 19—Compressor discharge temperature vs. pressure ratio

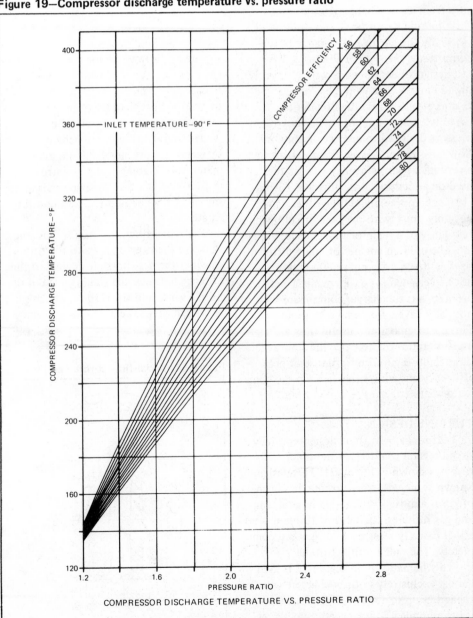

COMPRESSOR DISCHARGE TEMPERATURE VS. PRESSURE RATIO

If this method of calculating intake-manifold pressure is still too complicated, it can be done easier yet without any calculations by using the chart in Figure 19 prepared by Don Hubbard.

When discussing centrifugal compressors, the terms *broad range* or *narrow range* are often used. These terms could have several meanings, but in turbocharger work it is normally the width of the compressor map at about 2:1 pressure ratio. The width of a compressor map is taken from the surge line to the 60% efficiency line. Figure 20 includes examples of compressors with narrow, normal and broad ranges. The surge area on the left side of each map is a region of pressure and flow where the compressor is unstable. Depending on the compressor, this instability will vary from a sharp banging sound, to a slush-pump-like action, to no surge at all. Normally the narrower the range of the compressor, the sharper the surge. Why not design all compressors with extremely broad ranges? This would be fine except that as a general rule the broader the range, the lower the peak efficiency. Compressors designed to operate at only one flow have a very narrow characteristic and a very high peak efficiency such as that used on an industrial gas turbine. Turbocharger compressors, on the other hand, not only must work over the broad operating range of a reciprocating engine, but must be used on engines of many different sizes so that a different compressor need not be designed for each engine. To compromise, a turbocharger compressor will normally have a flow range of about 2:1. This means maximum useful flow at 2:1 pressure ratio will be twice the flow at the surge limit—a good compromise of peak efficiency and mild surge to keep the number of different sizes to a minimum.

TURBINE DESIGN

Textbooks on turbine design normally spend several chapters on the theory of turbines shown in Figure 21. This design, known as an *axial-flow turbine,* has been used for almost 100 years on large steam and gas turbines. Radial-flow turbines were either casually referred to or ignored completely. The radial-inflow turbine shown schematically in Figure 22 is used almost exclusively in turbochargers with capacities up to about 1,000 HP because it is economical to produce in small sizes.

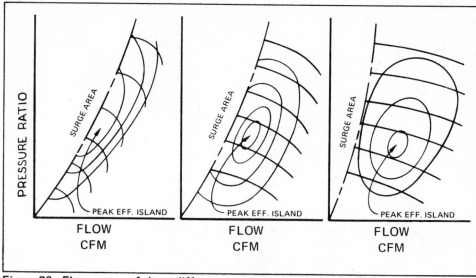

Figure 20—Flow ranges of three different type centrifugal compressors

The axial-flow turbine is used in most cases where the radial wheel is too large to cast in one piece. The normal method of manufacture is to make the disk of high-strength material and attach the turbine blades to the disk either mechanically or by welding. Turbine blades are made of material with great heat and corrosion resistance. Stationary nozzle vanes direct the gases at an angle to make the turbine rotate.

The radial-flow turbine also has a nozzle to direct the flow of gases to the turbine wheel at the best possible angle, but the distance between the trailing edge of the nozzle vanes and the turbine wheel is not as critical as for the axial-flow turbine

Figure 21—Axial-flow turbine and nozzle

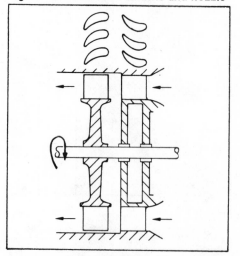

because the gases will continue on at approximately the same angle as directed by the nozzle vanes. This spiral flow of fluid—a free vortex—can be observed any time we watch water go down a drain. Because of this phenomenon, the number of nozzle vanes is not critical on a radial-flow turbine. By designing the turbine housing in a scroll or volute shape as shown in Figure 23, only one nozzle vane is needed. This considerably reduces the cost of building a radial-inflow turbine, although it is necessary to change turbine housings rather than nozzles when the turbine is used in different conditions. Changing turbine housings may be awkward but it is not expensive. A small turbine housing does not cost any more to manufacture than a small nozzle. This is not true with a large turbine, and large turbochargers usually have a separate nozzle with many vanes.

The nozzle area of either an axial-flow turbine or a radial-flow turbine with multiple nozzle vanes is the cross-section of a single nozzle opening multiplied by the number of nozzle vanes. In a turbocharger, the larger the nozzle area, the slower the turbocharger will run. Example: If a turbocharger has a 1.0 in.^{2} nozzle and is putting out too much boost at a given condition, the nozzle may be changed to an area with 1.2 in.^{2}, slowing down the turbine and reducing the boost from the compressor. If this is not enough, the area may be increased still farther to 1.4 in.^{2} which

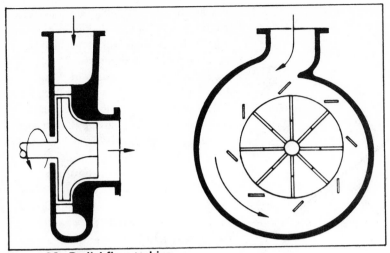

Figure 22—Radial-flow turbine

Figure 23—Vaneless turbine housing

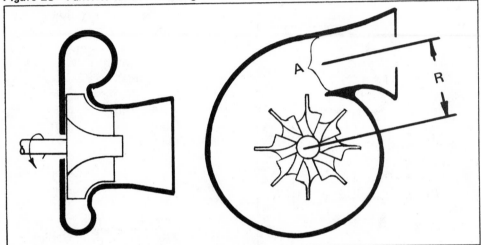

Figure 24—Vaneless turbine housing with larger R

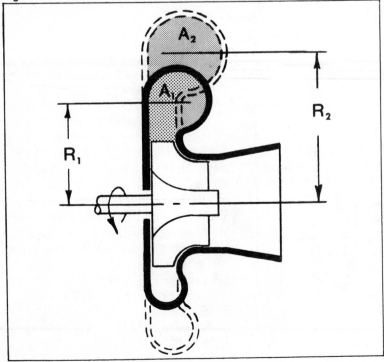

will further reduce the speed and therefore the compressor boost.

Nozzle area is measured a little differently when the single opening or vaneless turbine housing is used. In this case, the area alone shown as A in Figure 23 will not necessarily determine the amount of gas flow into the turbine. However, area A divided by R—the distance from the center of the turbine wheel to the centroid of area A—will determine the flow of the gas for a given turbine wheel. If A is increased, the turbine will slow down in the same manner as one with a multi-vane nozzle. If a housing is used with a larger R, as shown in Figure 24, A must be increased to retain the same A/R Ratio. This is important to the turbine designer but not to the user since the variations in R from housing to housing are usually insignificant. Not all turbocharger manufacturers use the A/R method of sizing turbine housings. Schwitzer uses area A only and because of this, their turbine housing sizes are not comparable to those of AiResearch or Rajay. This ratio or area is usually cast or stamped into the turbine housing by the manufacturer. The thing that is important to the user is if he has a turbocharger with a turbine housing A/R of .7 and he wants to run his turbocharger slower, he knows that a turbine housing designed to fit this same turbine wheel with an A/R of .9 will definitely cause his turbocharger to run slower. On the other hand, if he wants it to run faster, he knows a turbine housing with an A/R of .6 or .5 will cause the turbocharger to run faster and give it more boost. The same is true with area alone in the Schwitzer vaneless turbine housing or any turbocharger with a multi-vaned nozzle. This is discussed further in the chapter on sizing and matching and also in the chapter on kits and where to buy them. On most turbochargers, changing the turbine housing is a simple task involving a few bolts or a V-band clamp.

Turbine designers try to use the pulse energy of gases coming from the individual cylinders to increase the boost pressure at very low speeds. This is done on large axial-flow turbines by running a separate stack from each cylinder to the turbine nozzle. This is not practical on a radial-inflow turbine so housings are divided in 180° increments as shown in Figure 25. This makes some improvement at very

Figure 25—180° divided turbine housing

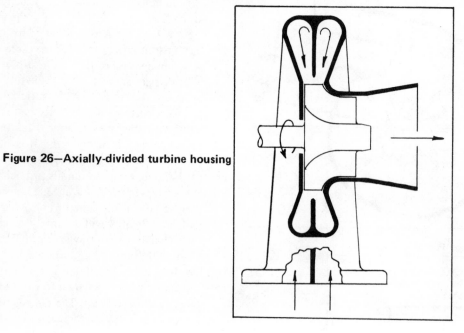

Figure 26—Axially-divided turbine housing

Figure 27—Contour relationship for different flows

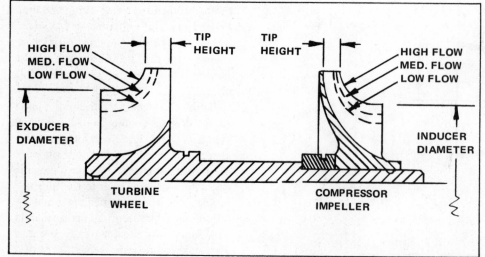

low engine speeds but the gas does have a tendency to reverse its flow due to centrifugal force when there is no high-pressure pulse in the housing.

Turbine-housing designs by John Cazier, Patents 3,292,364 and 3,383,092; D.H. Connor, 3,270,495; and Hugh MacInnes, 4,027,994 divide the turbine housing axially, Figure 26. This prevents the gas pulses from reversing and is used on engines where high torque is desired at low engine speed.

To use both turbine-wheel and compressor-impeller castings for more than one flow size turbocharger, different contours are machined on the wheels. Figure 27 shows three different contours on both turbine and compressor. Because the turbine is not as sensitive to flow changes as the compressor, it is common for a given turbocharger model to have many more compressor-impeller variations than turbine-wheel variations. Compressor maps usually specify both the blade-tip height and the inducer diameter so an impeller may be identified even if the part number has been obliterated.

Years ago, most turbine housings were made from ductile type Ni-Resist[R] cast iron which contained somewhere between 20% and 30% nickel. It is recommended where the engine is going to run continuously at extremely high temperature, as on a track type race car or an airplane. It is also recommended for marine use because it has better resistance to corrosion from sea water than other types of cast iron.

The high cost of nickel has made it almost prohibitive to use Ni-Resist[R] in diesel-engine turbochargers or those designed for intermittent use on passenger cars. For many years turbine housings for this type application were made from a cast iron similar to that used in exhaust manifolds of automobiles and diesel engines. This material worked fairly well, but about 1960 ductile iron became available at almost the same cost as gray iron. Most turbine housings are now manufactured from this material. Ductile iron not only machines well but it can be welded more readily than gray iron.

Some of the earlier automotive-type turbine wheels were made by machining the blades from solid forgings, and the curved or exducer portion was cast from a material such as Hastelloy[R] B and welded to the turbine wheel. The turbine exducer assembly was then bolted to the shaft. This method was expensive and time consuming so better methods had to be evolved for mass production.

The first change was to cast the turbine wheel and exducer as a single unit. This would have been done earlier but materials suitable for high stress at the temperatures encountered were not available at reasonable prices until about 1955.

The next step was to braze the turbine wheel to the shaft rather than bolt it. This method worked well but quality control was a problem because it was difficult to determine whether the braze was satisfactory until the turbocharger was run on an engine. If the braze was faulty, it was a little late to be finding out.

Since that time, several very satisfactory bonding processes have been developed, such as inert-gas welding, resistance welding and electron-beam welding. The latest method is friction welding—the turbine wheel is attached to a heavy flywheel and rotated at a high speed. The rough-turned shaft is held in a vise and simultaneously, as the motor which rotates the turbine wheel is turned off, the shaft is jammed against a stub on the center of the turbine wheel as shown in Figure 28. This whole process takes only a few seconds, and the tremendous heat generated in both the shaft and the turbine wheel weld them together solidly. Once the process time is worked out for a given wheel and shaft, the repeatability is excellent, and a good weld is achieved every time.

Another method in current use is to cast the shaft and turbine wheel in one piece. In the early days when turbochargers were run on bushings pressed into the housing, it was necessary to have extremely hard journals on the turbine shaft to keep them from wearing out quickly. With the floating-type bearings used on today's turbochargers, there is almost no contact between the bearings and the journals, and it is not necessary to have journal hardness in the range of Rockwell C60. Shafts cast integral with the turbine wheel have a hardness of about Rockwell C35 and do not seem to wear out any faster than those with harder journals. Several materials have been used in the past for turbine wheels such as 19-9 DL, Stellite 31[R] and Stellite 151[R] but nickel-based super

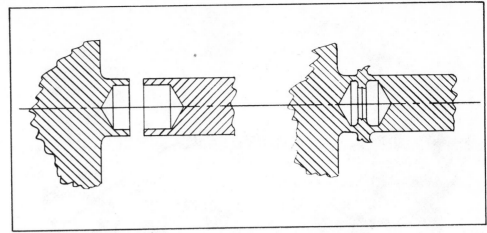

Figure 28A—Friction welding

alloys such as GMR 235[R] and Inco 713C[R] seem to be most popular. These alloys will not corrode or melt even under extreme conditions and will usually last until a nut, or bolt or valve goes through them or they have a bad rub on a housing due to a bearing failure.

BEARING HOUSING

The bearing housing is kind of a necessary evil between the compressor and the turbine to hold the whole thing together. Although bearing housings come in many shapes and sizes, they are basically all about the same. They have a bearing or

bearings in the bore and an oil seal at each end. Many years ago, bearing housings had internal water passages to keep the bearing temperature down because Babbitt was frequently used as a bearing material. If the engine was shut down from full load, heat soakback from the turbine wheel was enough to melt the Babbitt from the bearings unless there was a water jacket in the vicinity.

Turbochargers now use either aluminum or bronze bearings and heat soakback is not critical. Water jackets have been almost eliminated.

Figure 28B—Section through shaft friction-welded to turbine wheel

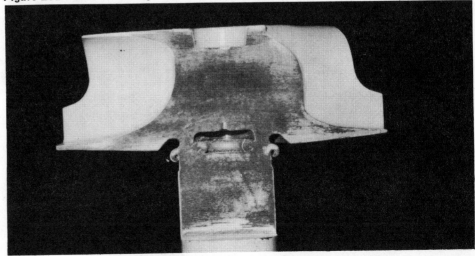

Figure 29—Cartridge assembly cross section. This is a Roto-Master replacement unit.

Figure 30—Cross section of T04 turbocharger

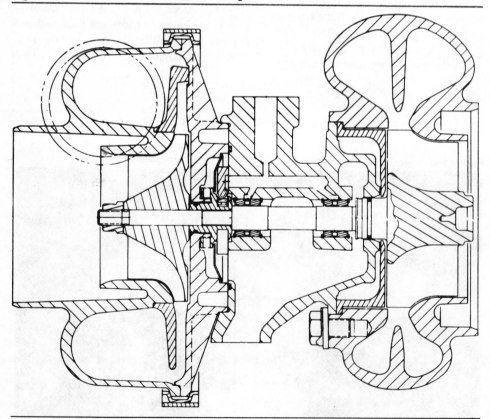

Figure 29 shows a turbocharger cross-section without the compressor or turbine housing in place. These components are usually referred to as a *cartridge* or *cartridge assembly*.

Pressurized oil enters the oil inlet and flows over and through the bearings. The clearance between the bearing and bearing housing and the bearing and the journal is about the same. Oil flowing between the bearing and the bearing housing tends to damp out vibration caused by imbalance in the turbine rotor. This imbalance, if it were great enough, would cause the journal to rub on the bearing. But the bearing has a slight bit of give due to the oil cushion, and contact between the journal and the bearing is practically eliminated. Thus, the life of the turbocharger is considerably extended.

In Figure 30, the cross-section of an AiResearch TO4 Turbocharger, some of the oil also enters the thrust bearing where it is ducted to the two thrust surfaces to lubricate the space between the thrust bearing and the thrust shoulders. After the oil has passed through the bearing, it flows by gravity to the bottom of the bearing housing where it is carried by a hose to the crankcase of the engine.

Oil enters the turbocharger from the engine at about 30 to 50 pounds pressure. After it is mixed up with air in passing through the bearings, it flows from the turbocharger with no pressure and looks like dirty whipped cream. For this reason, it is not only important to have a much larger oil-drain line than oil-inlet line but also to be sure this drain line has no kinks or traps. This subject is covered in detail in the lubrication chapter.

When the turbocharger is doing its job, i.e., supercharging the engine, the gas pressure behind the turbine wheel and that behind the compressor impeller is much greater than the pressure inside the bearing housing. Seals must be placed between the bearing housing and the other two housings. This is relatively easy on the turbine end in spite of the higher temperatures encountered because pressure in the turbine housing is always positive. The main job is to keep hot gases out of the bearing housing. This is normally done by using a piston ring in a groove at the turbine end of the shaft, Figure 31. This piston ring fits snugly in the bearing housing and does not rotate. The piston

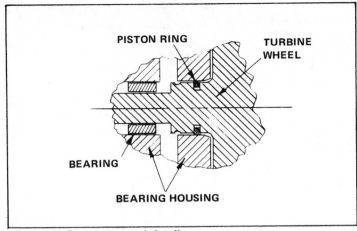

Figure 31—Piston-ring-seal detail

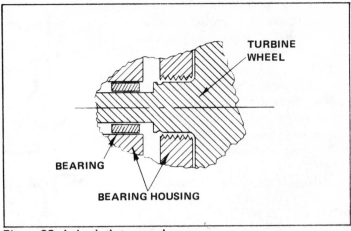

Figure 32—Labyrinth-type seal

ring is also a very close fit between the two walls of the piston ring groove and does a good job of preventing the hot gases from entering the bearing housing. Some turbochargers use a labyrinth-type seal on the turbine end. Here the hot gas is prevented from entering the bearing housing by a series of dams, Figure 32.

The seal at the compressor end is a slightly different problem. On a diesel engine at idle or at very low power, the compressor will be producing practically no boost. Pressure drop through the air cleaner, even if it is in good shape, will cause a slight vacuum behind the compressor impeller. This vacuum will tend to suck oil from the bearing housing into the compressor housing. Because the oil wets all the surfaces in the bearing housing, it is very difficult to prevent it from being in the area of the compressor end seal. Even a little oil leakage into the compressor housing makes things pretty messy in a hurry. The compressor end seal in Figure 33 is designed for use on a diesel engine and does a fairly good job. This seal has a piston ring and a small centrifugal pump built into the slinger which attempts to prevent oil from reaching the seal. This works fairly well on a diesel engine where the compressor-intake vacuum is in the order of a few inches mercury. However, when a carburetor for a gasoline engine is placed upstream of the compressor, it is possible to have almost total vacuum when the engine is running at high speed and the throttle is suddenly closed. A piston-ring type seal is not satisfactory under these conditions and

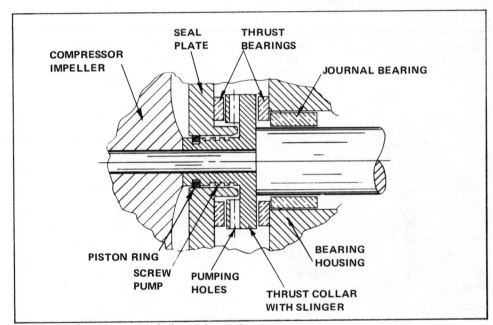

Figure 33—Compressor-end piston-ring seal

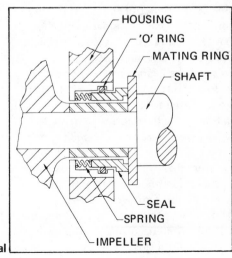

Figure 34—Mechanical face seal

will leak large quantities of oil into the intake manifold of the engine. It will work as long as the carburetor is downstream of the compressor.

Turbochargers designed to be used with the carburetor upstream of the compressor usually have a mechanical face seal similar to that shown in Figure 34. Rajay has chosen to make all their turbochargers with seals of this type while AiResearch usually uses mechanical face seals only on turbochargers specifically designed for use on gasoline engines. Schwitzer has chosen to stay with the piston-ring type seal for all applications. Crane Cams, which markets the Schwitzer Turbocharger for automotive use, recommends a second butterfly downstream of the compressor as used on the Ford-powered race cars. When properly connected to the carburetor butterfly, the second butterfly prevents the compressor housing from being subjected to a high vacuum, Figure 35.

As mentioned earlier in this chapter, the first automotive-type turbochargers had bearings which were pressed into the bearing housing in the same manner as a low-speed bushing. This type of bearing becomes unstable when used with a lightly-loaded, high-speed shaft. At extremely high speeds, the center of the shaft starts to move in its own orbit in the same direction of rotation as the shaft but at somewhere below half the shaft speed. This unstable condition, known as oil whirl or oil whip, usually occurs at a speed somewhere around the natural frequency of the shaft. This is often referred to as the *critical speed.* The motion becomes so violent that if the end of the rotor can be observed on a test stand, it will suddenly become a blur due to the violent excursion of the center of the shaft. It will sometimes appear to move as much as one sixteenth inch. This is impossible because the clearance between the journals and the bearing may only be three or four thousandths of an inch. Once this has occurred for any length of time, examination of the bearing and journals will show severe wear on both—indicating the center of the shaft was actually moving far more than was allowed by the clearance.

Bearings were designed with many different kinds of grooves and wedges to help stabilize the condition and prevent oil whirl from occurring. Nothing worked very well until floating bearings were

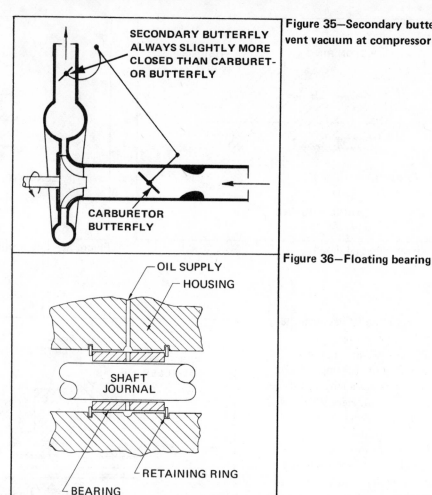

Figure 35—Secondary butterfly to prevent vacuum at compressor inlet

SECONDARY BUTTERFLY ALWAYS SLIGHTLY MORE CLOSED THAN CARBURETOR BUTTERFLY

CARBURETOR BUTTERFLY

Figure 36—Floating bearing

OIL SUPPLY

HOUSING

SHAFT JOURNAL

RETAINING RING

BEARING

adopted. As mentioned earlier in this chapter, floating bearings have about the same clearance on the outside of the bearings as they do on the inside, Figure 36. Without putting any special grooves in the bearing, it does a great job of damping vibrations caused by rotor imbalance. It is almost impossible to determine the critical speed of the rotor because there is practically no difference in the vibration level of the turbocharger when running at the critical speed. When turbochargers with fixed bearings were run on a test stand equipped with a vibration meter, .001 inch displacement was considered normal. When floating bearings were introduced, the vibration level dropped so low that the limits of acceptability were changed to about .0002-inch peak-to-peak displacement.

Because these bearings are loose in the housing, they are free to rotate and are kept from moving axially either by a snap ring or a shoulder in the bearing-housing bore. This rotation causes two problems—possible oil starvation and

bearing-housing wear. Because the bearing is rotating at approximately half the shaft speed, it will rotate at about 50,000 RPM when the rotor is turning at 100,000 RPM. In spite of the fact the bearing may only have a wall thickness of about 1/8 inch, holes through the bearing walls used to supply oil to its inner surface, will act as a centrifugal pump. At 50,000 RPM the pressure differential between the inner surface of the bearing and the outer surface of the bearing may be enough to overcome the oil pressure applied from the engine. If this should occur, no oil will flow through the bearing to the journal and rapid failure will occur.

Ways have been devised to prevent this, as shown in Figure 37, a cross-section of the Schwitzer Model 3LD Turbocharger. The area of the bearing where the oil enters has a thinner wall than the rest of the bearing, thereby minimizing the pumping action. In addition, holes in this area are relatively large compared to the wall thickness, making it a very inefficient pump. In Caterpillar[R] Patent 3,058,787

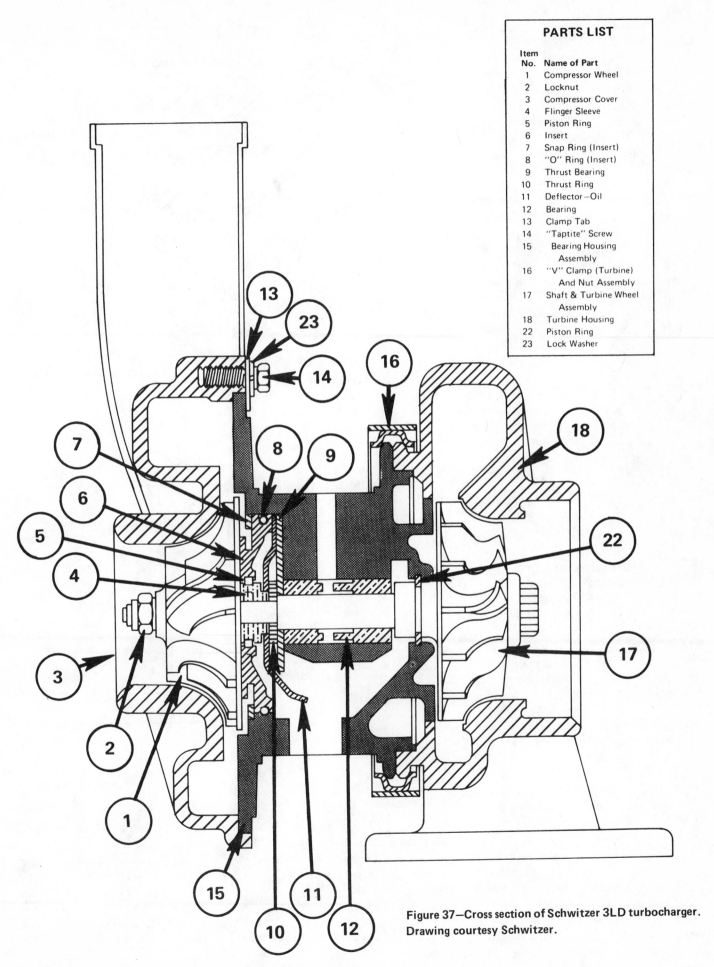

Figure 37—Cross section of Schwitzer 3LD turbocharger. Drawing courtesy Schwitzer.

E. R. Bernson attacked the problem in a different way. The oil passage which supplies the bearing has a wedge-shaped groove. This tends to increase the oil pressure as the oil is rotated from the oil-supply hole to the hole in the bearing, Figure 38.

The other problem—bearing-housing wear due to the rotating bearing—is partially solved by making the bearing housing from cast iron. Some bearing housings using full-floating bearings have been made from aluminum but they were equipped with a hardened steel sleeve in the bore. The cost of manufacturing and assembling a steel sleeve makes the use of an aluminum bearing housing prohibitive.

When floating bearings first came into general use in turbochargers, it was assumed they had to rotate, so all the units were made in this manner. Because oil flowing around the outside of the bearing does the damping rather than the rotation of the bearing, the semi-floating bearing, Rajay Patent 3,043,636 (Hugh MacInnes) is used by some manufacturers. It is kept from rotating by pinning a flange on the end of the bearing or matching the flange to an irregularly-shaped pocket in the bearing housing or the oil-seal plate, Figure 39. The flange prevents the bearing from rotating and also prevents it from moving axially. The wall thickness at the end of the bearing can be used for a thrust surface. Oil which passes through the bearing then passes between the shoulders on the shaft and the ends of the bearing to lubricate the thrust bearings.

Because the bearing does not rotate, it is possible to operate turbochargers of this type with very little oil pressure. Extremely low oil pressure is not a recommended procedure, but a turbocharger which will operate under adverse conditions has certain advantages. This type bearing works very well in an aluminum bearing housing—as it does not need a hard surface on the bore of the bearing housing.

Another design feature worth mentioning is some manufacturers press or shrink the compressor impeller on the shaft while others prefer a looser fit. If the turbocharger rotates counter-clockwise viewed from the compressor end, a right-hand nut on the compressor impeller will tend to tighten during operation of the turbocharger. If the turbocharger has a clockwise rotation, a right-hand nut will

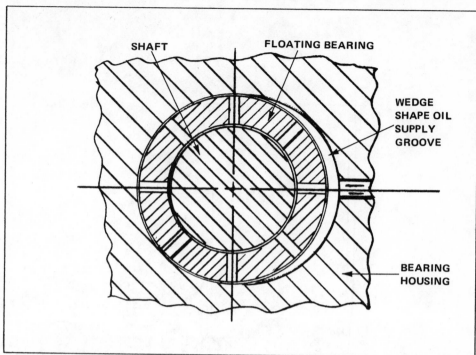

Figure 38—Bernson patent

Figure 39—Semi-floating bearing

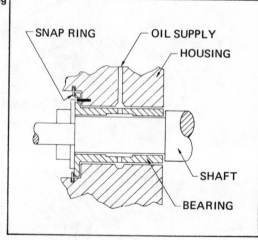

tend to loosen during operation. Clockwise-rotation turbochargers with right-hand nuts must be assembled with the nut very tight—even to the point of stretching the shaft.

Small turbochargers are all basically-simple, rugged devices and when treated properly, will last as long as the engine.

Jack Lufkin has run turbocharged cars at the S.C.T.A. Bonneville Salt Flats Speed Trials for many years, used the same turbocharger for six years without disassembling the unit. The turbo still works fine but the car was retired. On the other hand, a turbocharger which is not treated properly may only last ten seconds.

This 1929 Model A roadster has done more than its fair share of convincing hotrodders that turbos are the way to get lots of power. Built specifically for the Bonneville Nationals Speed Trials, this car ran 234 MPH at the 1976 meet. It holds the D Fuel Roadster record at 221 MPH two-way average. Crew includes Jerry Kugel at left, Red Holmes and Mac McGinnis. The engine is pictured on the next page. Photo courtesy Gray Baskerville/Hotrod Magazine.

One of the first questions usually asked by a person interested in doing turbocharging is, "Can I turbocharge my engine?" The answer is, of course, "Yes, regardless of the make or age of the engine." The next question is usually, "How much power can I get from it?" The answer to this one—"As much as the engine will stand." And this one is usually followed by, "At what speed will I start to get boost?" The answer here often startles the unknowledgeable, "At what-ever speed you want."

The fact is, any automobile or motorcycle engine from about 30 CID (500cc) can be turbocharged with presently available units, but results will depend on how strong the engine is and how well the installation is made. There isn't an engine built today which cannot be turbocharged beyond its physical capabilities. Turbochargers have already been staged to produce intake-manifold pressures above 100 psig and *this could be increased without*

AiResearch turbo on 170 CID Falcon. Note special distributor, Corvair air cleaner. Split-scroll control at turbine inlet keeps boost pressure from exceeding preset levels.

Shelby-Spearco kit on big-block Chevrolet in a pickup truck adds about 100 HP at 2300 RPM. Especially helpful for towing or use with big campers. Significant economy improvements are claimed.

Datsun 510 with Rajay turbo and LPG carburetor.

Reeves Callaway's A/SR SCCA road racer. The Alex Dearborn "Deserter" dune-buggy chassis is powered by a turbocharged Corvair engine with a Porsche 911 cooling fan. Rajay turbo is fed by a Crown-adapted Weber 45DCOE carburetor with Crown water injection. Corvairs are especially easy to turbocharge because stock and special equipment is readily available. Corvair engine hotrodding and chassis modifications are detailed in "How to Hotrod Corvair Engines," an H. P. Book.

258 CID Chevrolet small-block powerplant of the Kugel roadster shown on the previous page. Engine has Carillo rods, Venolia pistons, Iskenderian cam. Two AiResearch TO-4 turbos pressurize the Hilborn fuel injectors which feed straight methanol fuel to the engine. Photo courtesy Gray Baskerville/Hotrod Magazine.

Where and when maximum boost is achieved is covered in the chapter on Sizing and Matching. This should be done after it is decided what the use of the vehicle is going to be and how much time and money is to be invested. Because any engine can be turbocharged, it is not necessary to narrow the choice down to one or two models, although it is certainly easier to turbocharge an engine where a bolt-on type kit is available. However, the kit may not be designed to produce maximum horsepower at the speed you want for your application. Most kits are designed for street use and must be modified for such things as drag racing and/or track racing.

For someone turbocharging an engine for the first time, an in-line four-cylinder or six-cylinder engine presents the least problems. Those with the intake and exhaust manifolds on the same side of the head simplify the installation still further. When turbocharging an opposed or V engine, there's a problem in ducting half of the exhaust gases to the other side of the engine. Most V-6 Engines are too small to consider the use of two turbochargers but two small or medium-type turbochargers work very well on a V-8. A few years ago fours and sixes were more desirable than the eights from a cost viewpoint, because they usually had a low-compression ratio while the eights almost invariably had high-compression ratios up to 10:1. This has all changed recently because a low compression ratio is one of the ways the engine manufacturers have reduced emissions. The effect of turbochargers on engine emissions is covered in Chapter 19. When engines had high compression ratios they were designed to run well on 100-octane fuel. This limited the amount of power which could be gained easily with the addition of a turbocharger. Ak Miller's rule of thumb says, "The octane requirement of an engine goes up one point with each pound of boost from the turbocharger." For example, if an engine with 8:1 compression ratio runs well on 90-octane gasoline, it will require 98-octane to run with eight pounds of boost and no detonation. Anything above this may require water injection.

Because just about all production

Natural gas is often used to fuel truck engines connected to irrigation pumps. When one of these engines is turbocharged it can normally replace two naturally aspirated engines. This 542 CID International Harvester engine was converted for natural gas and dual turbos by Ak Miller Enterprises.

engines available in the mid-70's have low compression ratios, the choice of engines which can be highly turbocharged without any major modification is unlimited.

Flathead engines disappeared with the advent of the high-compression overhead-valve engines—probably because the extra volume of the combustion chamber did not lend itself to very high compression ratios. Most of these engines had crankshafts with only one main bearing for

every two throws, and therefore, are not recommended for a big horsepower increase. It would be interesting, on the other hand, to see the results of a turbocharged flathead engine compared to an overhead-valve engine of the same displacement. It would not be surprising if the flathead engines were able to produce about the same horsepower per cubic inch with the same amount of boost pressure because turbochargers tend to be equalizers with respect to the breathing ability of the engine.

120 CID Ford Pinto engine powered this streamliner to the E Class record of 203.84 MPH at the Bonneville National Speed Trials. Owned by Bennett & Ruiz of Santa Barbara, California, the engine relies on an AiResearch turbocharger for its outstanding performance.

Choosing between an air-cooled and a liquid-cooled engine is not much of a problem because most engines are liquid-cooled. The VW engine takes very well to turbocharging and a 100% power increase is possible with no other engine modifications. *Bullshit for hot* [handwritten annotation]

The biggest single problem with turbocharging air-cooled engines is keeping the heads cool. If the heads are allowed to get too hot, pre-ignition will occur which will destroy the engine in a matter of seconds. It is advisable to use a head-temperature indicator on a turbocharged air-cooled engine with some kind of a buzzer or light to provide a warning before pre-ignition occurs. Corvair Spyders had such a warning device.

The Wankel Engine has been turbocharged with good and bad results, the same as with reciprocating engines. In this case, detonation is to be avoided because of the detrimental effect on the apex seals.

TRANSMISSIONS

Modern three- and four-speed manual transmissions have resulted from many years of development and seem to stand up well under the increased torque produced by a turbocharged engine. It doesn't take long to find out that the turbocharged engine requires different shift points than the naturally-aspirated engine, and the manual transmission doesn't seem to care one way or the other.

Automatic transmissions are another story. These are frequently designed to accept the torque of the naturally-aspirated engine with gears and bearings strong enough to put up with considerably more horsepower. However, the shifting mechanism—internal clutches and brake bands—do not always have enough surface area to work without slipping when extra torque is available at the shift points.

A symptom of this problem occurs during a full-throttle acceleration where slippage occurs at each gear change. Slippage will get worse rather than better with time until the transmission will not even transmit the engine torque at road load. On a super highway at cruising speed, the car will suddenly slow down while the engine will speed up. One of the ways to prevent this is to tighten up the clutches and brake bands, after which a full-throttle shift becomes a real boot in the tail. This can sometimes be overcome by changing the shift points. The problem here is the naturally-aspirated engine/ transmission combination is designed to shift, if possible, where the torque delivered before and after the shift is equal. When this is done, the shift point is almost imperceptible. The turbocharged engine, however, is a different story. Assume the engine has revved up to say 4,500 PRM before the shift and the turbocharger is putting out seven pounds boost pressure. Then if the engine drops to 3,000, the turbocharger will still be producing at least seven pounds boost instantaneously. This boost at low RPM really produces a lot of torque and causes the transmission shifting mechanism to do things it was not designed to do.

When and how the transmission shifts is usually controlled by the mechanical linkage to the carburetor and a vacuum line to the intake manifold. In addition, the transmission has a governor to sense shaft speed. Any one or perhaps all may have to be modified when the engine is turbocharged. If these changes are done by a transmission expert, and if the transmission is capable of handling the extra power, it is possible to have a very responsive setup with outstanding performance.

Most automatic transmissions have what is known as a *vacuum modulator*. This device uses intake-manifold vacuum as a signal source to tell the transmission about engine load. Because boost pressure would confuse transmission operation, it is essential to include a one-way check valve on a T in the line to the vacuum modulator. The check valve will be closed when there is manifold vacuum and will bleed off pressure when the turbo is supplying boost. The check valve opening can be quite small—a 1/16-inch to 3/32-inch bleed hole will be adequate. The check valve outlet should be hose-connected to vent to the inside of the air cleaner or to the carburetor inlet.

If it runs, it can probably be turbocharged. But as with hopping up naturally-aspirated engines, some become considerably more popular than others because the parts are available and some engines can stand a lot more overload than others. Small-block Fords, Chevys and Chrysler V-8's are all popular.

28

Art Nolte of Scottsdale Automotive Specialists runs this turbocharged AA dragster. Triple turbos are AiResearch TO-4's with V-trim. Engine is a 481 CID Rodeck big-block Chevrolet with Delta crank, Childs & Albert rods, Aries pistons and Howard cam. Hilborn injectors feed straight methanol. Speed of 204 MPH and elapsed time of 6.90 seconds had been recorded early in 1978.

4 CHOOSING THE RIGHT TURBOCHARGER FOR THE APPLICATION

TABLE II

TURBOCHARGER APPLICATIONS

Category	Engine Speed Range For Maximum Torque	Duration of Power Burst	Maximum Boost Pressure psi	Fuel
I Street machine	As great as possible	10 seconds maximum	10	Gasoline or Propane
Truck or bus	Medium to high	Continuous	10	
Sport fishing boat	High	Continuous	10	
II Road racer	As great as possible	Some short, some long	20	Gasoline or Propane
Drag racer	Medium to high	10 seconds maximum	20	
Short-course racing boat	High	Off and on but almost continuous	20	
Drag racing boat	High	10 seconds maximum	20	
III SAME AS II ABOVE			30	Gasoline with water-alcohol injection
IV Oval track racer	Medium to high	Almost continuous	45	Methanol
Long-course racing boat	High	Continuous	45	
Drag-racing boat	High	10 seconds maximum	45	
V Farm tractor-pulling contest	Medium to high	2 minutes	40	Diesel
VI Farm tractor-pulling contest	Medium to high	2 minutes	110	Diesel

Author MacInnes holds a Rajay turbocharger for automotive use. These tiny 14-pound units can easily double the HP output of an engine, but it is important to select the unit with the correct compressor flow size for the engine. Matching the turbine housing to the engine is the other essential to get good performance, as explained in this chapter. MacInnes directed the design efforts at TRW where this line of turbochargers was originally created. He subsequently joined Rajay Industries as Chief Engineer where he developed the Rajay Die-Cast Bearing Housing, Patent No. 3941437. As this book went to press, he was Vice President and Chief Engineer of Roto-Master, a subsidiary of Echlin Co. This firm manufactures replacement turbochargers, parts, kits and wastegates.

Using the correct turbocharger on an engine creates more power than by any other means. However, putting any turbocharger on an engine does not guarantee good results. If a turbocharger is a good match for a 200 CID Engine at 4,000 RPM, it will probably not be a good match for a 400 CID Engine at 4,000 RPM. Some people have the notion that by running the turbocharger twice as fast, it will work on an engine twice as large. It just isn't so. A look at any of the compressor maps in the appendix of this book will show you the turbocharger speed lines are relatively horizontal in the operating range, and *increasing the speed of the turbocharger increases the pressure ratio rather than the flow.* Turbocharger speed is varied by changing the turbine-nozzle size but if the compressor is not sized correctly to the engine, changing

the turbine nozzle will not help. This process was described in my earlier H. P. Book, *How To Select and Install Turbochargers.* However, it is apparent from talking to many hot-rodders that they don't feel confident in doing it by this method. Therefore, I've included a selection of turbochargers to be used on most of the popular engines for different applications. It's at the end of this chapter. If your engine is not listed, pick the closest size available—you'll find it will be a good match.

For the sake of those willing to go through the process of choosing the right size turbocharger for their engine, it is covered in detail in the next few pages similar to that in the previous book but presented in a manner which should make it easier to follow. Don Hubbard suggests that turbocharged engines be classified by

application because the user will want to achieve maximum torque and horsepower at an engine speed dependent on the application as shown in Table II.

Table II is very useful in matching the correct compressor to the engine and takes into account whether the engine is to be run at steady power as in an offshore-racing boat or on-and-off as in a road-racing machine. This information is important when choosing the turbine-nozzle size or deciding whether or not to use a waste gate or other controls. Table II points out the engine-speed range necessary for various applications and the power-burst duration. The engine speed selected, plus the required intake-manifold pressure are the key factors in choosing the compressor for the engine. Figures 40 and 41 have been included so

John Goddard's 1928 8-liter Bentley resides in a 3.5-liter chassis. Antique engines are not ordinarily selected for turbocharging because components are not capable of handling high HP outputs. Two Ai-Research turbos with seals on the compressor side suck fuel from SU carburetors. "Blower Bentleys" are famous, but this is the only turbocharged one.

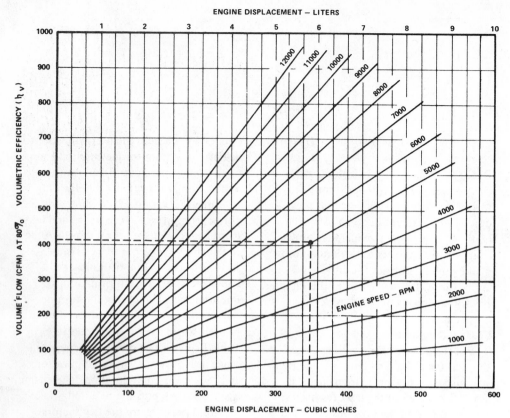

ENGINE DISPLACEMENT – LITERS

ENGINE SPEED – RPM

ENGINE DISPLACEMENT – CUBIC INCHES

Figure 40—Naturally-aspirated volume flow for 4-cycle engines. Dotted line is for a 350 CID engine at 5000 RPM. See text.

Figure 41—Density ratio vs. pressure ratio

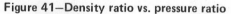
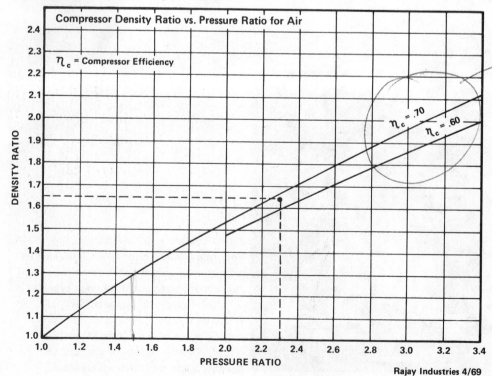

Compressor Density Ratio vs. Pressure Ratio for Air

η_c = Compressor Efficiency

η_c = .70 η_c = .60

DENSITY RATIO

PRESSURE RATIO

Rajay Industries 4/69

volume flow at the peak conditions may be calculated with the least effort. For example, start with 350 CID engine in Application II, running on gasoline with a 7:1 compression ratio at 18 psi boost. It is desired to meet these conditions at 5,000 PRM. On Figure 40, start at 350 CID as shown on the dotted line and draw a line vertically to intersect the 5,000-RPM line. At this point, draw a horizontal line left to intersect the volume-flow scale. In this case the engine will flow 410 CFM. This chart has been compensated for a volumetric efficiency of 80%, a good round figure for average engines. Figure 41 is Compressor Density Ratio vs. Pressure Ratio for Air. Because the turbocharger compressor squeezes the air down considerably from ambient conditions, this chart is necessary to determine the amount of air entering the compressor. All centrifugal-compressor maps are based on inlet conditions. To use the chart, it is first necessary to convert boost pressure to pressure ratio. Assuming the engine is to be run at approximately 1,000-feet altitude where the ambient pressure is 14.3 psia (Appendix page 173), the pressure ratio is computed:

$$\frac{\text{Ambient Pressure} + \text{Boost Pressure}}{\text{Ambient Pressure}} = \text{Pressure Ratio}$$

$$\frac{14.3 + 18}{14.3} = 2.26$$

Most of the running done on turbochargers available today will be between 60% to 70% compressor efficiency, and only these two lines are shown on the chart. Draw a vertical line from 2.26 pressure ratio until it intersects one of the efficiency lines. In this case, we will split the difference and bring it up to about 65%. From this point, draw a horizontal line to the left to intersect the density-ratio scale. The density ratio is 1.62. Going back to Figure 40, the naturally-aspirated volume-flow chart where we obtained 410 CFM, multiply 410 by 1.62 density ratio to get 664 CFM at 2.26 pressure ratio. Looking at the Rajay Model 300E Map, Figure 42, we see this point is off to the right of the map. Any point falling below 60% compressor efficiency is to be avoided. However, if two turbochargers were used on this engine with 332 CFM each at 2.26 pressure ratio, this point looks very good on Rajay 300F map, Figure 43, where it

Figure 42—Rajay Model 300E compressor map

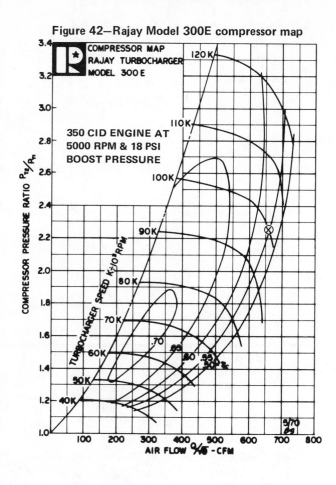

COMPRESSOR MAP
RAJAY TURBOCHARGER
MODEL 300 E

350 CID ENGINE AT
5000 RPM & 18 PSI
BOOST PRESSURE

DICO Company makes this neat turbocharged Honda installation in the sandbuggies they assemble. Chassis is called SKAT-TRAK or Sidewinder 1.

Figure 43—Rajay Model 300F compressor map

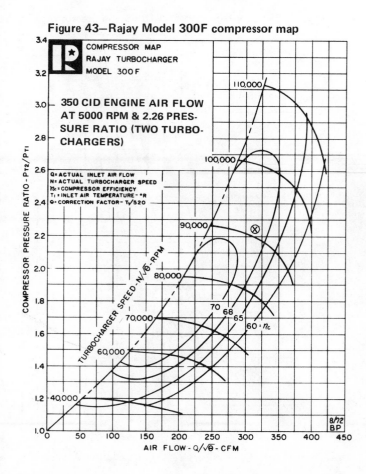

COMPRESSOR MAP
RAJAY TURBOCHARGER
MODEL 300 F

350 CID ENGINE AIR FLOW
AT 5000 RPM & 2.26 PRES-
SURE RATIO (TWO TURBO-
CHARGERS)

Q = ACTUAL INLET AIR FLOW
N = ACTUAL TURBOCHARGER SPEED
η_c = COMPRESSOR EFFICIENCY
T_1 = INLET AIR TEMPERATURE - °R
θ = CORRECTION FACTOR - $T_1/520$

Performance Systems makes this kit for the Alfa-Romeo 1750 and 2000cc engines. A Rajay turbo is used to pressurize the fuel-injection system.

Typical 159 CID Offenhauser engine with AiResearch turbocharger and waste gate.

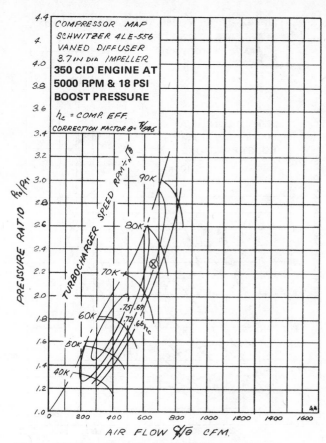

Figure 44—Schwitzer Model 4LF556 compressor map

Figure 45—Schwitzer Model 4MD459 compressor map

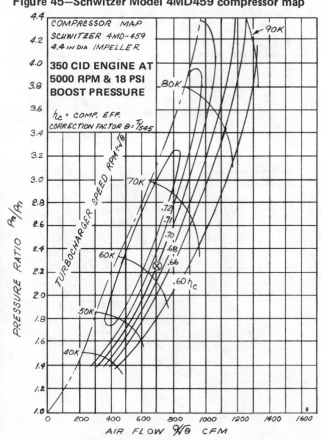

Miller-Norburn offers this kit for the 530i and 630i BMW coupes and sedans. Space-saving turbo design is by Reeves Callaway of Callaway Cars. A Miller-Norburn kit is also available for the 320i.

Figure 46—Schwitzer Model 4LE444 compressor map

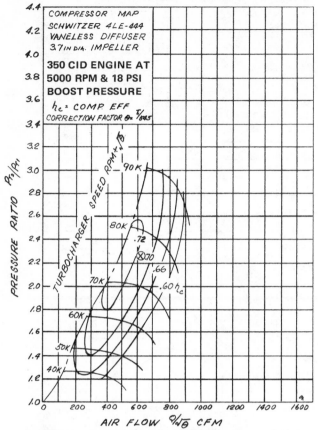

Figure 47—Schwitzer Model 3LD305 compressor map

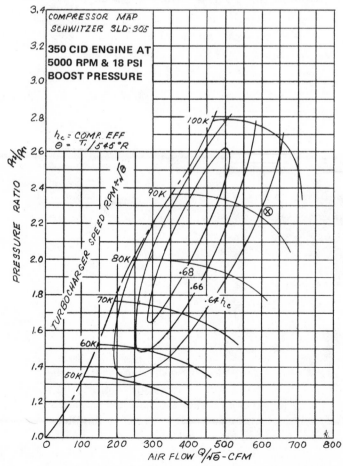

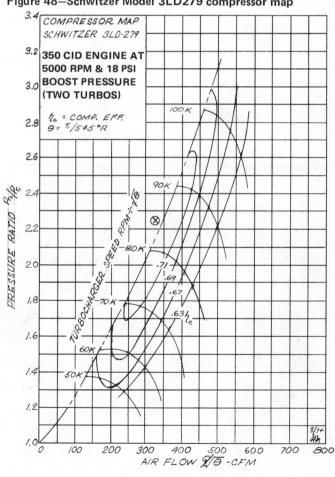

Lloyd Capanna's Pontiac Firebird is powered by this Rajay turbocharged 3.3-liter Nissan 6-cylinder diesel. Five-speed transmission has 20% overdrive. Car gets 30 MPG in town, 45 MPG on highway, yet provides 0—60 MPH acceleration in 12 seconds.

Figure 48—Schwitzer Model 3LD279 compressor map

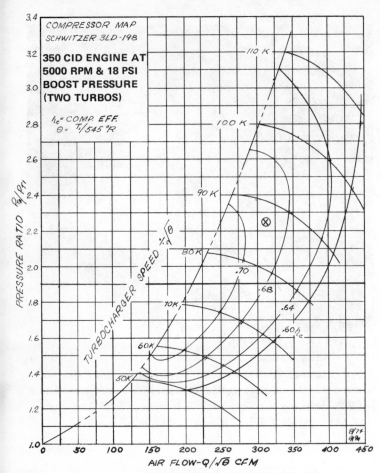

Figure 49—Schwitzer Model 3LD198 compressor map

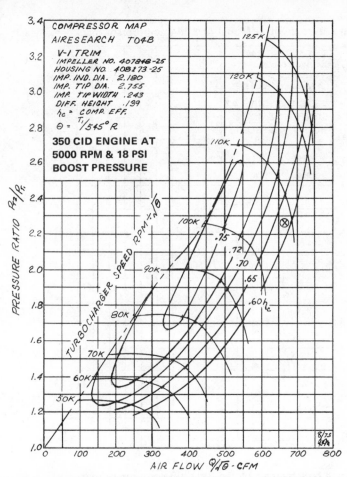

Figure 50—AiResearch TO4B V-1 Trim compressor map

Sometimes it is really tough to fit a turbo-charger in a tight engine compartment such as that of the Buick Skyhawk. Doug Roe managed it quite well in this Buick V-6 kit offered by Kenne-Bell. Carburetor is an SU or Dellorto.

falls in an area of better than 68% efficiency. Plotting this point on the Schwitzer Map, shows a single Schwitzer Model 4LE556—Figure 44, or 4MD459—Figure 45, or 4LE444—Figure 46, would all work very well. The 4LE444 is probably the best match because the point is well away from the surge line but still in a high-efficiency area. The 3LD-305 in Figure 47 would be borderline and anything smaller in the three-inch size could not be considered as a single unit. Here again if we decide to use two turbochargers where only 332 CFM is required per turbocharger, all the Schwitzer four-inch sizes shown here would be too large. The operating point would fall on the surge line of the 3LD279—Figure 48. In this case, the 3LD-198—Figure 49 would be ideal for a dual installation.

If the AiResearch T04B Model is used, the V-1 trim, Figure 50 is borderline for a single installation. However, an S-3— Figure 51 or E-1—Figure 52 trim will work very well on a dual installation.

What this points out is: More than one model or make of turbocharger will frequently do a good job for a specific application and the engine builder is not limited to one particular size and is not forced to compromise and choose a turbocharger which is not a good match for the engine.

Another decision to be made is whether to use one or two turbochargers. If the engine is a small in-line four, it is easy to decide on one. Even an in-line six looks good with one unless the desired output is very high. When it comes to a V or opposed engine other factors must be considered. If one unit is to be used, you have to pipe the exhaust gases from one side to the other, or at least join the two exhaust manifolds. Because the exhaust pipes get considerably hotter than the rest of the engine, they will expand more and unless some sort of flexibility is built in, they will eventually crack and leak exhaust pressure. Using two smaller units eliminates this problem because the system need be connected only on the compressor side. In addition to this, it is often easier to fit two small turbochargers under the hood than one large one.

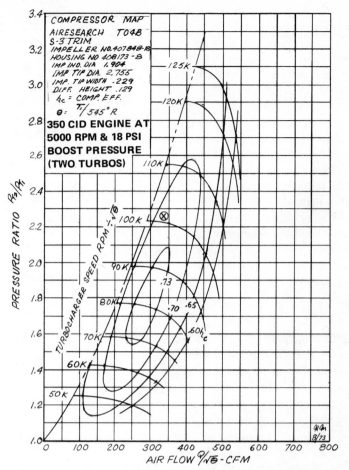

Figure 51—AiResearch TO4B S-3 Trim compressor map

Figure 52—AiResearch TO4 E-1 Trim compressor map

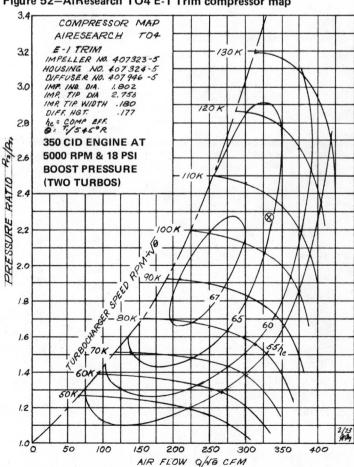

Besides installation problems, the inertia of the rotor should also be considered. One of the standard complaints about the turbochargers is, "They lag behind the engine." This can occur due to poor carburetion or ignition timing but reducing rotor inertia is a step in the right direction.

As soon as the throttle is opened there is a sudden increase in exhaust-gas volume and the turbocharger accelerates rapidly. Total time required to reach maximum speed is a function of overall turbocharger efficiency and the polar moment of inertia of the rotating group. Moment of inertia is the resistance of a rotating body to a change in speed, represented by the letter I

$$I = K^2 M$$

where K is the radius of gyration and M is the mass of the body. Radius of gyration is the distance from the rotating axis to point where all the mass of the body could be located to have the same I as the body itself. In other words, a turbine wheel one foot in diameter might be represented by a ring with a diameter of 7 inches. In this case, $K = 3.5$ inches, Figure 53.

For good rotor acceleration it is essential to have the lowest possible moment of inertia. Turbine wheels are designed with a minimum of material near the outside diameter to reduce K because the moment varies as the square of K.

Because of this, it is often advantageous to use two small turbochargers rather than one larger one. As an example, a 3-inch diameter turbine weighing one pound with a K of 1-inch will have a moment of inertia

$$I = K^2 M$$
$$= K^2 \frac{W}{G}$$

were G is the acceleration of gravity and W is the weight

$$I = 1 \times \frac{1}{386}$$
$$= .00259 \text{ in. lb. sec.}^2$$

If one larger turbocharger is used instead of two small ones, it may have a turbine diameter of 3.5 inches and a rotor weight of about 1.5 lbs. Assuming a radius K of 1.25 inches, the moment of inertia will be

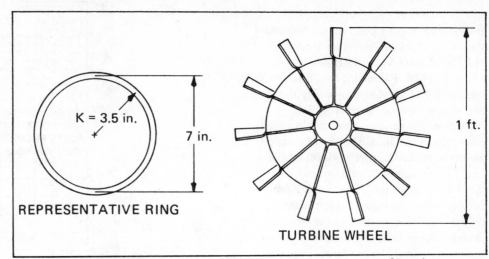

Figure 53—Turbine wheel and representative ring with same moment of inertia

$$I = K^2 \frac{W}{G}$$
$$= \frac{1.25^2 \times 1.5}{386}$$
$$= \frac{1.56 \times 1.5}{386}$$
$$I = .00607 \text{ in. lb. sec.}^2$$

This is about 2 1/2 times as great as the smaller turbocharger. Where turbocharger acceleration is important, I recommend you use two small units instead of one large one.

One of the toughest applications is that of the road racer. There are times when the car is making a turn with the throttle closed and the turbo running at low RPM. The throttle will then be opened wide and the engine will immediately demand, for example, 100 CFM of air. As shown on the compressor map in Figure 54, this will happen with no boost. The turbocharger will immediately accelerate but will not catch up with the engine until steady-state conditions are achieved, which may not occur if the

time between maximum acceleration and shut-off is very short.

The fact that the turbocharger is not mechanically connected to the engine and must overcome inertia has some advantages as well as disadvantages. Many applications, including drag racing, require gear shifting. This time we will look at the path on the compressor map Figure 55, which represents this application.

The vehicle will be on the line with no boost and start out similar to the previous illustration. When the shift is made, the engine speed will drop off while turbocharger speed remains constant. Because the compressor puts out more boost at the lower flows, there will be an immediate increase in manifold pressure. This occurs at each shift point and gives the car a noticeable push. Dotted lines parallel to the turbocharger speed lines are drawn to show how much boost increase will occur at each shift point. These curves are general and the actual amount will depend on the engine/turbocharger/gear combination.

Sizing and matching a turbocharger for a short-duration application must take into account both the maximum boost desired and turbocharger acceleration. A bus or truck engine must be matched so the engine can live with the maximum boost which will occur when climbing a long hill. A drag-race engine has to produce full power for only a few seconds, and the turbocharger must be matched not only for a higher boost but for the acceleration lag as well.

There is no set rule on how to arrive at a perfect match, and each application must be matched either by "cut and try" or experience. This is where the selection chart at the end of this chapter will prove very useful. The fellows who supplied the information have done it based on actual experience. The main thing is to know which way to go after some results have been obtained.

The first requirement is to find out how much air will flow through the engine at maximum speed. This leads to the question: What is the maximum speed? In general, the cam will determine the best engine speed and the turbocharger is matched to increase output at that speed. One comment along this line is that a turbocharged engine does not always require as much valve overlap as a naturally-aspirated engine. Too much overlap can actually reduce the output by cooling down the exhaust gases, which in turn will slow down the turbine and therefore produce less boost.

As mentioned earlier in this chapter, many turbocharger enthusiasts don't like the idea of going through a lot of calculations to determine which size unit to use for their particular application. For those who are interested, the following example goes through the whole process longhand and I used this kind of calculation to derive the charts at the end of the chapter.

First of all, we must start with some known quantities:

Engine Size	250 CID
Four-Stroke Cycle	
Maximum Speed	5,000 RPM
Maximum Boost Pressure	10 psig
Ambient Temperature	70°F. (530°R)
Barometer	29.0 in HG

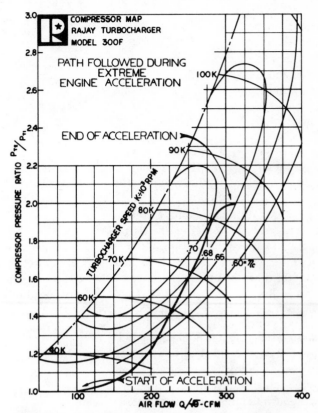

Figure 54—Path followed during extreme acceleration

Figure 55—Path followed during upshifting

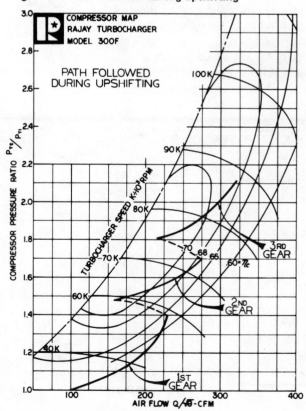

Start by converting the displacement to cubic feet per revolution.

$$\frac{250 \text{ cu. in.}}{1728 \text{ cu. in./cu. ft.}} = .145 \text{ cu. ft.}$$

Next calculate the ideal volume flow through the engine.

$$\frac{.145 \text{ cu. ft.}}{\text{Rev.}} \times \frac{5,000 \text{ RPM}}{2} = 362.5 \text{ CFM}$$

Speed is divided by 2 because this is a four-stroke-cycle engine. This engine should flow 362.5 CFM if the volumetric efficiency (η_{vol}) is 100%.

Because of restrictions through the ports and residual gases left in the clearance space between the piston and the head, this engine will probably flow only about 80% of its theoretical capacity, known as $.8\eta_{vol}$.

362.5 CFM x $.8\eta_{vol}$ = 290 CFM Actual

Because air entering the intake manifold will not be at standard conditions (29.92 in. Hg and 60°F.), it is necessary to compute the actual density to determine air flow through the turbocharger compressor. All compressors are rated on inlet flow so the outlet flow (engine flow) must be multiplied by the density ratio across the compressor to determine the inlet flow. It would be nice if we could just multiply the outlet flow by the pressure ratio but unfortunately the temperature rise which accompanies the pressure rise makes the gas less dense than it would be if the temperature remained constant. This is discussed in detail in the chapter on Intercooling.

Assuming 65% compressor efficiency, calculate the density of the intake manifold air:

$$\text{Pressure Ratio} = \frac{\text{Manifold Pressure Abs}}{\text{Inlet Pressure Abs}}$$
$$= \frac{10 \text{ psig} + \text{Barometer}}{\text{Barometer}}$$
$$= \frac{(10 \times 2.03) + 29.0}{29.0}$$
$$= 1.7$$

From Table I Page 17
Where   R = 1.7
                Y = .162
Ideal Temp. Rise ΔT_{ideal}
                = Y x T_1
Because inlet temp. is 70°F.
                ΔT_{ideal} = .162 x (70° + 460°)

It is necessary to add 460° to the temperature because this calculation must be in absolute temperature; i.e., degrees Rankine.

ΔT_{ideal} = 85.9°

Actual Temp. Rise,

$$\Delta T_{actual} = \frac{\Delta T_{ideal}}{\text{Comp. Eff.}}$$
$$\Delta T_{actual} = \frac{85.9}{.65}$$
$$\Delta T_{actual} = 132°$$

Intake-manifold Temp.
                = compressor inlet temp. + ΔT_{actual}
                = 70° + 132°
                = 202°F.

Air in the intake manifold will not actually get this hot because fuel has a cooling effect. Hopefully, there will also be some heat loss through the ducting.

Comparing this to the air at the compressor inlet will result in the density ratio.

Density Ratio

$$= \frac{\text{Comp. Inlet Abs. Temp.}}{\text{Comp. Outlet Abs. Temp.}}$$
$$\times \frac{\text{Comp. Outlet Abs. Press}}{\text{Comp. Inlet Abs. Press.}}$$
$$= \frac{70 + 460}{202 + 460} \times \frac{20.3 + 29.0}{29.0}$$
$$= \frac{530}{662} \times \frac{49.3}{29.0}$$

Density Ratio
                = 1.36

Comp. Inlet Flow
                = Comp. Outlet Flow (Engine Flow)
                x Density Ratio
                = 290 CFM x 1.36
                = 394.4 CFM

If you are using a compressor map scaled in Lbs./Min. rather than CFM it is necessary to convert by multiplying by .069 to obtain the correct flow because most Lbs./Min. compressor maps are run at 85°F. and 28.4 in. Hg.

For convenience reasons, all the maps in this book are scaled in cubic feet per minute.

The above calculations show 394.4 CFM flowing through the compressor at 1.7:1 pressure ratio. It would be desirable to have this point on the right (high-flow) side of the map because it will occur at maximum engine RPM. Try plotting this point on several maps to determine which is best. No doubt any one of several will do the

job so the user will have a choice. Starting in alphabetical order, the AiResearch TO4B V-1 trim looks very good because it will produce this flow and pressure ratio at about 73% compressor efficiency.

A Rajay 300E flow will also work well with airflow to spare.

Schwitzer's 3LD-279 is a little on the small side, but the 4LE-556 should work very well.

This is not an attempt to limit the user to these makes of turbochargers but it is very difficult to match one to an engine without a compressor map or from previous experience with another engine.

It is best to start with a large turbine housing A/R or nozzle area because one too small might overboost on the first run and destroy the engine. If the housing is too large, the boost pressure will be low but at least the engine will be intact.

An engine operated with the largest-possible carburetor and the lowest-possible exhaust restrictions has a wide-open-throttle acceleration line like the solid line on the Figure 56 map. This leaves something to be desired at the mid-range but if a smaller turbine nozzle is used, the engine will be overboosted at maximum RPM. This can be overcome by using a control device such as a waste-gate. Until recently, these were expensive and hard to obtain. Controls are covered in Chapter 9.

It is possible to have a more desirable wide-open-throttle operating line, as shown by a dotted line in Figure 56, without using a movable control. Any one or a combination of the methods described here will improve the mid-range torque without over boosting at maximum engine speed.

CARBURETOR VENTURI SIZE LIMITATION

If a carburetor is used which has a pressure drop of about 4 in. Hg at the 5,000-RPM point, the depression at the compressor inlet will make it necessary to use a smaller turbine housing of perhaps A/R .8 to achieve the original boost level of 10 psi. This carburetor will have a lower pressure drop at the lower speeds and the smaller turbine housing will still deliver adequate boost. This arrangement would follow a speed line similar to the dotted line on Figure 56. The use of a smaller A/R turbine housing will cause more back pressure on the engine, which might raise exhaust-valve temperature. This is only critical when the engine is used for steady-state high-output.

EXHAUST MUFFLER RESTRICTION

A similar result may be obtained by restricting the turbine exhaust, causing a back pressure on the turbine of about 4 in. Hg at maximum speed. Although a turbocharged engine is relatively quiet without the use of a muffler, this will result in an even quieter running engine.

VALVE TIMING AND DURATION

A valve cam profile which favors a certain engine speed naturally aspirated, will have the same tendency turbocharged. Our theoretical engine will reach peak boost at 5,000 RPM but if the cam and valve train are designed to favor 4,000 RPM, it is possible to match the turbine housing so the boost again will follow the dotted line on the compressor map, Figure 56.

One of the measures of overall turbocharger performance is the amount of positive differential across the engine. This differential occurs when intake-manifold pressure is higher than exhaust-manifold pressure and it is extremely beneficial to the engine. In the case of a diesel engine, when both intake and exhaust valves are open, this positive differential blows clean—relatively cold—air through the clearance area over the piston and drives out any unburned exhaust gases which might still be there. As a result, it cools the engine and provides extra air—which in turn allows more fuel to be burned without increasing exhaust-gas temperature. This contributes to longer turbo life. No raw fuel is ever blown into the exhaust system because all diesels have cylinder-type fuel injection.

Gasoline engines, on the other hand, seldom have cylinder injection. Almost all gasoline and LPG engines have either carburetors or port injection.

Either of these systems work well with a moderately turbocharged engine because the combination of intake and exhaust restrictions and the fact that most turbocharging takes place only under extreme acceleration conditions causes the exhaust-manifold pressure to be higher than intake-manifold pressure at all times.

If steady-state conditions of high-pressure turbocharging occur with a carburetor

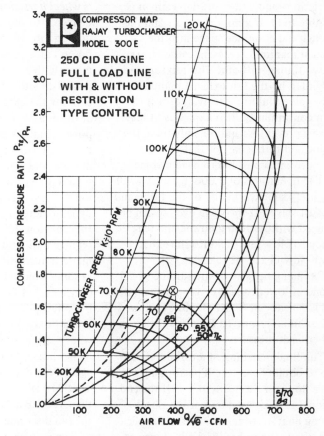

Figure 56—300 CID engine on compressor map

Sid Cook turbocharged his 390 CID Ford engine in a motorhome. Hobbs switch at left side of carburetor senses manifold pressure. Fuel is supplied directly from pump into venturis under boost. See page 51 for more details on this method.

and exhaust system having a very low restriction—and a high-overlap cam—it is possible to blow a mixture of air and fuel through the clearance space into the exhaust manifold. This can cause either of two things—or both! This mixture can be ignited by the hot exhaust manifold and explode intermittently and/or it can burn continuously. If it explodes, it may cause a power loss and possibly harm the engine and turbocharger. If it burns continuously, it is possible to have turbine-inlet temperatures of 2,000°F., which will definitely shorten the life of the turbo and exhaust valves. If the valve overlap can be reduced without losing power, the tendency to blow raw fuel into the exhaust manifold will also be reduced.

Reducing the size of the turbine wheel to one of lower capacity may also help if it is large enough to handle the gas flow at maximum engine RPM with a little higher back pressure.

The final matching of a turbine nozzle size to obtain best overall performance is often done on a dynamometer. If the end product is to be used on a truck, sport-fishing boat, or other steady-state application, this is undoubtedly the best way to go. There are a couple of drawbacks for most of us, namely cost, and the application is not steady-state. The larger engine manufacturers have dynamometers which can be programmed to simulate acceleration conditions. These are not usually available to the average hot rodder and even if they were, the cost would be prohibitive.

They say, "Necessity is the mother of invention," so naturally somebody has come up with an accurate method of measuring horsepower in the vehicle and depending on the amount of information desired, this can be a simple or rather elaborate set-up. In either case, it is far less costly than a programmed dynamometer. I call it the Griffin System because Dick Griffin was the first to tell me how to do it.

The basic idea is to mount a reliable accelerometer in the vehicle and use the weight of the vehicle to resist the acceleration. An aircraft-type accelerometer won't work because the divisions are too small. The maximum scale reading should not be greater than 1 G. and most readings will be below .3 G if the vehicle is a street machine.

Horsepower measured by this method is *wheel horsepower* or that actually delivered to the road. Many enthusiasts don't go for the method because it doesn't give as high a reading as a dynamometer with a needle which reads horsepower directly. The method often used is to rev the engine and catch the needle at the end of its swing. This gives great power readings but they are less than reliable. Even when reliable readings are made at the rear wheels, there is a tendency to add 30% or more for "power train losses." Having run the same engine on a dynamometer and in a car with manual transmission, I found only about 4% difference in the output. Even with an automatic transmission, losses are not as great as some would like us to believe. Passenger cars are rated fairly honestly these days but a few years ago, the 210 HP car you bought only put out about 117 at the rear wheels. Because we liked to believe the higher horsepower, we charged the loss against the drive train. It just wasn't so! That 210 HP engine never saw much more than 150 HP at the flywheel—even with the fan disconnected!

The point here is, don't be disappointed if your rear-wheel horsepower is not as great as you expected but if the power obtained after the turbocharger has been added is twice as much as before, the increase is 100% no matter how you measure it.

A few years ago when we turbocharged a 4,000-lb. Oldsmobile with an automatic transmission and were able to turn the quarter at better than 103 MPH on factory tires, charts showed this required almost 400 HP. We never measured more than 275 HP at the rear wheels.

How to measure horsepower:

1. Weigh the car and occupants accurately.
2. Install a tachometer.
3. Calibrate the speedometer.
4. Install an accelerometer.

The car and occupants may be weighed at any public scale. The tachometer can be calibrated by a strobe light or a revolution counter. The speedometer is easy to calibrate by driving at a constant speed on any highway equipped with mile posts. A stopwatch is used to measure the exact time for a given distance. The longer the distance, the more accurate the calibration. The actual speed is obtained by dividing the distance by the time.

After all the calibrations have been completed, the same two people included with the weight of the car will run the tests. Many tests will have to be run to obtain a power curve but we will go through the process completely for only one because the rest will be done in the same manner.

To find maximum horsepower at 4,000 RPM, first determine the road speed necessary to obtain that engine speed in high gear. If it is above the legal limit, drop down a gear.

Starting at a speed well below that required, open the throttle all the way. The driver keeps one eye on the speedometer and when it reaches the required speed, he calls out *mark* or some other predetermined word. The other occupant then reads and records the reading on the accelerometer. After a speed of about 5 MPH above the required speed is reached, the driver puts the transmission in neutral and starts coasting. When the speed again reaches the required MPH he again calls out *mark*. This time the deceleration is read and recorded. The second reading is taken to measure windage and road loads. The two readings are added to determine the total acceleration delivered by the tires to the road.

These readings will be accurate so long as there is no change in grade or wind direction during the interval between the readings. It is desirable to make several runs and average the readings.

If the road-load-horsepower readings are to be done regularly and extreme accuracy is desired, it will be worthwhile to invest in some additional equipment.

In this case, a surplus 16mm movie camera was mounted in the car to photograph the instruments during acceleration runs. Film was viewed on a small screen used for editing. Instruments used measured compressor inlet and outlet pressure, turbocharger speed, time in 1/100 seconds, acceleration, engine speed and road speed. The turbocharger tachometer is very expensive and not required except in turbocharger-development work. The rest of the instruments are commercially available and the results obtained will be as good as from a high-quality recorder at considerably less cost.

An 8mm camera is not recommended because the definition is not sharp enough to read the dials accurately without eyestrain. Super-8 cameras may work, but I've never tried them.

The biggest single advantage of the camera method over direct observation is that the camera will not slant readings in the direction desired by the observer. Everyone who is making modifications to his engine has the tendency of reading higher figures than actually occur.

The next step is to make use of the readings. To do this, it is necessary to go back to a couple of formulas from high-school physics.

$$F = MA$$

or, Force = Mass x Acceleration

and Mass = $\dfrac{\text{Weight}}{\text{Acceleration of Gravity}}$

If the accelerometer readings are in G units which is

$$\dfrac{\text{Acceleration of Vehicle}}{\text{Acceleration of Gravity}}$$

F = Weight x Accelerometer Reading

This force is the actual effort applied to the road by the tires. If the speedometer reading is converted to ft./sec., horsepower can be calculated directly.

Velocity (ft./sec.)
= Velocity (MPH) x $\dfrac{5280}{3600}$

Because 1 horsepower equals 550 ft.lb./sec., the road horsepower is then:

$$HP = \dfrac{\text{Force x Velocity}}{550}$$

A small calculation shows how simple this is:

Weight of car and occupants	3650 lbs.
Corrected road speed	60 MPH
Engine speed	2800 RPM
Full throttle acceleration	.12G
Neutral deceleration	.06G
Total acceleration	.18G

$$F = MA$$
$$= \dfrac{3650 \times .18 \times 32.2}{32.2}$$
$$F = 657 \text{ lbs.}$$
Velocity = $60 \times \dfrac{5280}{3600}$
$$V = 88 \text{ ft./sec.}$$
$$HP = \dfrac{657 \times 88}{550}$$
$$HP = 105.1 @ 2800 \text{ RPM}$$

Engine torque can then be calculated from

$$HP = \dfrac{T \times RPM}{5250}$$
or T $= \dfrac{5250 \times HP}{RPM}$
$$= \dfrac{5250 \times 105.1}{2800}$$
Torque = 197 lbs. ft.

Results of several speeds can then be plotted to let us look at the horsepower and torque curves, Figure 57.

If possible, readings should first be taken and plotted in the naturally-aspirated condition so a base line can be established before the engine is turbocharged.

After the installation has been made and the necessary settings have been established for idle speed and ignition timing, the acceleration test should be rerun to determine if there has been a power gain and how much.

If the power curve looks like Figure 58, it means the compressor is the right size, but the turbine housing has been matched for increase in power at the top end only.

Using a turbine housing with a smaller A/R should give more boost at the low-speed end, Figure 59.

Too small a turbine housing may push the boost out of sight at high speeds. This is often fatal to engines and should be avoided. One of the various types of restrictions mentioned previously should be used. When this is done correctly, an HP curve similar to Figure 60 can be established. Please remember these curves are for comparison only and do not represent a specific engine. An increase of 100% in road horsepower with a broad speed range is not only possible, but has been demonstrated many times.

This method of matching is fine for cars and trucks which are to be used on

Figure 57—Road horsepower

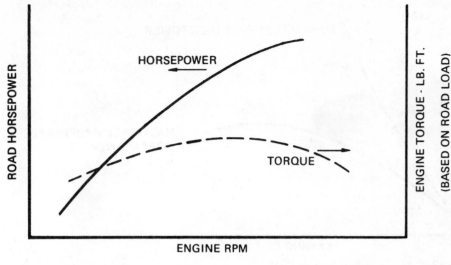

Figure 58—Turbo matched for high RPM

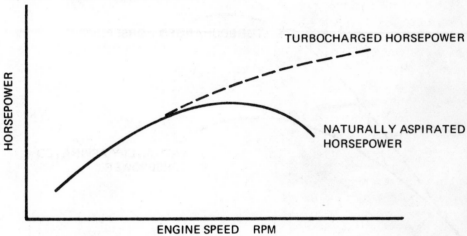

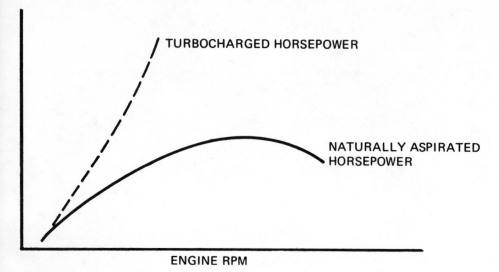

Figure 59—Turbo matched for low RPM

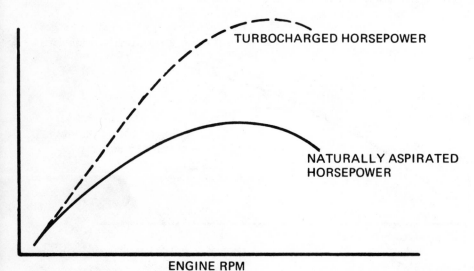

Figure 60—Turbo matched for broad speed range

the street but is impractical for road or track racers.

After the size of compressor has been established, the turbine housing should be matched to the track conditions just as final gear ratios are matched. Changing turbine housings on turbochargers takes about five minutes, including disconnecting and connecting the inlet and outlet ducting. Asbestos gloves are recommended. If "V" band inlet and outlet connections are used along with quick disconnects on the oil supply and drain, the whole turbocharger can be replaced in less than a minute.

To summarize, the compressor should be picked which will flow air or air-fuel mixture in the area of the map between the surge line and the 60% efficiency line. The turbine housing A/R should be matched to produce the required boost at the required speed and if necessary, means should be provided to prevent overboosting at maximum engine speed.

If boost pressure is too high, use a turbine housing with a larger A/R. Tuning the installation with the correct turbine-housing A/R is essential to make the turbocharger work correctly. Novice installers of turbos have nearly always blamed the unit for producing too much or too little boost when all they had to do to make it right was to change the turbine housing. Because the information has not been common knowledge in the past, this part of making the turbocharger installation work has been completely

TABLE III

Suggested turbochargers for low-boost (10psi Maximum) V-8 engines
Use 1 or 2 turbos, with boost control.

CID	RPM	CFM @ 1.4 PRESSURE RATIO	SCHWITZER MODEL	TURBINE AREA	RAJAY MODEL	AIRESEARCH TO4 TRIM	TURBINE A/R	ROTO-MASTER TO4 TRIM	TURBINE A/R
283	5000	430	2-3LD-279	1.10	2-375F70	2-E-1 or 1-V-1	0-.69 P-.81	2-Y-4 or 1-V-2	N-.69 P-.58
305	5000	462	2-3LD-279	1.25	2-375F80	2-E-1 or 1-V-1	0-.81 P-.81	2-Y-4 or 1-V-2	N-.69 P-.58
327	5000	496	2-3LD-279	1.79	2-375F90	2-E-1 or 1-V-1	0-.96 P-.96	2-Y-4 or 1-V-2	N-.69 P-.69
350	4000	425	2-3LD-279	1.10	2-375F90	2-E-1 or 1-V-1	0-.81 P-.96	2-S-4 or 1-V-2	0-.40 P-.81
400	4000	484	2-3LD-279	1.25	2-375E80	2-S-3	0-.81	2-S-4 or 1-V-2	0-.58 P-.96
396	4000	482	2-3LD-279	1.25	2-375E80	2-S-3	0-.81		
427	4000	520	2-3LD-279	1.79	2-375E90	2-S-3	0-.96	2-S-4 or 1-R-11	0-.69 P-.96
454	4000	551	2-3LD-305	2.00	2-375E90	2-S-3	0-.96		
500	4000	609	2-3LD-305	2.45	2-375E10	2-S-3	0-.96		

For me (handwritten, next to 283)
26-3000 econ (handwritten)
for chris (handwritten, next to 350)

TABLE IV

Suggested turbochargers for moderate-output (20 psi Maximum) V-8 engines
Use 1 or 2 turbos with boost control.

DISPL	RPM	CFM @ 2.3 PRESSURE RATIO	SCHWITZER MODEL	TURBINE AREA	RAJAY MODEL	AIRESEARCH TO4 TRIM	TURBINE A/R	ROTO-MASTER TO4 TRIM	TURBINE A/R
283	7000	759	2-3LD-279	2.00	2.375F80	2-S-3	0-.81	2-S-4	0-.81
305	7000	808	2-3LD-279	2.45	2.375F80	2-S-3	0-.81	2-S-4	0-.81
327	7000	858	2-3LD-279	3.02	2.375E70	2-S-3	0-.96	2-S-4	0-.96
350	6500	858	2-3LD-279	3.02	2.375E70	2-S-3	0-.96	2-S-4	0-.96
396	6500	957	2-3LD-305	3.02*	2.375E80	2-V-1	P-.81	2-V-2	P-.81
400	6500	973	2-3LD-305	3.02*	2.375E80	2-V-1	P-.81	2-V-2	P-.81
427	6500	1031	2-3LD-305	3.02*	2-375E10*	2-V-1	P-.96	2-V-2	P-.96
454	6500	1072	2-3LD-305	3.02*	2-375E10*	2-V-1	P-.96	2-V-2	P-.96
500	6500	1221	2-3LD-305	3.02*	2-375E10*	2-V-1	P-.96	2-V-2	P-.96

TABLE V

Suggested turbochargers for high-output (25 psi MAXIMUM) V-8 engines
Use 2 turbos with boost control.

DISPL	RPM	CFM @ 2.7 PRESSURE RATIO	SCHWITZER MODEL	TURBINE AREA	RAJAY MODEL	AIRESEARCH TO4 TRIM	TURBINE A/R	ROTO-MASTER TO4 TRIM	TURBINE A/R
283	7000	822	2-3LD-305	3.02	2-375E10	2-S-3	0-.96	2-S-4	0-.96
305	7000	883	2-3LD-305	3.02	2-375E10	2-S-3	0-.96	2-S-4	0-.96
327	7000	935	2-3LD-305	3.02	2-375E10	2-S-3	0-.96	2-S-4	0-.96
350	6500	936	2-3LD-305	3.02	2-375E10	2-S-3	0-.96	2-S-4	0-.96
396	6500	1068	2-3LD-305	3.02	2-375E10	2-V-1	P-.96	2-V-2	P-.96
400	6500	1078	2-3LD-305	3.02	2-375E10	2-V-1	P-.96	2-V-2	P-.96
427	6500	1148	2-3LD-305	3.02	2-375E10	2-V-1	P-.96	2-V-2	P-.96
454	6500	1212	2-3LD-305	3.02	2-375E10	2-V-1	P-.96	2-V-2	P-.96
500	6500	1349	2-3LD-305	3.02	2-375E10	2-V-1	P-.96	2-V-2	P-.96

overlooked unless the tuner was able to get help from someone with turbo experience. Thus, it is important to buy your turbo from an organization which has the various turbine housings in stock and will agree to work with you by swapping turbine housings until the installation is exactly right.

As mentioned at the beginning of this chapter, a good percentage of potential turbocharger users will look over this method and say, "But how do I know which turbocharger to use for my application?"

The people who sell turbochargers for special applications are anxious to make money so they have gone through the process for just about any engine or application they could imagine. These men, Don Hubbard, Paul Uitti, and Chuck McInerney have all spent years matching turbochargers to engines. They have contributed information on matching turbochargers to various engines depending on the application. This is shown in Tables III, IV, V, VI and VII.

No doubt, someone will ask why such and such a Schwitzer or AiResearch turbocharger is not shown on the list. Both manufacturers make many models of turbochargers but only certain ones are readily available, so if you have a model not on these tables and it needs overhaul, you might have trouble finding parts. Those shown on the tables are available *and* repairable.

If you cannot find your engine among those on the tables, one of the same size and method of valving will normally take the same size turbocharger.

Small diesel turbo was seen on a Buick-powered competition roadster in Flint, Michigan in 1962. Two large 4-bbl. carbs mounted on a "trunk" manifold to the compressor inlet. Diesel-type turbo had no seals to protect against gasoline flowing through compressor into turbo bearing, so turbo bearing failure resulted. Junction box connected right and left exhaust manifolds next to turbo. This is another example of mismating — in the turbo sizing and construction — and in carburetion requirements.

TABLE VI
Suggested turbochargers for 4-cylinder engines: 1 turbo per engine with boost control.

VEHICLE	CID	SCHWITZER MODEL	TURBINE AREA	RAJAY MODEL	AIRESEARCH TO4 TRIM	AIRESEARCH TO4 TURBINE A/R	ROTO-MASTER TO4 TRIM	ROTO-MASTER TO4 TURBINE A/R
Chevrolet Vega	140	3LD-198	1.25	375B60	E-1	0-.69	Y-4	N-.69
Dodge Colt	98	3LD-168	.87	377B25	J-1	N-.58	Y-4	N-.40
Ford Pinto	98	3LD-168	.87	377B25	J-1	N-.58	Y-4	N-.40
Ford Pinto	121	3LD-198	1.25	377B40	E-1	0-.69	Y-4	N-.58
Alfa Romeo	96,120	3LD-168	.87	377B40	E-1	0-.69	Y-4	N-.58
Audi	103,114	3LD-168	.87	377B40	E-1	N-.58	Y-4	N-.58
Austin Healey Sprite	67,78	3LD-168	.68	377B25	J-1	N-.32 or N-.58	Y-4	N-.30
BMW	108,121	3LD-198	1.25	377B40	E-1	N-.58	Y-4	N-.58
Datsun	79,87,97,108	3LD-168	.87	377B25	J-1	N-.58 or N-.50	Y-4	N-.40
Ford	91,103	3LD-168	.87	377B25	J-1	N-.58 or N-.50	Y-4	N-.40
Honda 750	46	3LD-168	.68	377B25	J-1	N-.58 or N-.32	Y-4	N-.30
Mercedes	121	3LD-168	.87	377B25	J-1	N-.58	Y-4	N-.58
Mercedes	134	3LD-168	.87	377B25	E-1	0-.69	Y-4	N-.58
MG	78,99,110	3LD-168	.87	377B25	J-1	N-.58 or N-.32	Y-4	N-.40
Opel	66	3LD-168	.68	377B25	J-1	N-.32	Y-4	N-.30
Opel	91,103,116	3LD-168	.87	377B40	E-1	N-.58 or N-.50	Y-4	N-.40
Porsche	96,121	3LD-168	.87	377B40	E-1	N-.58	Y-4	N-.58
Renault	96,101	3LD-168	.87	377B25	J-1	N-.58	Y-4	N-.40
Saab	104,121	3LD-198	1.25	377B40	E-1	N-.58	Y-4	N-.58
Toyota	71,86	3LD-168	.87	377B25	J-1	N-.32	Y-4	N-.40
Toyota	97,120	3LD-168	.87	377B25	E-1	N-.58	Y-4	N-.40
Triumph	70,79,91	3LD-168	.87	377B25	J-1	N-.58 or W-.32	Y-4	N-.30
VW	78,91,97,102	3LD-168	.68	377B25	J-1	N-.58 or N-.32	Y-4	N-.40
Volvo	108,121	3LD-168	.87	377B40	E-1	N-.58	Y-4	N-.58

TABLE VII
Suggested turbochargers for 6-cylinder engines: 1 turbo per engine with boost control.

VEHICLE	CID	SCHWITZER MODEL	TURBINE AREA	RAJAY MODEL	AIRESEARCH TO4 TRIM	AIRESEARCH TO4 TURBINE A/R	ROTO-MASTER TO4 TRIM	ROTO-MASTER TO4 TURBINE A/R
Am. Motors	199,232,258	3LD-279	1.79	375E80	S-3	0-.81	S-4	0-.69
Buick	198,231	3LD-279	1.79	375E80	S-3	0-.81	S-4	0-.69
Chevrolet	200,230,250	3LD-279	1.79	375E80	S-3	0-.81	S-4	0-.69
Chevrolet	292	3LD-305	2.00	375E10	V-1	P-.96	V-2	P-.58
Ford	144,170	3LD-198	1.79	375F60 (144)	S-3	0-.69	S-4	0-.40
				375F70 (170)	S-3	0-.69	S-4	A-.40
Ford	200,250	3LD-279	1.79	375E80	S-3	0-.81	S-4	0-.69
Ford	240	3LD-279	1.79	375E80	S-3	0-.81	S-4	0-.69
Ford	300	3LD-305	2.00	375E10	V-1	P-.96	V-2	P-.58
Dodge, Plymouth	170,225	3LD-279	1.79	375F70 (170)	S-3	0-.81	S-4	0-.58
				375E70 (225)	S-3	0-.81	S-4	0-.69
GMC	270,302	3LD-305	2.00	375E10	V-1	P-.96	V-2	P-.58
Aston Martin	244	3LD-279	1.79	375E80	V-1	P-.81	S-4	0-.69
Austin Healey	178	3LD-198	1.79	375F80	S-3	0-.81	S-4	0-.40
BMW	182	3LD-198	1.79	375F80	S-3	0-.81	S-4	0-.40
Datsun	146	3LD-198	1.25	375F60	S-3	0-.58	Y-4	N-.69
Ford V-6	155	3LD-198	1.79	375F70	S-3	0-.69	Y-4	N-.69
Jaguar	151	3LD-198	1.79	375F60	S-3	0-.69	Y-4	N-.69
Jaguar	210,231,258	3LD-279	1.79	375E80	V-1	P-.81	S-4	0-.81
Porsche	143	3LD-198	1.79	375F60	S-3	0-.69	Y-4	N-.69
Toyota	121,137,156	3LD-198	1.79	377B40 (121)	E-1	N-.58	Y-4	N-.58
				375B60 (137)	E-1	N-.58	Y-4	N-.58
				375F60 (156)	S-3	0-.58	Y-4	N-.69
Triumph	122,152	3LD		377B40 (122)	S-3	0-5.8	Y-4	N-.58
				375F60 (152)	S-3	0-.58	Y-4	N-.69

McLaren CanAm car with a 465 CID big-block Chevrolet aluminum engine. Two AiResearch TEO-670 turbos with wastegated exhaust produce 1,200 HP at 60 inches Hg manifold pressure. Lucas timed mechanical fuel injection with 2.25-inch throttle bores has blow-off valves for closed throttle manifold-pressure relief. **Photo by Bill Howell.**

The purpose of a carburetor or fuel-injection system is to add fuel to the air entering the engine at the correct ratio so it will burn efficiently in the combustion chamber and, at the same time, not create too hot a fire which would cause early destruction of the engine. The duty is the same for a naturally-aspirated or turbocharged engine except in a turbocharged engine one more problem is added, that of the supercharged condition where the intake-manifold pressure is higher than ambient.

Modern carburetors differ in the way they do their job but, in general, all have systems to cover the following modes of operation:

1. An enriching system to enable the engine to start and run when it is cold. This is the choke system.
2. An idle system to provide the correct air-fuel ratio to the engine when it is idling with no output.
3. A main fuel system which is in operation at cruise.
4. A power system which enriches the fuel air mixture under extreme power or acceleration conditions.
5. An accelerator pump which gives an extra shot of fuel to the mixture each time the throttle is opened so there will not be a lag between the idle circuit and the main circuit or the main circuit and the power circuit.

These carburetor circuits—duplicated in a good fuel-injection system—have been developed over the past 75 years to a point where the average carburetor is a very reliable device needing little attention. Progressive carburetors such as the two-barrel type used on the Pinto and Vega and the four-barrel type used on just about every V-8 built are basically the same as the single barrel except that the secondary barrels are added to reduce the pressure drop at extremely high engine speeds so the engine can achieve its maximum power. The secondary barrels will usually only contain as many systems as necessary for their operation. For instance, the secondaries ordinarily do not have a choke circuit, and may not

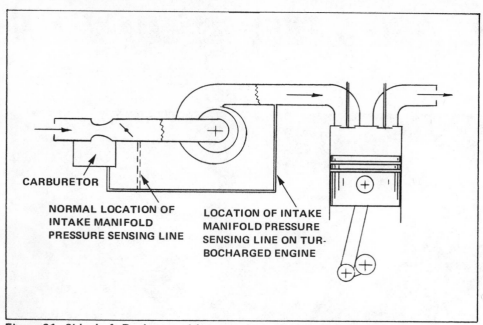

Figure 61—Side draft Rochester with external manifold-pressure sensing line

Figure 62—Carburetor power circuit, showing power valve open

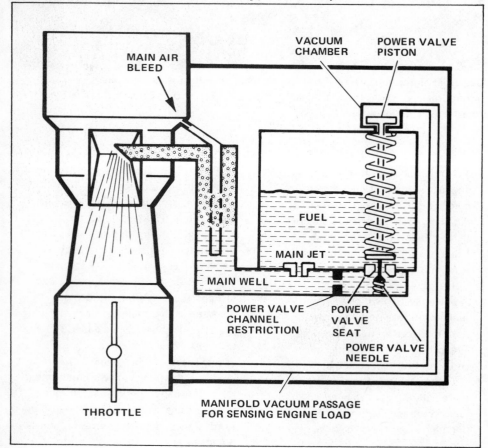

include a power system, accelerator pump or idle system.

The main problems with carburetors and fuel-injection systems are: They were invented before the turbocharger became readily available for gasoline engines, and, therefore, do not take into account the fact that it is necessary to run richer when the intake manifold pressure is above 15 psia than it is on a naturally-aspirated engine where this condition cannot occur.

Looking back over the years when the Corvair was first turbocharged, Chevrolet used a carburetor (Carter YH) which was already available because it had been used on an early-model Corvette. This carburetor did not have any way to sense intake-manifold pressure so two things were necessary to keep the engine out of trouble when the boost went up to about 7 or 8 psig. One thing was to choose a metering rod and jet which resulted in an overrich condition at full throttle. The other was to put a pressure-retard diaphragm rather than a vacuum-advanced diaphragm on the distributor. This diaphragm actually retarded the spark about 10 crankshaft degrees when the intake manifold pressure reached 2 psig. The system worked fairly well but was a compromise and never had the feel desired by many hot rodders.

At the same time Oldsmobile was developing its Jetfire, a turbocharged version of its 215 CID V-8 F85 Cutlass Engine. Oldsmobile's approach was quite different in that they started with a high-compression ratio engine, but they did develop a carburetor particularly for this application. This carburetor had two features which were in the right direction for a turbocharged engine. First the power piston was not connected to the downstream side of the butterfly but had an external line which enabled it to be connected to the intake manifold of the engine downstream of the turbocharger. See Figure 61. With an ordinary carburetor, where the power piston or diaphragm senses pressure immediately downstream of the throttle, it is possible to have a partially closed throttle plate creating a good vacuum at the power-valve port while the turbocharger is turning this vacuum into pressure and the engine sees pressure above atmospheric. When this happens, the engine will run lean and probably

48

detonate. The other thing Oldsmobile did was add anti-detonant fluid to the carburetor when the engine ran in the supercharged condition. It was necessary to add this anti-detonant because of the engine's high compression ratio. This same system works well with a low-compression-ratio engine where the anti-detonant can be added at a much higher manifold pressure.

Because we have to live with carburetors designed for naturally-aspirated engines, several things can be done to modify them to do a better job on a turbocharged engine. Figure 62 shows the power circuit of a typical carburetor. Note the sensing line, as described previously, senses pressure just downstream of the throttle valve. If this sensing line, normally a drilled internal passage, is plugged up and a new line connected to the power diaphragm, it can be routed to the intake manifold with a short length of copper tubing. On some carburetors there is enough material in the wall to drill and tap for a tube fitting. On others it is necessary to drill a hole about the size of the tubing and then epoxy the tubing in place. This modification only solves one problem, that of giving the correct signal to the carburetor power system when operating with a turbocharger downstream of the carburetor. It does not, however, do anything for enriching the fuel/air mixture when the intake manifold is above atmospheric. There are several ways to do this without redesigning the carburetor. The device in Figure 63 can be added to the carburetor with the least effort. I have run this system on a turbocharged Corvair with good results. Get the Hobbs pressure switch at an automotive parts supply house for a nominal price. These come in various pressure ranges but mine has a 0-4 psi range. The actual point where the switch closes is adjustable with a small screw driver. The solenoid valve may be a little harder to come by but should be available at a recreational-vehicle outlet. Make sure the valve seat is made from a gasoline-resistant material. The size of the orifice which adds the extra fuel to the carburetor will vary with the engine but I have found .040" works pretty well in my case. The use of this fuel-enriching device allows the carburetor power valve to be set at a fuel/air ratio which would be too lean for a supercharged engine. As soon as the intake manifold pressure reaches

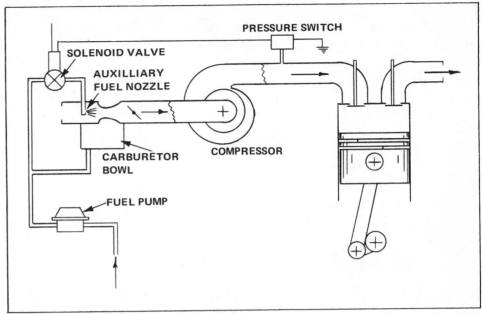

Figure 63—Pressure-sensitive enriching device

1976 Indianapolis Pace Car was a Buick V-6. The engine was turbocharged with a single Rajay 301E10 turbo limited to 22 psi boost by a Rajay 337-156 wastegate valve. 231 CID engine produced over 315 HP at 4600 RPM and 370 lbs. ft. torque at 3900 RPM.

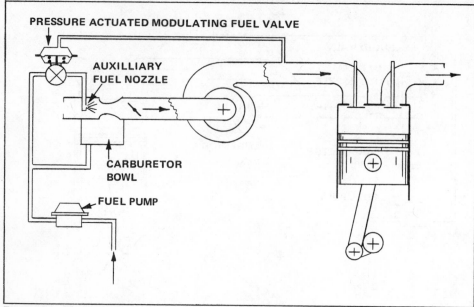

Figure 64—Modulating pressure-sensitive enriching device

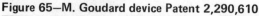

Figure 65—M. Goudard device Patent 2,290,610

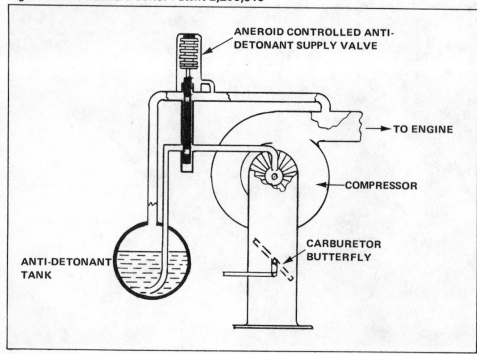

about 2 psi, extra fuel is sprayed into the carburetor, cooling the engine down and preventing detonation. Because it is possible to drive all day without ever reaching the supercharged condition, this modification is also a good fuel-saving device. It is an off-and-on system, so it is also a compromise where the engine will still be running too rich at 2 or 3 pounds boost pressure and too lean at 8 to 10 pounds boost pressure. It can be carried one step further by building a system shown in Figure 64. In this case, added fuel is controlled by a diaphragm which senses intake-manifold pressure. This system which will modulate the added fuel can be designed to enrich the mixture gradually as a function of the intake-manifold pressure. Although it can be made to do a better job than the pressure switch and solenoid, it will require considerably more development.

Just to make sure we don't think we are inventing the wheel again, Figure 65 shows a device patented by Maurice Goudard in 1942, Patent 2,290,610. This device was designed for an aircraft engine but not exclusively limited to one.

Even before that, two Englishmen, Fedden and Anderson designed a method of introducing anti-detonant to a supercharged engine. A schematic drawing of British Patent 458, 611 issued in 1936 is shown in Figure 66. These are shown for historical reasons but point out that supercharging had the same thermodynamic problems 40 years ago as it does today.

If a progressive two-barrel or four-barrel carburetor is used, the problem can be approached in a completely different manner. The power-valve modification is still valid but the extra fuel enriching can be done completely in the secondary. When a progressive type of carburetor is used, the primary barrel or barrels have all the systems necessary to run the engine and, as mentioned before, the secondary is used to get the maximum out of an engine at very high RPM. This problem does not exist on a turbocharged engine because any pressure drop through the carburetor within reason can be made up by the compressor of the turbocharger. On a naturally-aspirated engine if the ambient pressure is 30 inches Hg, the engine can only put out $\frac{30-4}{30}$ or 87% of its potential. When the secondaries of a progressive carburetor open and drop this restriction down to practically nothing, the engine can then achieve its full potential as far as breathing capacity is concerned. The case is quite different with a turbocharged engine because it is possible to have even 8 inches drop through the carburetor and still have a manifold pressure of 10 or 15 psig. The point I am making is, the use of a progressive carburetor on a turbocharged engine is not significant from a power viewpoint. But, its two separate fuel/air systems can be utilized very well to give the correct fuel-air ratio to the engine under both naturally-aspirated and supercharged conditions. Secondary butterfly/s on a progressive carburetor can be actuated by several different methods. A simple mechanical linkage can start to open the secondary when the primary is three-quarters open or the secondaries may be diaphragm-operated using the vacuum drop through the primary venturi as a vacuum source. These carburetors usually have an interlock to prevent the secondaries from opening at part load. This type of actuation as used on the Holley 4150 Series carburetors lends itself to modification, Figure 67. The modification is as follows: The interlock between the primaries and secondaries was removed completely. The diaphragm assembly was taken apart and the spring moved to the opposite side of the diaphragm. The linkage was reworked so that pressure on the diaphragm would open the secondary while the spring would tend to close it. When a carburetor is modified in this way, there is no mechanical linkage between the primary and the secondary butterflies. All modes of engine operation take place using the primaries only until the intake-manifold pressure overcomes the spring in the diaphragm and opens the secondary butterflies. Because this can only occur in the supercharged condition, it is possible to select main and power jets for the primary to give the ideal air-fuel ratio at naturally-aspirated conditions. The jets in the secondary system can be sized for a rich condition which is more compatible with high intake-manifold pressures. If the diaphragm were connected to the intake manifold without any other modifications, the secondaries would not close when the

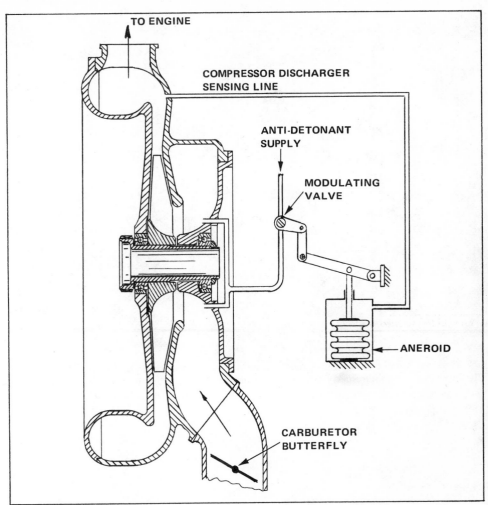

Figure 66—Fedden and Anderson anti-detonant, British Patent 458,611

Figure 67—Schematic of progressive carburetor with pressure-operated secondary

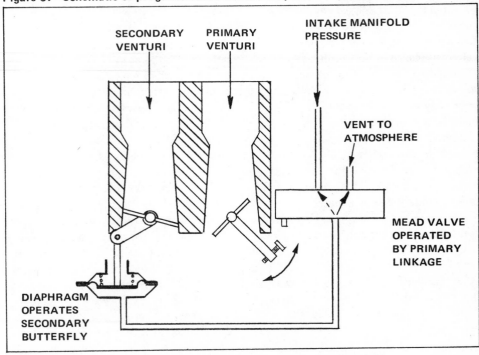

Author's twin turbocharged Corvair engine before it was installed shows diaphragm actuator for secondary throttles rearranged to open them with manifold pressure rather than primary vacuum.

driver's foot was removed from the accelerator pedal; the engine would continue to run in the supercharged condition on the secondaries alone. To prevent this from happening, a small three-way Mead valve was placed in the sensing line and mounted on the side of the carburetor so the valve actuated only when the primaries were fully opened. As soon as the primaries close, the Mead valve vents the secondary diaphragm to the atmosphere causing the secondaries to close immediately. This Mead valve is the same size and shape as a standard Microswitch and is actuated in the same manner.

This carburetor set-up gives a different feeling to the car than the standard set-up because the secondaries will not open until manifold pressure has reached about 1 psig. When this happens, there is not only a sudden jump in the manifold pressure but a definite feeling of being pushed from the rear.

Ever since turbochargers have been available for use on carbureted engines, the question as to whether it is better to suck or blow through the carburetor comes up. There are advantages and disadvantages either way and before we start knocking one or the other remember excellent results have been obtained with both methods. The biggest advantage of blowing through the carburetor is that it requires the least modification to the engine intake system. Fuel lines, choke mechanism and accelerator linkage may all be left as is. Some people say that blowing through the carburetor makes the turbocharger more efficient but this is *not* so. The efficiency of the turbocharger is a function of the design of the turbocharger and cannot be changed by carburetor location. If the peak adiabatic efficiency of a compressor is 75%, it will be 75% regardless of whether the carburetor is upstream or downstream of it. When people say this, I think they actually mean capacity rather

than efficiency. Because there will always be a pressure drop through the carburetor, a turbocharger compressor downstream of the carburetor sees air below atmospheric pressure. Because the centrifugal compressor is a CFM device, the maximum flow which it can handle will be the same but the maximum pounds per minute will be greater when the intake conditions never go below ambient. Saying this in a different way, a slightly higher capacity compressor is needed when sucking through the carburetor to achieve the same maximum horsepower. If a large enough carburetor is used, this size difference is insignificant.

One big advantage of blowing through the carburetor is it is not necessary to have a positive seal on the compressor end of the turbocharger. If a turbocharger is scrounged from a farm tractor or a piece of construction equipment, chances are it will have a piston-ring seal on the compressor end. This type of seal is not recommended for use downstream from a carburetor because it will not seal oil much beyond 5 inches Hg, vacuum. Because it may have to see vacuum as high as 29 inches Hg, an engine with this type turbocharger sucking through the carburetor will have a lot of blue smoke come out of the exhaust. In addition, it won't take long to use up all the oil in the crank case. Don Hubbard suggests adding a second butterfly downstream of the compressor as was done on Schwitzer Turbochargers used on Indianapolis-type race cars. This second butterfly is linked to the main butterfly so the compressor seal never sees a high vacuum.

Getting back to the advantages of blowing through the carburetor, the people who designed the original engine, in the case of a passenger car, did a pretty good job of designing the intake manifold to conduct the air fuel mixture from the carburetor to the cylinders. When this system is left intact, the distribution remains about the same. If this system is changed, as when the carburetor is removed from the intake manifold and a turbocharger placed between the carburetor and the manifold, the connections from the compressor to the intake manifold become very critical. The fuel/air mixture comes out of the compressor discharge in a swirl which must be broken

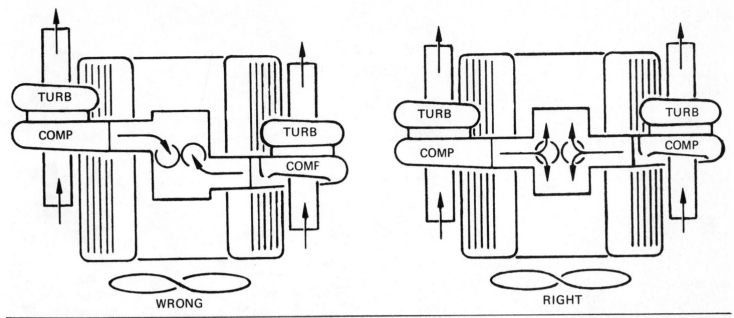

Figure 68—Method of ducting compressor outlets when using two turbochargers

up before it enters the intake manifold. This is usually done by having a square-cornered plenum at the junction of the compressor-discharge pipe and the intake manifold. If two turbochargers are used, as on a V-8, the square plenum chamber is not only important, but in addition the compressor discharges should be mounted to enter the plenum head-to-head rather than tangentially. Looking at Figure 68, the left sketch shows two compressors mounted with their discharge entering the plenum tangentially. When this happens, some of the cylinders will run lean while others will run rich. This situation can cause the engine to fail by burning holes in some of the pistons while the spark plugs are fouled from an over-rich condition in other cylinders. In one case when this happened, the inlets were changed to the configuration shown in the right sketch and no further distribution problems were encountered.

Similar problems have occurred where only one turbo was used. Duke Hallock's 289-CID Ford installation directed the turbo outlet into a *doghouse* atop the intake-manifold carb flange. A plate with 1/4-inch holes had to be added to restore turbulent flow for equal mixture distribution. An intercooler or a slightly longer tube between the turbo and the manifold might have accomplished the same end result. Any device between the turbo and

the engine which will break up swirls or laminar flow into turbulent flow is definitely recommended.

Cast manifolds usually have enough sharp bends to promote turbulence but fabricated intake manifolds must be carefully designed to prevent some fuel separation. Tuning the inlet system with individual runners of specific lengths to get a ram effect at a certain engine RPM is not recommended. The turbocharger compressor should provide all the air needed. Chances are a tuned system will work well at one speed only and could be a detriment at other speeds. Most turbochargers are designed to be run with the shaft horizontal. Because of this, a sidedraft carburetor is ideal for mounting purposes. There are, however, a few drawbacks to using them. For every sidedraft built there must have been a million downdrafts. By sheer numbers, the average downdraft carburetor is further developed, easier to procure and easier to service. There are a few exceptionally good sidedraft carburetors, but they are usually quite expensive. "One drawback with most U.S. passenger-car downdraft carbs is that they are subject to mixture changes due to G forces in one direction or another," says Ted Trevor. He developed kits to adapt the Weber 40 and 45 DCOE sidedraft carbs to Rajay turbos. Trevor claims only a little effort is required to get the Webers to provide

correct mixtures under G loads imposed by slaloms, road racing, hill climbs—or even the fast manuevering required for evasive action in everyday driving. As you will note from some of the accompanying photos, several engine builders have made good use of the Weber and SU-type sidedraft carburetors in various turbocharged applications.

Another advantage to blowing through the carburetor is all carburetors on passenger cars have some method of warming to prevent icing conditions. It is usually accomplished on an in-line engine by bolting the exhaust manifold directly to the intake manifold underneath the carburetor. On some in-line engines, a water-heated spacer is placed between the carburetor and the intake manifold, or the intake manifold is heated by jacket water.

On a V engine, the two exhaust manifolds are often connected by a heat-riser passage through the intake manifold to allow hot exhaust gases to heat the intake manifold in the carburetor area. Some V engines have jacket water passages in the intake manifold to keep it warm and some have both a heat riser and a water jacket. When the turbocharger compressor is placed between the carburetor and the intake manifold, it is possible for the carburetor to "ice up" and also for fuel to condense in the compressor housing. Some turbochargers have been designed with water-jacketed compressor housings, but most are designed to keep the compressor housing as cool as possible to increase the volumetric efficiency. To prevent carburetor icing, a spacer should be placed between the carburetor and the compressor similar to Figure 69. A drilled or cored passage through the spacer should be connected in series with the heater to allow hot water to flow through the passage. If the carburetor-discharge temperature remains about 60°F., neither icing nor condensation will normally take place.

If a downdraft carburetor is used, a water passage should be drilled or cored on the bottom of the elbow, Figure 70. If fuel is allowed to collect anywhere in the induction system, a liquid slug will be carried into the cylinder when the throttle is opened. This can cause anything from stalling to overspeed.

One of the disadvantages of blowing through the carburetor is fuel pressure. The average fuel pump will not produce more than about 5 psig fuel pressure to the carburetor. This is fine on a naturally-aspirated engine but will not work on a blown carburetor. If the turbocharger is delivering 10 psi to the carburetor, it is impossible for fuel to flow. One way to overcome this problem is to add a high-pressure electric pump in series with the engine-driven pump, but located between the mechanical pump and the carburetor. Otherwise, the mechanical pump will act as a regulator. This will deliver enough fuel pressure when the engine is super-charged but will also deliver high pressure at part load. If the additional pressure is great enough to overcome the buoyancy of the inlet valve float, fuel will pour through the carburetor and flood the engine. In some cases the exhaust pipe will act like a blow torch.

Duke Hallock, former high-performance coordinator and test-lab supervisor for AiResearch, has been driving the same 1937 Ford pickup since it was new. 292 CID engine with AiResearch T-7 turbo is one of many engines he has installed in the chassis over the years. A plate perforated with 1/4-inch holes is used at the original manifold flange to get turbulent flow and good mixture distribution.

Dyno-test set-up at M & W gear with blow-through carburetor and water-cooled turbine housings on Ford 302 CID V-8 for marine use.

Overpressure can be prevented by operating the electric fuel pump with a pressure switch. The switch should be set to start the pump only when the manifold pressure goes above atmospheric. This will work but it costs money, adds another potential source of trouble, and does not control the fuel pressure smoothly.

The high-performance Holley electric fuel pump has a remote regulator which is mounted near the carburetor. One side of this remote regulator is vented to atmospheric pressure through a set-screw factory-set to give 6 psi outlet from the regulator. The pump itself is factory-adjusted to give 12 psi through the fuel line to the regulator. The regulator vent can be hose-connected to the duct which feeds air to the carburetor from the turbo so that any boost pressure will automatically raise the outlet pressure by the amount of the boost. In the normally aspirated condition, the fuel pressure will remain at 6 psi. Because the Holley pump produces 12 psi pressure, the maximum boost that can be accommodated with the pump/regulator combination is 6 psi. At any boost above 6 psi, the effective fuel pressure will be reduced by the amount that the boost exceeds 6 psi. For example, 8 psi boost will lower the fuel pressure to 4 psi. However, these pumps and regulators can be used with boost pressures in excess of 6 psi by reworking the pump to operate at a higher pressure.

Looking at the cross section of a typical fuel pump in Figure 71, it is apparent the rocker shaft, operated by the engine cam, serves only to compress a spring which is the force used to pump the fuel. The fuel pressure will remain constant so long as the flow is less than pump capacity. The pressure can be increased by putting in a stiffer spring; but, as in the case of the electric pump, it will deliver the higher pressure even when not needed.

Figure 72 and Figure 73 are cross sections of Corvair and Volkswagen fuel pumps. The Corvair pump has its operating spring located on the top side of the diaphragm. In this case, if a fitting is attached to the vent hole and a line connected to the compressor discharge, the spring will be assisted by the compressor-discharge pressure and will always deliver standard pump pressure *plus* supercharge pressure. The pump in effect becomes a pressure regulator.

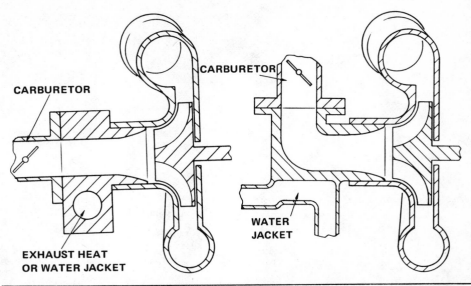

CARBURETOR

CARBURETOR

EXHAUST HEAT OR WATER JACKET

WATER JACKET

Figure 69—Sidedraft carburetor adapter with built-in heater

Figure 70—Downdraft carburetor adapter with built-in heater

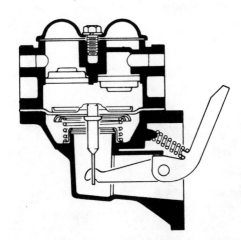

Figure 71—Typical automotive fuel pump

Figure 72—Corvair fuel pump

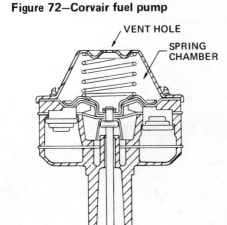

VENT HOLE

SPRING CHAMBER

The Volkswagen fuel pump has the spring on the bottom of the diaphragm but the rocker arm is driven by a push-rod, which is in turn driven by the engine cam. The pushrod fits loosely in a plastic guide. If the pushrod is replaced with one which fits snugly in the guide, the lower chamber of the pump may be pressurized by connecting an air line from the compressor discharge. Then the pump will always deliver adequate fuel pressure. The rod can also stick in the up position, causing the pump to cease operating. However, when running supercharged, pressure will tend to prevent sticking if the rod is very smooth.

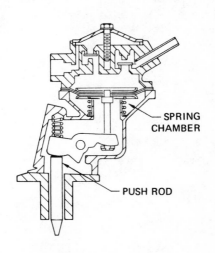

SPRING CHAMBER

PUSH ROD

Figure 73—Cross section VW fuel pump

TRW made this installation on a 1963 Corvair with a prototype Rochester fuel-injection system. Performance was phenomenal but high cost kept this one out of production.

V-6 Ford turbocharged by engineer Eric Fuchs of Ford's Advanced Vehicle Operations. This is a blow-through-the-carburetor installation. Photo courtesy Ford of England.

Car & Driver magazine staffers turbocharged this Opel and wrote an article on it. Turbo is a Rajay unit. Note how neatly everything works together, even with all of the emission controls kept intact. Pat Bedard photo.

Another tight-fit problem solved: Corvettes are hard to turbocharge because of underhood space limitations. Larson Engineering offers this blow-through system with an AiResearch turbo, Blake wastegate, water injection and a special pressure-relief valve in the cast aluminum adapter atop the carburetor. Stainless-steel exhaust system is featured as part of the kit. Lower photo shows a dual turbo kit by the same company. It fits under the Corvette hood, but only if your desire for neck-snapping performance exceeds your need to stay cool, as the second turbo takes up the spot ordinarily occupied by the air-conditioning compressor.

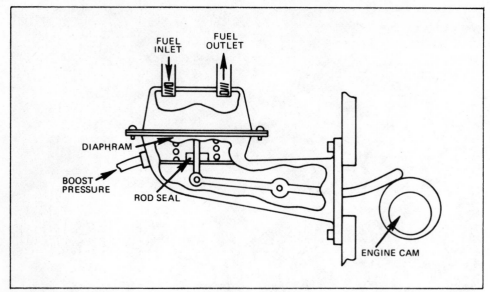

Figure 74—Diaphragm-type fuel pump with rod seal

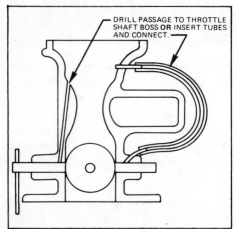

Figure 75—Air-sealed throttle shaft

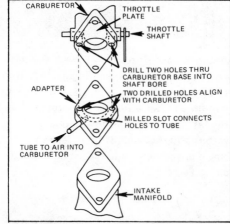

Figure 76—Adapter for carburetor-flange air seal

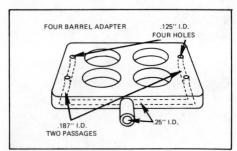

Figure 77—Adapter for 4-barrel carburetor flange

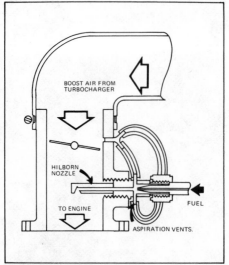

Figure 78—Fuel injection aspriation venting

NOTE: Figures 74 through 78 are from Crane Cams' Turbocharger book, courtesy Crane Cams.

This method may be used on any fuel pump where the spring chamber can be sealed from the crankcase, Figure 74, but will not work on a fuel pump where the spring chamber is essentially open to the crankcase. It is neither practical nor safe to supercharge the engine crankcase on a four-cycle engine.

After all these problems have been solved, it may still be impossible to pressurize a carburetor because the design of the carburetor may not lend itself to being sealed. In this case, it will be necessary to build a box around the carburetor and run the linkage through a seal in the box.

Don Hubbard has done quite a bit of turbocharging by blowing through the carburetor and makes the following suggestions: The carburetor needs to be inspected to make sure that all float bowl and other vents are vented into the air-horn area so that air or air fuel mixture cannot be blown outside the carburetor if the carburetor is to be pressurized from the air-cleaner flange. The next thing needed is to get a foam-plastic or Nitrophyl float. Brass floats with flat sides may collapse under pressure or accidental back firing and then sink and flood the engine. A brass float can have a small hole drilled in it and the plastic foaming liquid poured in. After the plastic foam has hardened, the hole can be resealed. Many modern carburetors come with foam floats or replacements are available. Brass SU cylindrical floats are usually strong enough to withstand boost pressure. Don then suggests sealing the throttle shafts. The choke shaft only leaks dry air so it needs no seal. If the throttle shaft has no linkage required on one end, it can be shortened and a plug pressed into the end of the bore. Mechanical seals are not the best way to seal a throttle shaft because of friction. The best way is an air seal. Take dry air from above the venturi and duct it into the throttle shaft boss. The air pressure above the venturi is slightly higher than that below so some dry air leaks out. But also, some leaks into the throttle bore carrying the fuel/air mixture with it. This also creates no extra friction. Some carburetor castings can be merely drilled while some may require drilling and pressing in small tubing connected with flexible tubing, Figure 75.

Don also suggests another method of sealing the carburetor throttle shafts by

58

machining a special adapter flange, Figures 76, 77, and drilling holes through the bottom of the carburetor flange directly into the throttle shaft. In a two-shaft carburetor—four barrel or staged two-barrel—be sure to balance the drilled hole areas so that one hole will not rob pressure from the other holes.

Turbocharging a fuel-injected engine has many of the same problems as blowing through a carburetor because the injection nozzles are always on the pressure side of the compressor. Port fuel injections such as used on the Chevrolet Corvette Engines have aspirated nozzles. This is done mostly to prevent vacuum from sucking fuel from the nozzle at idle or very low load conditions. When engines with this type fuel injection are supercharged, pressurized air is forced out through the nozzle preventing the fuel from entering. To eliminate this problem, the aspiration vents must be connected to the compressor discharge, Figure 78, suggested by Don Hubbard. In addition to this, it is necessary to increase the fuel-injection pressure to ensure good fuel flow at supercharged conditions.

One of the modifications made to carburetors in an effort to reduce air pollution is a vent from the fuel bowl to a charcoal canister. This same canister is usually connected to the fuel tank to capture gasoline fumes from that source, too. The fellows who invented this system did not have turbocharged cars in mind—or at least those which blow through the carburetor—because pressure from the compressor will supercharge the float-bowl chamber. And, unless a check valve is placed in the vent line to the charcoal canister, it will also supercharge the canister and the fuel tank. A simple blowoff line which opens at 1/4-pound pressure and connected to the air cleaner should do the job.

In general, a high-output turbocharged engine requires the same or even less CFM carburetion capacity than a high-output naturally-aspirated engine. As an example, when Rajay turbocharged a 1971 Oldsmobile 350 CID engine which normally aspirated had a 725-CFM Quadra-jet, they got best results with a single Holley 600-CFM double-pumper. Crown Manufacturing's Datsun 240Z installation uses only one of the two SU-Type carburetors provided on the engine, yet gets near 100-MPH performance in the 1/4 mile.

Some people think an air cleaner is a waste of time and power on a high-performance engine. The compressor impeller in Figure 79 is a good example of what can happen when an air cleaner is not used. Ted Trevor says, "There may be instances where an air cleaner is not desired—like a boat which never comes to port—or an airplane which never lands. All other applications of internal combustion engines need air cleaners." A small rock or a piece of metal such as a screw or nut will wipe out a compressor impeller. Parts of the impeller will then pass through the engine, perhaps causing extreme damage.

Carburetor butterfly screws should be staked in place to prevent them from backing out. This should be done very carefully using a backup anvil on the opposite side of the shaft so there will be no chance of bending the shaft.

Table VIII was compiled to show the advantages and disadvantages of blowing

Figure 79—Compressor impeller with chopped-up blades

and sucking through the carburetor. As you can see neither method is perfect but, on the other hand, either method will do a good job when done correctly.

TABLE VIII
Advantages and disadvantages of blowing or sucking through the carburetor

FEATURE	BLOW THROUGH	SUCK THROUGH
1. Location of carburetor and linkage	No change	Must be moved
2. Fuel pump	Requires either extra pump or one compensated for compressor discharge pressure	No change
3. Positive crankcase ventilation	Must be moved to compressor inlet	No change
4. Fuel evaporation system	Must be equipped with check valve to prevent supercharging fuel tank	No change
5. Carburetor leakage	All holes and shafts must be sealed or complete carburetor boxed	No change
6. Distance from carburetor to cylinder	No change	Much longer
7. Carburetor float	Might collapse unless made of closed-cell plastic	No change
8. Turbocharger oil seal	Nothing special required	Must have positive seal on compressor end
9. Compressor surge	Can be a problem on deceleration	Not ordinarily a problem
10. Compressor size	Inlet pressure always atmospheric so maximum capacity always available	Inlet pressure below atmospheric so slightly larger physical size is required in some cases
11. Carburetor inlet temperature	Low temperature at low load, high temperature at high load	Constant temperature, regardless of load
12. Vacuum source for brakes, air-conditioning etc.	Sporadic, requires check valve	No change

Porsche's Turbo Carrera coupe was introduced to the world market in 1975. Car is a true race-bred machine offering outstanding appeal to the motoring enthusiast. 1978 models feature an intercooler in the whale-tale rear spoiler.

Schematic of exhaust and intake plumbing on the 1978 Porsche Turbo Carrera six-cylinder engine. Item 9 is the intercooler. Drawing and photos courtesy Porsche-Audi Public Relations.

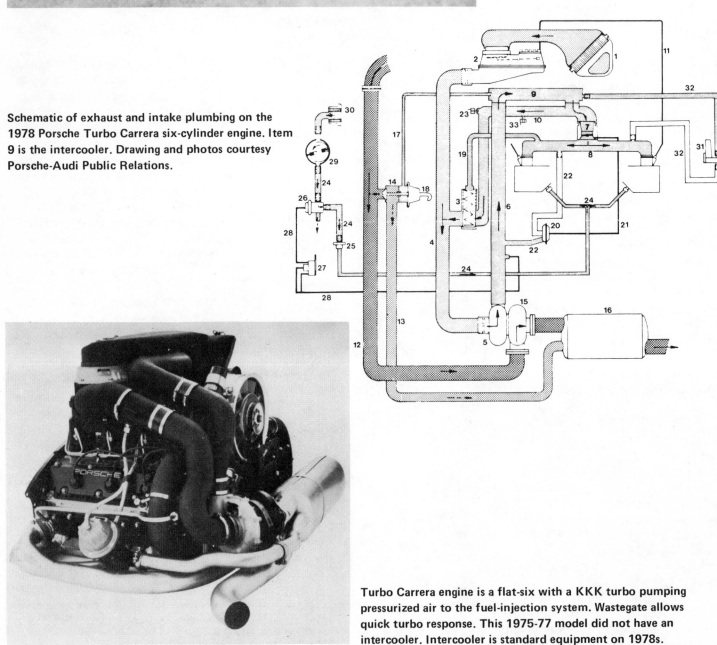

Turbo Carrera engine is a flat-six with a KKK turbo pumping pressurized air to the fuel-injection system. Wastegate allows quick turbo response. This 1975-77 model did not have an intercooler. Intercooler is standard equipment on 1978s.

The ignition system for a turbocharged engine is not much different than that for a high-performance naturally-aspirated engine. It has to make a spark at the right time to fire the charge and the things going on outside the combustion chamber are about the same in either case, although higher pressures inside the combustion chambers create a few extra problems for the turbocharged engine.

When spark plugs are cleaned by sand blasting, there is usually a little chamber in the machine where the spark plug can be inserted and pressure applied to see if it will fire under pressure as well as at atmospheric conditions. This chamber has a little glass window so the actual spark may be observed. A little experimentation will show as the pressure in the chamber is increased, the spark gap on the plug must be decreased to make it fire. This same problem exists in a turbocharged engine. The combustion-chamber pressure at the time of ignition will be considerably higher than on a naturally-aspirated engine of the same compression ratio and, therefore, it is necessary to reduce the spark gap to ensure positive ignition when maximum boost is developed. The recommended gap on most naturally-aspirated passenger cars is around 0.035 inches. It is a good idea to reduce this to 0.025 inches when adding a turbocharger.

Plug heat range—as in a naturally-aspirated engine—is determined by the use of the engine. However, even in ordinary street use, one range colder than production is recommended. Don't go too cold or you will have the same plug-fouling problems on a turbocharged engine as you would have on a naturally-aspirated engine.

Some ignition cables consist of cotton or similar material impregnated with carbon. This is done to reduce radio and TV interference and the wires are called *TVR*. On a typical passenger car where the plugs are changed maybe once a year, the cable could last the life of the car. In the hands of a hot rodder or enthusiast, it's a different story. The whole harness might be removed and replaced dozens of times. This will cause flexing of the cables and possibly an increase in the resistance. In one instance, an engine was missing badly for no apparent reason. After trying everything else, it was decided to check the resistance of the spark-plug leads. The resistance was supposed to be 20,000 ohms but one lead had 200,000 ohms. The whole wiring harness was replaced and the engine ran without missing.

TVR-type wires should be replaced with steel-core wires or with the MSW Magnetic-Suppression Wire. The MSW type should be installed if the vehicle is radio-equipped or if there is any reason to be concerned about radio/TV interference. It has all of the advantages of the resistance-type wire with none of the disadvantages. In addition, it should be noted that resistance-type wire cannot be used with capacitive-discharge ignition systems. These systems will quickly destroy the TVR wire.

Ignition systems on present day passenger cars are equipped with several mechanisms to prevent spark advance any time when such advance might increase NO_x in the engine exhaust. These devices vary from car to car but, in general, they consist of no vacuum advance in the lower gears, no vacuum advance until the engine has come up to temperature and no vacuum advance

before a preset engine speed. Some also have spark retard during deceleration and at engine idle.

As bad as these things sound, a turbocharger may be applied to an engine with these ignition devices and still get very good performance. *A turbocharger is one of the few ways of getting a large increase in engine performance without disturbing the emission-control devices.*

When turbocharging an older engine not equipped with these emission devices, the spark curve should be adjusted to get the maximum out of the engine either in the naturally aspirated or the turbocharged mode. Because a turbocharged engine is normally a low-compression-ratio engine running on high-octane gasoline, it is able to accept extremely advanced timing at the lower speeds when no turbocharging takes place. This was done on the Corvair Spyder where the distributor was set with an initial advance of 24° BTDC. This 24° advance gave pretty good performance until about 2,000 RPM when the intake-manifold pressure became positive. At this point, the pressure-retard device—used instead of a vacuum-advance device on the distributor—retarded the spark approximately 10 crankshaft degrees at 2 psig boost. At 3,800 RPM the engine was able to stand more spark advance even with the high intake-manifold pressure. The centrifugal advance of the distributor came into effect at this speed and advanced the spark another 12 degrees by 4,500 RPM. This combination of centrifugal advance and pressure retard was worked out on the dynamometer and, at the time, seemed to be the best compromise to get maximum power from the

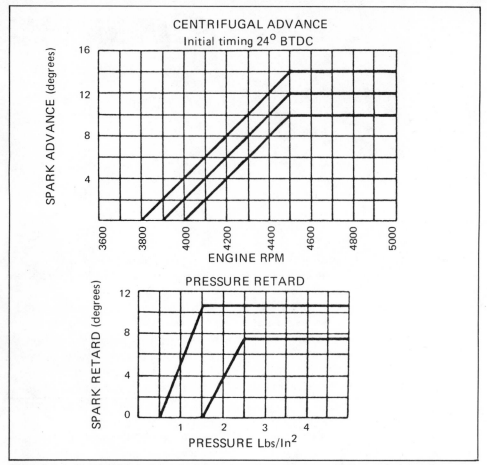

CENTRIFUGAL ADVANCE
Initial timing 24° BTDC

(graph: SPARK ADVANCE (degrees) vs ENGINE RPM)

PRESSURE RETARD

(graph: SPARK RETARD (degrees) vs PRESSURE Lbs/In²)

Corvair Spyder distributors used a pressure-retard unit instead of a vacuum-advance unit. Spark retards when manifold sees boost, partially opposing the effects of centrifugal advance. Initial distributor setting is 24° BTDC. Curves show advance/retard production tolerances of the centrifugal and pressure-retard mechanisms.

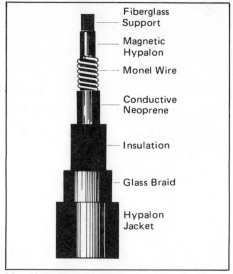

Magnetic-suppression wire construction details.

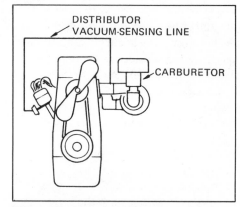

Figure 80—Vacuum-advance sensing line location

engine without detonation problems. As mentioned in the carburetion chapter, the carburetor used on this engine had no provision to add extra fuel to the mixture when the engine was running in the turbocharged condition. Using either a fuel-enriching device or some type of water or water/alcohol injection eliminates the need for the pressure-retard device and good results have been obtained with a vacuum-advance device although it is recommended to attach the vacuum line to the intake manifold where it will sense manifold pressure rather than pressure at the spark-advance port, for the same reason the power valve sensing line of the carburetor should be connected to the intake manifold instead of sensing butterfly pressure, Figure 80.

The pressure-retard diaphragm from the Corvair Spyder fits other four- and six-cylinder distributors used by General Motors from 1962–74.

The centrifugal-advance curve and pressure retard for the Corvair may not neces-

sarily be the best for another engine and the best spark curve must be worked out either on a dynamometer or on the road. For example, in the case of 1,600cc Volkswagen, the engine seemed to operate best at 26° spark advance at 4,000 RPM. When the spark was advanced beyond this, the exhaust temperature cooled down, resulting in lower boost pressure and less horsepower. On the other hand, with less than 26° spark advance, boost pressure went up a little but the engine lost power due to the late ignition. Retarded timing also caused a sizable increase in head temperature.

Bill Reiste has had good success with some of the newer combination vacuum-advance/vacuum-retard mechanisms used on emission-controlled engines. He connects one port to the intake manifold and the other to the carburetor, Figure 81. By doing this he can have retard at idle, advance at part load and retard when supercharged.

Liquid-cooled engines do not seem to

be as sensitive to spark timing and can usually stand more advance at less than 3,800 RPM.

As in the case of naturally-aspirated engines, there is no best ignition timing for all turbocharged engines and the ideal timing for any engine will probably be the result of a lot of cutting and trying.

The difference between a transistor-switched ignition and the ordinary distributor and coil type is that with the conventional type of ignition, whenever the points are closed, the primary on the spark coil receives a charge of current from the battery. When the points open, this charge is immediately discharged through the condenser causing a high voltage in the secondary which fires the spark plugs. The faster the engine runs, the less time the coil has to build up a charge and if the engine speed gets too high, the secondary voltage will not be great enough to fire across the spark plug.

In the transistor system, the points are used merely as a trigger of a high-voltage electronic device which steps up the battery voltage before it enters the coil and therefore does not need as much time to build up a charge in the coil. Some ignition systems have been built with the higher voltage going through the points but this has a tendency to burn out the points very quickly. As long as the points are used only as a low-voltage, low-current triggering device, they should last a long time. In a breakerless ignition system, the triggering device is magnetic or optical rather than a mechanical switch. Starting and stopping of the current flow is accomplished by a solid-state diode.

Some turbocharged engines running at high speed and high boost pressures will suddenly backfire for no apparent reason. This is sometimes caused by too lean a mixture but can be the result of not enough secondary voltage. A good solid-state ignition system is sometimes the answer when this problem occurs.

To summarize, ignition does not pose any more difficult problems on a turbo-charged engine than on a naturally-aspirated engine but the timing is quite different and enough effort should be spent on this item or the results might be disappointing.

When I was reviewing this section in mid-1978 to see what needed to be added, it was obvious that Buick's unusual approach to ignition-timing control on their turbocharged V-6 should be included. This system, pictured in the schematic at right, reacts so quickly that you can usually hear only one or two "rattles" before the Electronic Spark Control (ESC) module has retarded the ignition and completely eliminated detonation. This system has been made possible by the rapid advances in electronics technology and is probably a forerunner of more sophisticated systems which will appear in future years.

The ESC approach allows using near-optimum spark advance at all times, even though gasoline octane may vary considerably. This provides a good boost toward obtaining best economy. It also eliminates the possibility of an unaware owner burying his or her foot in the throttle and leaving it there while the engine is destroyed by the ravages of detonation.

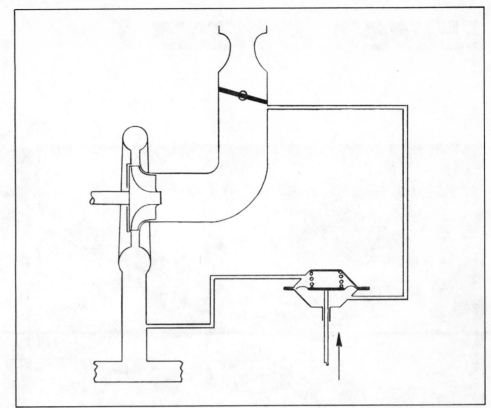

Figure 81—Bill Reiste's double-acting diaphragm

Buick's approach toward positive control of detonation is accomplished by an electronic spark control (ESC) which accepts a signal from the detonation sensor. When detonation occurs, the controller retards the spark electronically up to 22 degrees (crankshaft). This system was introduced on the 1978 Buick turbocharged V-6.

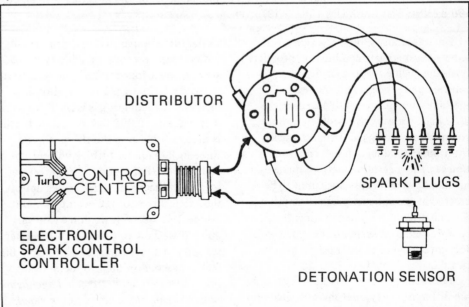

Fastest stock-block-based engine ever to run at Indianapolis. Smokey Yunick's small-block Chevrolet qualified for the 1973 race at 190.8 MPH; best finish was 13th in 1975. **Photo by Herb Fishel.**

On a naturally-aspirated engine, the exhaust system gets combustion products from the engine to the rear of the vehicle and reduces the noise level. At the same time it is desirable to create as little back pressure as possible on the engine. On a racing car, exhaust stacks from the individual cylinders are sometimes cut to a certain length to make use of the pulses and cause a vacuum to be created at the exhaust port at the instant the exhaust valve is opened. In either case, the exhaust system is designed to rob the engine of as little power as possible.

Turbocharged engine exhaust systems are different. They duct the hot, high-pressure, high-velocity gases from the engine

to the turbocharger without reducing its temperature, pressure or velocity if possible. As mentioned in the chapter about turbocharger design, a turbine housing increases the exhaust-gas velocity to somewhere around 2,000 feet per second. This is necessary because the tip speed of a three-inch-diameter turbine wheel rotating at 120,000 RPM is about 1,600 feet per second. If the exhaust gas comes out of the exhaust port of the engine at about 300 feet per second, we don't gain very much if we slow it down to 100 feet per second just so we can speed it up to 2,000 feet per second in the turbine housing. For this reason, *an extremely large-diameter exhaust manifold is not recommended.*

The area of the exhaust port is about right for the manifold.

There is nothing wrong with smooth flowing exhaust headers with beautiful swerving bends, but in the case of turbocharged engines, their use is more esthetic than power-increasing. This is evident when comparing turbocharged and non-turbocharged race cars. Turbocharged engines have relatively simple exhaust systems while the naturally-aspirated or mechanically supercharged engines usually have exhaust headers designed to eliminate all back pressure if possible.

One of the drawbacks of most V-8 engines is they have 90° crankshafts. This causes two adjacent cylinders on each bank to fire 90° apart. This overlap of exhaust pulses is not important unless the engine is used for all-out racing. To obtain maximum performance, the gases from the two ports should be ducted separately, rather than through a collector.

The problem is easily solved by using a 180° crankshaft if you can stand the vibration—and the cost of having one specially made.

On some engines, particularly V-8 engines with one turbocharger, it is desirable to have a slip joint in the exhaust duct between the two heads. Don Hubbard suggests the joint shown in Figure 83. This type has been used on aircraft engines for many years and surprisingly little leakage takes place because the inside pipe always gets hotter than the outside, causing the joint to become very tight. Don suggests 0.004 to 0.005-inch diametral clearance for mild steel and 0.005 to 0.008-inch on stainless steel.

It is not uncommon to insulate an exhaust pipe on a turbocharged engine as a means of keeping as much heat as possible in the exhaust gases. This insulation can cause other problems.

When a pipe is insulated, it becomes considerably hotter and may even get hot enough to burn out. Even if the pipe does not burn out, it tends to grow longer because of the higher temperature. If the ends of the pipe are restrained, this tendency to grow longer will put excessive stress on any bends and may cause the pipe to crack. This problem is particularly evident with the Volkswagen type exhuast.

Many passenger cars today do not have gaskets between the exhaust manifold and the head. This is not important as far as engine power is concerned although a leak could be dangerous to the passengers. A small leak at this joint on a turbocharged engine could cause a considerable boost loss. The effect is double because the turbine will slow down, not only from the lower volume flowing through it due to the leak, but also because the compressor will now be putting out less pressure due to the lower turbine speed making less pressure available to the turbine as well.

A good sandwich-type metal asbestos gasket should be used if available. The next best thing to use is a gasket cut from asbestos material backed with perforated metal. Straight asbestos-compound material is not satisfactory and will blow out in a short time. Embossed stainless

steel gaskets work well if both surfaces are very flat but are not recommended for use with stamped-steel flanges.

Even the best gaskets will not work if the exhaust manifold is warped. Check the mating surfaces for warpage and if any is evident have them machined to restore flatness.

When two or more turbochargers are used on an engine, best results can be obtained only if all of the turbochargers put out the same boost pressure. For this reason, it is desirable to use some type of balance tube between the two manifolds. A V-8 engine ordinarily has a heat riser which passes through the intake manifold to prevent fuel condensation in the manifold and icing in the carburetor. The heat riser should be left open because it will ensure equal pressures in both exhaust manifolds. If a heat riser is not available, exhaust manifolds should be joined with a balance tube of not less than 3/4-inch diameter.

In-line engines with intake and exhaust manifolds on the same side of the head ordinarily have a hot spot in the intake manifold over an opening in the exhaust manifold. It is used for the same purpose as the V-8 engine heat riser. Because minor exhaust leaks are not important on a naturally-aspirated engine, the joint between the exhaust and intake manifold may not be perfect and will allow exhaust-gas leakage if used on a turbocharged engine. Figure 84 shows how the opening in the exhaust manifold can be blocked by welding a plate in place and machining it flat so it will not interfere with the intake manifold.

Spent exhaust gases coming out of the turbocharger ideally should be flow-

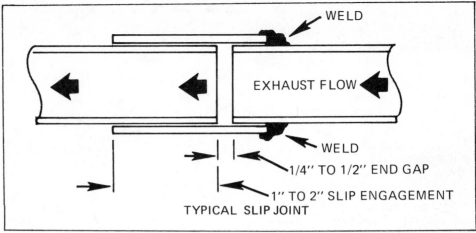

Figure 83—Typical slip joint for exhaust.

Figure 84—One way to close off in-line engine heat riser

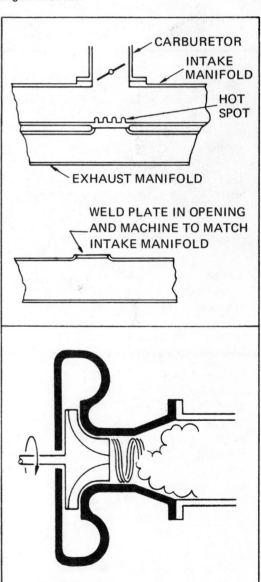

Figure 85—Turbine discharge with rapid expansion to convert swirl to turbulent flow

ing axially but actually will be rotating like a helix, Figure 85. The reason for this is the turbocharger is used over a broad range of engine speed and power and therefore the exhaust gases will sometimes be going faster than the turbine-wheel exducer—and sometimes slower. When they are going faster than the turbine wheel they will rotate in the opposite direction from the rotation of the turbine. When they are going slower than the turbine wheel they will rotate in the same direction as the turbine. In either case, the path for the exhaust gases will be considerably longer than if they were coming out axially. For this reason, it is desirable to break up the swirl and change the gases to turbulent flow as soon as possible after they leave the turbine housing. One way to do this is to have a sharp diffuser angle on the turbine housing, Figure 85. This requires a large-diameter exhaust pipe from the turbine housing. Once turbulent flow is established, it is not important for the exhaust pipe to be that big and after about eighteen to twenty-four inches, a smooth reduction in the cross section of the exhaust pipe will not create much additional back pressure and will help quiet exhaust noise. In some cases it will do such a good job that a muffler will not be required.

When a muffler is used, don't be misled by the amount of noise you hear at the back of the vehicle. The original Corvair Spyder muffler was extremely quiet but added very little back pressure to the system. When comparing one muffler to the other it is best to have a pressure gage between the turbine exhaust and the muffler.

Sometimes installation considerations cause the turbocharger to end up with the exhaust very close to an obstacle such as the engine-compartment firewall. When this happens, there may not be enough room to get an elbow between the turbine outlet and the exhaust pipe. Figure 86 shows a banjo-type turbine discharge sometimes used in close quarters.

Actual exhaust-pipe diameter used on a turbocharger system often depends on the application. Even on an all-out racing engine it may not be desirable to use as large an exhaust pipe as possible because a slight restriction in the exhaust pipe will be much more effective at high engine

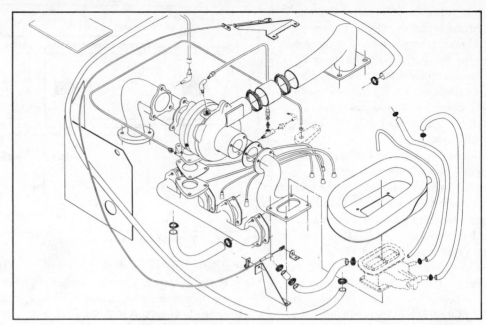

Exploded parts drawing of Car Corp. Pinto 2000cc kit components with cast exhaust manifold. Simple exhaust design is all that is required for the turbo. Free-flowing or "tuned" headers are not necessary and sometimes actually detract from the performance of the engine. Turbo Systems now makes this kit.

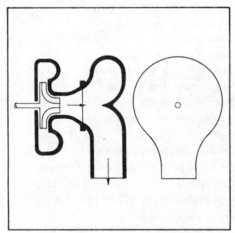

Figure 86—Banjo-type turbine discharge.

Duke Hallock wrapped the exhaust pipe coming from the turbine to reduce underhood temperature.

speeds than at lower speeds. This can be used as a fail-safe method of limiting manifold pressure without paying any power penalty at low and medium engine speed.

A leak in the engine-exhaust system large enough to cause considerable loss of boost may not be detectable to the ear because it will not necessarily leak at idle conditions, and at high engine speed everything makes so much noise even a large leak between the engine and turbine is hard to find. Ths can be very aggravating

because the turbocharger will not produce full boost and maximum power. The easiest way to check this is to block off the turbocharger exhaust completely while the engine is idling. If the engine continues to run, the leak is too big. When an engine does not deliver full power, the turbocharger will always be blamed. If the turbine and compressor wheels are intact and the shaft can be rotated, chances are 100 to 1 there is a leak in the exhaust system leading to the turbo.

1971 Olds 350 Cutlass turbocharged with two Rajay units was initially equipped with two special Rochester sidedraft carburetors. Turbo outlets oppose each other in connector above manifold opening. Car turned 105.41 MPH at 13.82 seconds ET at Orange County Raceway.

455 numbers? JT

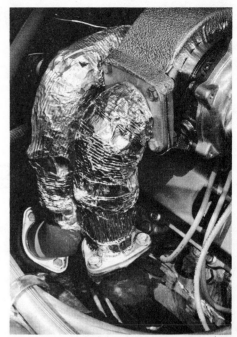

Experimental Oldsmobile 350 Cutlass installation by Rajay had new outlet welded onto each stock exhaust manifold. Aluminum foil on turbine inlet reduces heat loss so turbine operates with best efficiency. Wrapping the turbine housing and outlet pipe is done for safety and to reduce heating of the engine compartment. Two turbos were used in this installation.
Photos by Bill Fisher.

Mallicoat Brothers' 2400-pound glass-bodied BB Altered Gas class car turned 172.45 MPH at an 8.31-second ET in 1971. Chrysler hemi 467 CID engine produced 843 HP with a fully blueprinted Roots-type blower; 1,130 HP at 7000 RPM with two AiResearch TE06 turbos. Car was 10 MPH faster in turbocharged form. Note simple exhaust manifolding. Intake manifolds and injectors are Hilborn units.

Ak Miller displays his Pinto kit exhaust manifold. Manifold locates turbo so battery must be moved to left side. Gasoline and LPG kits are available.

8 LUBRICATION

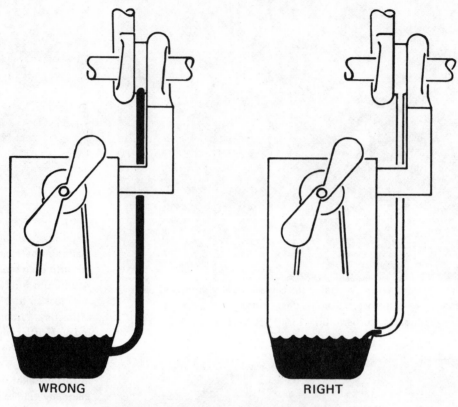

WRONG   RIGHT

OIL SHOULD DRAIN INTO CRANKCASE
ABOVE THE OIL LEVEL

Figure 87—Right and wrong way of draining oil from turbocharger

Turbocharger bearing and seal design was covered in Chapter 2, Turbocharger Design, but that is only half the story. A means must be provided to get clean lubricating oil to the bearings, and just as important, to get the spent oil back to the engine crankcase.

All turbochargers described in this book are designed to use engine lubricating oil. The actual type and viscosity will be dictated by the engine but, in general, a turbocharger will operate well on any oil that will work in the engine.

It is not necessary to install a special oil filter in the turbocharger oil line if the engine is equipped with an oil filter which passes particles of 30 microns or less. If an engine is not equipped with a full-flow oil filter, then a filter is definitely recommended in the oil-inlet line and it should be of the type with a built-in

bypass so oil will still get to the turbocharger even if the filter is clogged with dirt. It is not uncommon for a turbocharger to fail from lack of oil because the user has not serviced his oil filter. On the other hand, the life of a turbocharger running on dirty oil can be measured in hours.

It is usually safe to draw oil for the turbocharger from the opening where the low-oil-pressure light or pressure gage is normally connected. A tee should be placed in the line at the turbocharger end and the switch or pressure gage connected there. If there is a restriction at the point where the oil was taken off the engine, this will show up as low oil pressure as soon as the engine is started. Another test which should be made to ensure adequate oil to the unit is to disconnect the oil line from the turbocharger while the

engine is idling and measure the oil flow by running it into a bucket. At least .5 gallon per minute are required for each three-inch turbocharger and about 1.0 gallon per minute for each three and one half or four inch turbocharger.

Quarter-inch OD tubing is sufficient for a three-inch turbocharger while at least 5/16-inch OD tubing should be used for a three and a half or four-inch turbocharger. These tubing sizes are adequate if the engine is running on hot oil with at least 30 psi pressure. If the oil viscosity in the engine is too high for the ambient temperature conditions, no oil will flow to the turbocharger when the engine is first started. Here again, the low-oil-pressure switch or pressure-gage connection at the turbocharger will show this. If the engine is started and driven off under power before oil gets to the turbocharger, the bearings can be wiped out in a matter of minutes. Never use a screen or restrictor orifice in the turbocharger oil-supply line. Either will clog quickly and cause early turbocharger failure. If the oil pressure is so high the added flow causes drainage problems, it is better to place a pressure-reducing valve in the line than an orifice.

Oil entering the turbocharger from the engine is relatively air free but after passing through the bearings running as high as 130,000 RPM, it looks like dirty whipped cream. For this reason, it is necessary to have a much larger drain line on the turbocharger than on the oil-intake line. It is also necessary to have the line slant downward at all points without any kinks or sink traps. The drain line must dump oil to the crankcase above the oil level in the crankcase. Looking at Figure 87, the sketch on the left shows the oil line entering the crankcase below the oil level. This causes foamy oil to build up in the line and back up into the bearing housing of the turbocharger. The only place it can go from there is out through the seals. Many people have torn down turbochargers to replace leaking seals only to find they appeared as good as new. Chances are they *were* as good as new.

Before the days of emission-control devices on engines, the crankcase was normally equipped with a breather to prevent pressure from building up in the crankcase. This pressure is caused by blowby which occurs in all engines and is the result of high-pressure gases leaking by the piston rings of the engine. The breather allowed the blowby gases to escape but contained some kind of a filter element to prevent dirt from entering the engine. These breathers should be serviced regularly or they will become partially clogged and pressure will build up in the crankcase, preventing a free flow of drain oil from the turbocharger.

All passenger-car engines built today are equipped with a positive crankcase ventilation (PCV) device. The PCV design will vary with the engine but usually it will have one line going from the valve covers to the air cleaner and another line from the valve covers to the intake manifold. The line to the intake manifold is normally equipped with a PCV valve. This valve is designed to restrict flow from the crankcase when intake-manifold

vacuum is high and blowby is low. On the other hand, it has low restriction at full power when the intake manifold vacuum is low and the blowby is high. If the PCV valve is not serviced regularly, it will stick and cause pressure to build up in the crankcase. This, of course, will prevent the oil from draining properly from the turbocharger and cause leakage through the seals.

If your turbocharger shows signs of leaking oil into either the turbine housing or the compressor housing, be sure to check all these points before tearing it down only to find nothing is wrong.

When installing a turbocharger on an engine—particularly if it is part of a bolt-on kit—most people do not want to remove the engine from the vehicle unless absolutely necessary. Attaching the oil drain to the pan is rather difficult unless the pan is removed from the engine. In many cases, this can only be done by removing the engine from the vehicle. Because of this, it is desirable to find some other place to drain the oil back to the engine. If the turbocharger or turbochargers are mounted high enough, the oil may be drained back to one or both of the rocker-box covers. This will work on some engines but not on others because some have a problem of getting rid of the small amount of oil used to lubricate the rocker arms. Additional oil coming from the turbochargers can flood the rocker housing and back up into the turbocharger. On in-line engines, the plate which covers the valve push rods is often a good place to drain the turbocharger oil. Some V engines have either a hole through the intake manifold into the valley between the heads or, at least, there is a place in the intake manifold which has neither an air or water passage which can be drilled for draining oil back to the valley.

If the turbocharger is mounted so low it is not practical to drain the oil back to the engine, a scavenge pump must be used. This is often the case on an airplane engine where the only practical place to mount the turbocharger is beneath the engine. Remember the scavenge pump must have a much greater capacity than the amount of oil used by the turbocharger because of the air which gets mixed with the oil as it passes through the turbocharger. A scavenge pump for a

3-inch turbocharger should have a capacity of 1.5 gallons per minute. Aviaid Metal Products Company manufactures a scavenge pump specifically for turbocharged engines. This mechanical unit literally sucks the oil out of the turbocharger and pumps it into the engine sump. They are made in several sizes.

Most engines have an oil pump with enough capacity to handle a turbocharger as well as the engine. As mentioned earlier, if the oil-pressure gage at the turbocharger has a low reading, it is probably because of a restriction at the oil source rather than lack of oil-pump capacity. If it is established that there is no restriction on the oil supply and the oil pressure is still low, then a larger oil pump should be used. High-capacity pumps interchangeable with stock pumps are available for many engines but chances are one won't be necessary.

Innumerable high-capacity oil pumps available for Volkswagen engines are usually advertised for the purpose of lengthening the life of the crankshaft. Many turbocharged Volkswagens have been driven for what would be considered a high number of miles on a naturally-aspirated engine without excessive crankshaft wear. These engines were equipped with an oil filter which was probably more important than the high-capacity pump.

A turbocharger running at design speed will add about 80°F. to the oil as it passes through the bearings. Because the turbocharger is idling most of the time it is on a passenger car, this additional heat occurs only occasionally and the oil does not run much hotter than it would if the engine was naturally aspirated. This is not necessarily true on a truck, bus or a motor home where the turbocharger may be used for extended periods. On any of these applications I recommend installing an oil-temperature gage on the engine. If the oil temperature goes above 250°F. install an oil-cooler. These come in many shapes and sizes depending on the engine and the application but the important thing is to keep the oil cool to prevent oxidation.

A turbocharger lubricated with clean oil at engine pressure can be run for many years without any visible signs of wear on the bearing journals. On the other hand, if dirty oil or no oil at all is supplied to the turbocharger even for a short period of time, the chances are the unit will be short-lived.

9 CONTROLS

George Spears provided photos of two controlled turbocharger installations. Top one is a Porsche 911 with fuel injection. An IMPCO control is used to regulate boost to 11 psi for about 300 HP with a Rajay 375E.7 turbo. This installation was made in 1975, prior to the time when inexpensive exhaust-gas wastegate valves became available. A wastegate is preferable to the IMPCO "spoiler-type" control because there would be no heating of the fuel-air mixture by a restrictive control. MG Midget shows an installation where boost is controlled by the carburetor size and exhaust restrictions. Original rear-wheel HP was doubled to 70 HP with 11 psi boost. Rajay 301B.25 turbo installed by Shelby-Spearco.

Given enough time and money, it is possible to design a turbocharger engine combination to match the operating conditions—assuming they are known—and achieve optimum performance without any movable controls. The problem is, most of us do not have either the time or the money to do this and unless some type of control is used, the turbocharged engine will have to be a compromise and not achieve either maximum available horsepower or peak response. For street use or perhaps even for a Bonneville-type racer, a turbocharger can be matched to an engine without the use of controls and still give excellent performance.

This is not necessarily true in the case of a racing engine, whether it be for track, drag or boat racing. As an example, when a race driver is qualifying his car, he must get maximum horsepower from the engine but is not particularly concerned with durability. After the qualification is over and the race is run, then horsepower and reliability are equally important. If an adjustable control were not used here, then it would probably be necessary to use a different turbocharger for qualification than for the race. A similar situation could occur with a drag racer or a drag boat where adjustment of the maximum boost available could be made easily for maximum overall engine performance. It certainly would not be practical to change turbine-housing sizes between each run.

Another advantage of a turbocharger control is that it allows the turbocharger to be run at or near its maximum speed without bursting so long as the control works properly.

Turbocharger controls can generally be divided into two categories. Those which limit the speed of the turbocharger to prevent it from destroying itself; and those which limit the compressor-outlet pressure to keep it from destroying the engine. Because modern turbochargers will normally produce more pressure than the engine can stand, most controls are designed to limit compressor-outlet pressure.

The blowoff valve in Figure 88 is the simplest and also the least precise method of sensing turbocharger speed and controlling it at the same time. Although the valve itself might be either a poppet or flapper type, it will be subject to flutter-

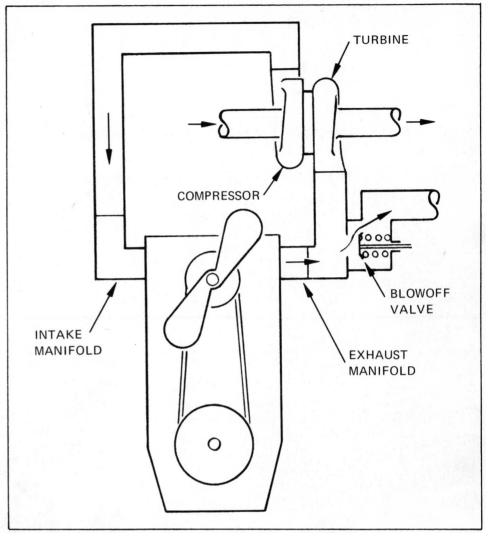

Figure 88—Turbocharged engine with simple exhaust-blowoff valve

ing unless a damper is attached. The valve will be opened by turbine-inlet pressure only, and although this will have a relationship to compressor-discharge pressure and rotor speed, neither will be exact. If flutter does occur, the valve will destroy itself in a short time.

It is possible to locate a blowoff valve on the compressor-discharge duct, Figure 89, but this is only recommended on a fuel-injected engine or where the compressor blows through the carburetor. This again is not an exact control and is subject to flutter. This type control has been tried as a manifold-pressure-limiting device by some racing officials, but racers are smart people and it did not take long for them to figure out it could be fooled by using a larger compressor. When the flow

of the compressor is much larger than the valve capacity, the valve no longer limits manifold pressure. BAE uses this type control on their installations and kits, calling it APC (absolute pressure control).

Figure 90 shows a compressor-inlet-controlled system. This system places a butterfly between the carburetor and the compressor. The valve reduces the air flow to the compressor and limits the manifold pressure. It has the advantage of the valve being on the cold end. The disadvantage is the manifold pressure is limited while the rotor speed might increase. It is not a good way of controlling maximum turbocharger speed. This higher speed also results in higher intake-manifold temperature while the pressure is being controlled.

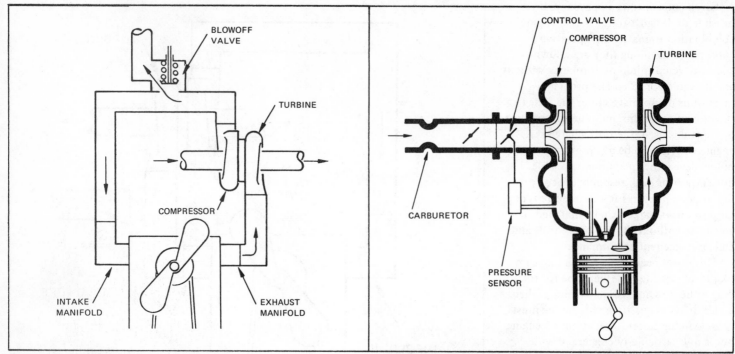

Figure 89—Turbocharged engine with compressor-blowoff valve

Figure 90—Compressor inlet-control system

BAE installation on 924 Porsche uses blow-off-type relief valve on feed duct from turbo to fuel injection. This is similar to Figure 89.

From a performance and efficiency standpoint, a variable-area nozzle as shown in Figure 91 is the best way to control turbocharger speed. With this method, all the gas goes through the turbine at all times and none is dumped overboard. The nozzle is opened and closed by an actuator controlled by the sensor. This method is often used on air turbines but is too expensive and unreliable for turbochargers because of the hot inlet gases. The mechanism must be made from materials which have good strength and corrosion resistance at elevated temperatures. Even then, combustion products will tend to jam the vanes and prevent reliable operation.

The most popular method of controlling turbocharger speed is with a wastegate or turbine-bypass valve. It can be either a butterfly—Figure 92; or poppet valve—Figure 93. The valve may be operated manually, Figure 94; by intake-manifold pressure, Figure 95; or by a servo motor, Figure 96. The servo in turn may be controlled manually or by a device which senses turbocharger speed, pressure ratio, gage pressure, absolute pressure, density, or air flow.

Figure 91—Turbine with variable-area nozzle

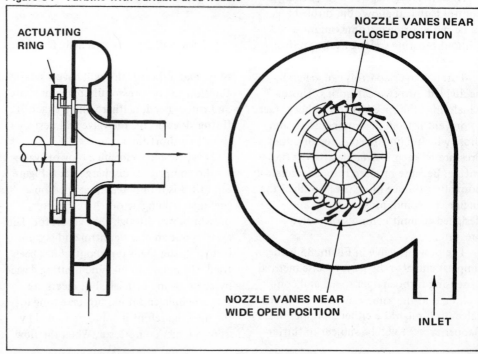

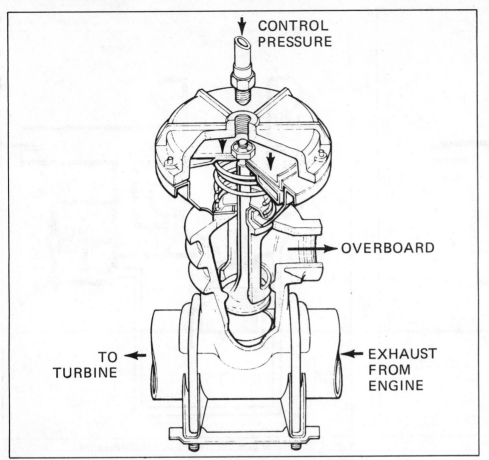

Roto-Master TurboSonic BPR (Boost Pressure Regulator) is a simple and inexpensive poppet-type wastegate. Its operational point is adjustable from 4 to 11 lbs. boost by changing color-coded springs. Or, the valve can be made adjustable as shown in the drawing on page 77. The saddle-mount version is shown in this drawing. A sandwich-type mount is shown in the photo at right. The control cartridge can also be screwed into the user's adapter.

Roto-Master BPR wastegate cartridge in sandwich-type adapter fits turbine inlet of AiResearch and Roto-Master TO4 models and Rajay turbochargers.

Figure 93—Poppet-type waste gate

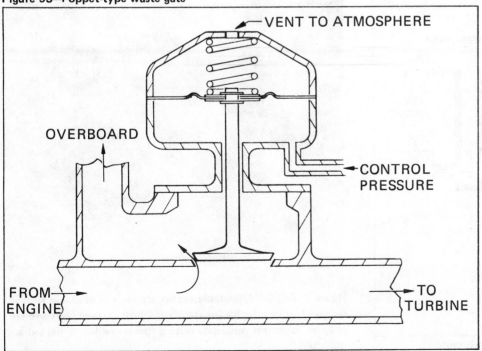

Figure 92—Butterfly-type waste gate.

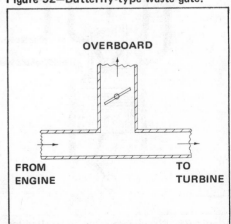

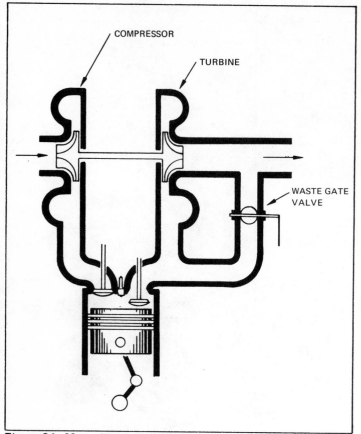

Figure 94—Manually-operated waste-gate valve

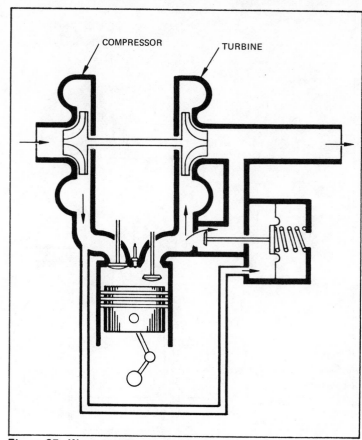

Figure 95—Waste gate controlled by intake-manifold pressure

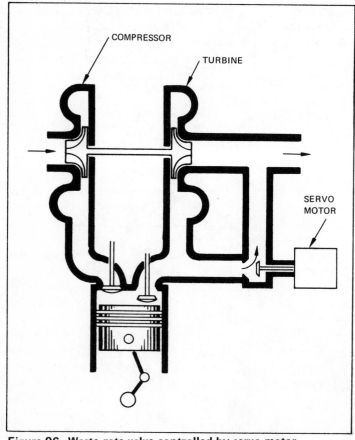

Figure 96—Waste-gate valve controlled by servo motor

Rajay 337-156A Adjustable Wastegate valve is available with sandwich-type adapter for standard 4-bolt turbine inlet and an adapter to mount wastegate onto a flange welded to the exhaust manifold.

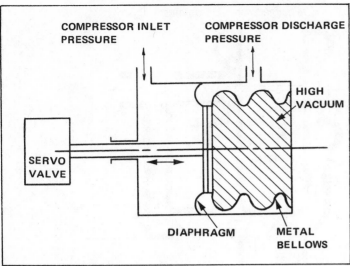

Figure 97—Pressure-ratio sensor

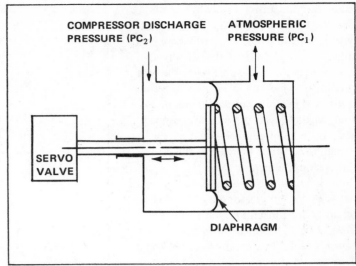

Figure 98—Differential-pressure sensor

Figure 99—Absolute-pressure sensor

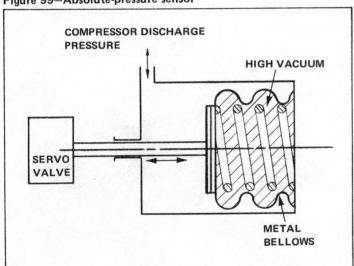

Figure 100—Density sensor

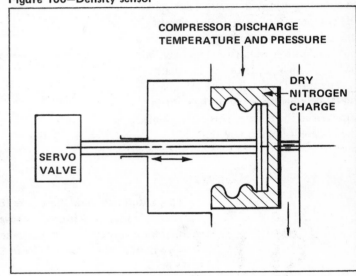

Turbocharger speed can be sensed by an electronic device and through the use of proper amplifiers operate a wastegate to control turbocharger speed. Because this requires not only an electric power source but rather elaborate electronic equipment, turbocharger speed is normally sensed by means of a pressure-ratio sensor because the pressure ratio on any specific installation is a direct function of speed. A pressure-ratio sensor is shown in Figure 97. This type sensor was used extensively years ago when turbochargers were run at the physical limits of the compressor impeller. If an engine equipped with a turbocharger were moved from sea level to some higher altitude, the turbocharger speed would increase if it were not controlled. The pressure-ratio sensor prevented this speed increase and allowed the engine

to be operated at high altitudes without requiring any changes in the engine or turbocharger.

A differential-pressure sensor in Figure 98 will sense the pressure differential across the compressor if PC_1 is connected to the compressor inlet and PC_2 is connected to the compressor outlet. If, however, PC_1 is vented to atmosphere, then it becomes a gage-pressure sensor, the most popular type used on engines operated mainly at one altitude. This type sensor connected to a wastegate will start dumping exhaust gas when a preset intake-manifold pressure is reached and will hold this pressure constant as the engine speed and power increases as long as the capacity of the wastegate is adequate.

An absolute-pressure sensor shown in Figure 99 is similar to the differential-

pressure sensor except that the volume around the spring is enclosed in a bellows evacuated of air. This vacuum not only gives an absolute-pressure reference but is not affected by air-temperature changes. This sensor type is desirable when the engine is to be used at many different altitudes such as an airplane engine. It has the big advantage of limiting the intake-manifold pressure to the same absolute value regardless of altitude of barometric conditions.

A density sensor, Figure 100, must be placed in the discharge-air stream of the compressor because it senses compressor-discharge temperature as well as pressure. It is a little fancy for the type of control we are talking about here and normally would not be used in a racing type of application.

A flow-control sensor, Figure 101, senses compressor-inlet flow by the differential pressure across the venturi. This type of control would be used where maximum torque is required at relatively low speed and it is possible with this type of control to have a higher boost pressure at low and medium speeds than at maximum engine speed. An engine equipped with this type of control would have a tremendous torque increase as the engine is slowed down.

A rather simple device can be placed between the compressor outlet and engine on an existing installion. Called the *IMPCO TC2 Turbocharger Pressure Control Valve,* its operation is shown in This valve is shown on several of the installation photos elsewhere in this book.

This valve should be very reliable because it is on the cold side and has only two moving parts. However, it can cause the compressor to surge if the operating line is too close to the surge line. This is a rather remote possibility and probably will not occur on a passenger-car installation.

The IMPCO valve is a restriction and therefore causes heating of the mixture supplied to the engine. This can increase the possibility of detonation.

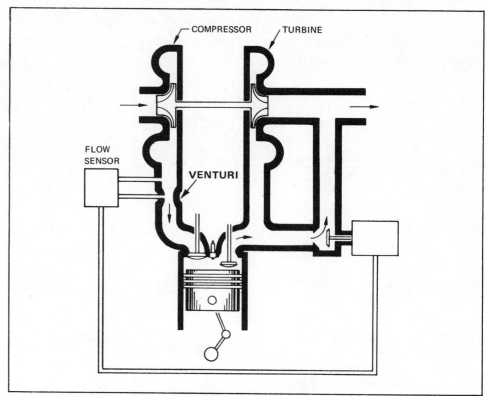

Figure 101—Waste-gate valve controlled by flow sensor

Blake Enterprises BPM Wastegate (Boost Pressure Modulator), is used by several other kit manufacturers and installers. Valve is infinitely adjustable from 6 to 18 psi boost.

HOW THE TC2 OPERATES

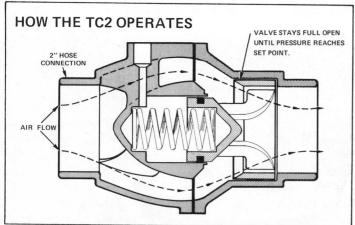

Figure 103—TC2 control valve has spring-loaded piston/sleeve valve in an enclosed housing. Spring pressure keeps piston/sleeve valve in open position as shown. This allows full pressure from turbo to flow through.

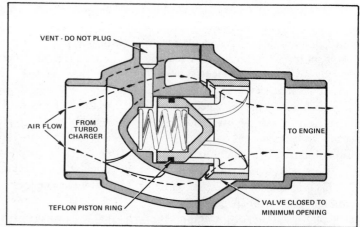

As pressure from the turbo increases, it works against the cone-shaped face of the piston. When pressure reaches the predetermined control point the spring will be compressed as shown. Piston/sleeve valve can move to close passage almost completely. This type of valve also limits RPM as it reduces volume of mixture supplied to engine.

Non-adjustable AiResearch wastegate is actuated by boost pressure from intake manifold. Arrow indicates connection for control piping. Valve typically opens less than 1/8 inch to bypass exhaust and reduce turbine speed and boost pressures. Adjustable wastegates have a screw in the cover to adjust the spring height and thereby boost pressure.

AiResearch T-3 turbocharger is used on the Buick V-6 and Ford Mustang and was being considered for a number of other automotive applications when this edition went to press in mid-1978.

Here is the simplest and least-expensive way I know to make a wastegate adjustable. The valve can be a simple needle valve.

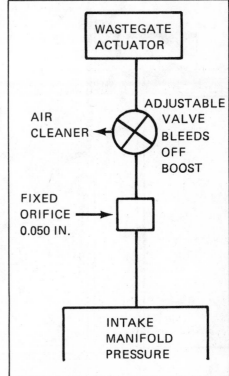

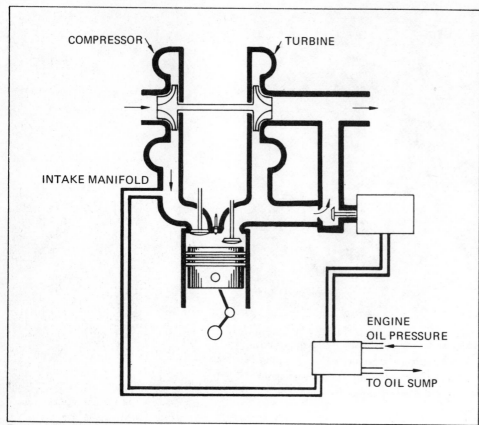

Figure 105—Waste gate operated by hydraulic servo

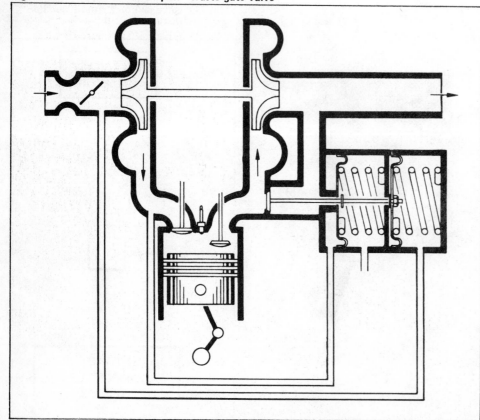

Figure 106—"Part-throttle open" waste gate valve

The combination of a device which senses intake-manifold gage pressure and a poppet-type wastegate valve is the most common method of controlling turbo-charger speed. Where ambient conditions are not likely to change abruptly, such as a racetrack, this type device is simple and fairly reliable. If the ambient conditions will change considerably such as the Pike's Peak Hill Climb, Ted Trevor has found the gage-pressure sensor is not adequate and suggests using an absolute-pressure sensor if one is available.

Most wastegates of this type use the intake-manifold pressure to open the wastegate against the force of a spring, Figure 95. A more exact method is shown in Figure 105 where the intake-manifold pressure operates a small hydraulic valve which allows engine oil pressure to flow through the wastegate servo and open the valve. This system has two advantages over the direct-operating wastegate in that it can use a smaller diaphragm on the wastegate because the oil pressure is usually much higher than the intake manifold pressure to be controlled. Also, since the oil is incompressible, the possibility of the wastegate valve chattering is eliminated.

On the other hand, the added complication of the hydro-pneumatic-servo leaves something else to go wrong. It can be made fail-safe by being spring-loaded. If the oil-pressure line fails, the valve will move to the full-open position.

When an engine such as that used in a passenger car is equipped with a free-floating turbocharger system which will not overboost the engine even at maximum conditions, back pressure on the engine at ordinary road loads is often less than that with a normal muffler system. To make a wastegate effective, it is always accompanied by a smaller turbine-housing area. This smaller turbine housing will cause more back pressure on the engine, particularly at road load. For this reason, automobiles equipped with a wastegate will ordinarily get poorer fuel mileage than one without wastegate. It is desirable to have the wastegate open at all conditions except when the turbocharger is needed for extreme acceleration or top speed. The part-throttle-open-valve shown in Figure 106, Patent 3257796, invented by Stanley Updike, does this and without complicated linkage. Looking at

Figure 106, notice that the upper diaphragm is connected solidly to the valve stem while the lower diaphragm is free to slide on the stem. A snap ring on the valve stem causes the lower diaphragm to open the valve but this diaphragm cannot close the valve. The chamber above the upper diaphragm is connected to the compressor inlet where it senses the pressure drop through the carburetor. The chamber below the lower diaphragm is connected to the intake manifold and senses both vacuum and pressure. At cruising power, the pressure drop through the carburetor will create a vacuum in the upper chamber which overcomes the spring and causes the valve to open when the pressure drop to the carburetor is greater than three inches Hg gage. During acceleration and at very low vehicle speeds, there will be little or no drop through the carburetor and the upper spring will cause the wastegate valve to remain closed. When the maximum desired manifold pressure is reached, the pressure underneath the lower diaphragm will overcome both the lower and upper springs and open the wastegate to maintain a relatively constant intake-manifold pressure. When connected to a small turbine housing, this type control has the same good low-end performance as a simple wastegate and still prevents the engine from being over-boosted at high engine speed. Because the turbine is bypassed at normal cruising speed, the engine has very little back pressure and will get better fuel mileage. Another advantage of the PTO Valve is it opens and closes every time the engine is accelerated and goes from the full-close to the full-open position every time the engine is started. An ordinary wastegate, on the other hand, may be operated for weeks without opening if the engine is never pushed hard enough to reach maximum intake-manifold pressure. This inactivity is frequently the cause of a wastegate valve sticking.

The use of a control not only improves the low-end performance of a turbocharged engine but makes the job of choosing a carburetor and tailpipe much easier. The carburetor can be much larger because it will not be used to limit boost pressure. Duke Hallock has found when a large carburetor is used in conjunction with a wastegate-controlled turbocharger, he uses a

Chevy small-block V-8 installation in a Ford Ranchero used exclusively for speed runs at Bonneville Salt Flats. Cragar machinist Bill Edwards owns the car and made the installation of two AiResearch TE0659 turbos with waste gates. Note plenums, Bosch fuel injection.

Setup similar to that on Chevy II on author's 230 CID Chevelle. Carburetor venturi was enlarged to 1-1/2-inch diameter and the waste-gate diaphragm diameter was increased for more positive actuation. Car was driven over 70,000 miles without removing the head.

Figure 108—Roto-Master's TurboSonic Turbo Module includes the priority valve, carburetor adapter and turbocharger so it can be bolted onto the engine as a unit.

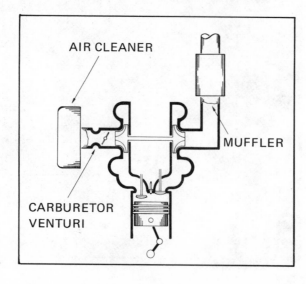

Figure 109—Boost pressure limited by fixed restrictions.

compressor with 10% to 15% less flow capacity than he would use with a free-floating turbocharger. One of the reasons for this is the smaller turbine nozzle A/R normally used with a wastegate system could drive a compressor into surge which would never occur with a free-floating system. This problem would be remote in a light sports car but could definitely happen on a heavy vehicle climbing a long hill.

Charles McInerney has found that a turbine housing which works best on a dynamometer will nearly always be about 10% too large for driving. This means about 1 A/R ratio.

For any given turbine as the A/R ratio decreases, the turbine speed increases up to a point. If the A/R is too small, it will cause a large drop in the efficiency of the turbine and the added back pressure on the engine may cause more losses in power than the added intake-manifold pressure achieved. If this condition should occur, it is advisable to use the next smaller size turbine wheel and go back to a larger A/R.

Bob Keller has come up with a neat idea called a priority valve, Figure 107. This device, when assembled with the TurboSonic Turbo-Module in Figure 108, allows the engine to run naturally aspirated until the compressor has a positive discharge pressure. At this point the priority valve closes the bypass between the carburetor and the intake manifold causing the air-fuel-mixture to pass through the compressor and become supercharged. This device allows the engine to act as if it were naturally aspirated until the throttle is open far enough to ask for help from the turbocharger compressor.

Bill Reiste and Jim Deatsch have come up with a similar device except the valve is a free-floating flapper actuated by the pressure differential inside the carburetor box.

As a general statement, I would say a free-floating turbocharger engine combination, Figure 109, can give low-cost performance to an engine which is outstanding for the amount of work required. However, for the ultimate in performance, whether it be a dragster, a track racer, sports car, boat or airplane, some type of control is necessary and is worth the added expense.

Air-to-water intercooler for turbocharged gasoline marine engine by Harrison Division of GM. Used on Daytona Marine engines and numerous marine conversions.

Figure 110—Turbocharged engine with intercooler

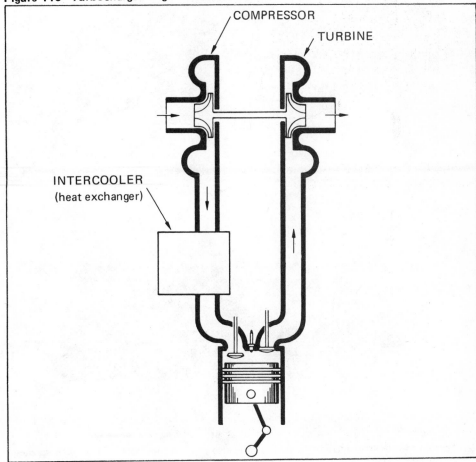

Whenever a group of engine men get together and someone brings up the subject of intercooling, invariably someone else says you mean *aftercooling* or if someone discusses aftercooling, someone else says *intercooling*. In any case they are usually referring to cooling the air or air-fuel mixture somewhere between the compressor discharge and the engine. Many engineers use the all inclusive term *charge-air cooling*.

The charge is cooled by ducting it to a heat exchanger which may use ambient air, ice water, sea water, or engine jacket water as a cooling medium, Figure 110. The temperature drop of the charge air passing through the heat exchanger will be a function of several factors. It will vary with heat-exchanger size, the temperature of the cooling medium and the available flow rate of the cooling medium. There will always be a pressure drop of the charge as it goes through the heat exchanger and the amount of the pressure drop must be weighed against the temperature drop as there would be no advantage to lowering the charge temperature say 100°F and then losing half the pressure. If the charge air passing through the heat

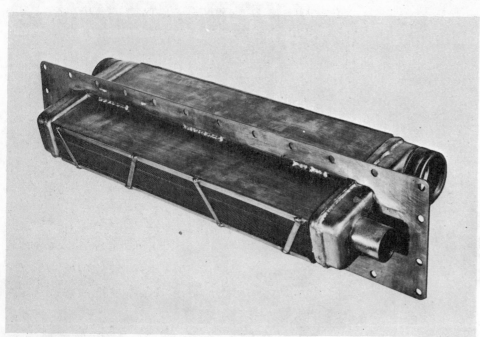

Modine air-to-water intercooler bolts into intake manifold of Caterpillar 0336-V8 diesel engine. Two are used to cool charge air approximately 150°F, using engine jacket water as the cooling medium.

Typical air-to-water intercooler made by Harrison Division of GM. This unit is used on some International Harvester engines.

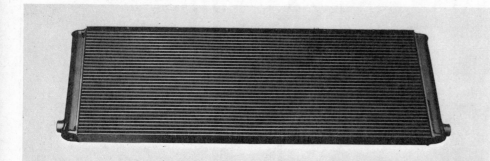

Modine air-to-air intercooler allows cooling charge air to within approximately 20°F of ambient temperature. Air that can be ducted to such an intercooler reduces the charge temperature more than a water-to-air unit because a greater temperature difference can usually be achieved than provided by 180°F jacket water.

exchanger does not become considerably more dense, then the heat exchanger is doing only half its job. As a rule of thumb, 1°F. decrease in intake-manifold temperature will result in 1°F. drop in exhaust temperature. For example, if an engine has an exhaust temperature of 1500°F. and through the use of an intercooler we are able to reduce the intake manifold temperature by 100°F., we will also lower the exhaust temperature to 1400°F. at the same time. This not only makes it easier on the exhaust valves, but cuts down on the heat-rejection requirement of the engine unless jacket water is used as the cooling medium.

Besides reducing the heat load on the engine, the higher charge density will allow more mass of air per minute to flow through the engine at any given intake-manifold pressure. This means more fuel can be burned and the engine can produce more horsepower. As an example, suppose a 151 CID engine running at 10,000 RPM with an absolute intake-manifold pressure of 120 inches Hg Abs produces 900 HP. The intake-manifold temperature, assuming 65% compressor efficiency will be 487°F., and the mass air flow through the engine will be about 900 pounds per hour.

If a heat exchanger is placed between the compressor discharge and the engine with only 50% effectiveness on a 100°F. day, the intake-manifold temperature will be reduced to 293°F. and even if the intake-manifold pressure is lowered to 100 inches Hg Abs, mass flow will increase to 941 pounds per hour. In addition, for the same horsepower and air/fuel ratio, exhaust temperature will be reduced by approximately 194°F.

The advantages to the engine are two-fold. First the overall operating temperature of the engine will be reduced and secondly the combustion-chamber pressure for a given BMEP will also be reduced, lessening stress on the engine.

If we had a perfect heat exchanger, the temperature of the charge air could be reduced to that of the cooling medium without any drop in pressure. This, of course, is not possible because there will always be a pressure drop through the heat exchanger and it is not possible to lower the charge temperature to the cooling-medium temperature.

If the charge-air temperature is 200°F. and the cooling-medium temperature is 100°F. and we are able to lower the charge temperature to 150°F., the heat exchanger has an effectiveness of 50%.

$$\frac{200° - 150°}{200° - 100°} = \frac{50°}{100} = .5$$

If a better heat exchanger is used which can drop the charge temperature to 130°F., the effectiveness is 70%.

$$\frac{200° - 130°}{200° - 100°} = \frac{70°}{100} = .7$$

Seventy-percent effectiveness is a reasonable value and will be used for examples in this chapter.

Assuming a compressor-discharge temperature of 250°F. and an ambient temperature of 75°F., a 70% effective air-to-air heat exchanger will reduce the charge air temperature (250 - 75) x .7 = 122.5°F. The charge temperature leaving the intercooler will be 250 - 122.5 = 127.5°F.

If jacket water is used at 180°F., the drop in temperature will be (250 - 180) x .7 = 49°F. This will result in a charge-air temperature of 201°F. This small decrease makes it impractical to use jacket water unless the compressor-discharge temperature is at least 300°F.

Using a low-temperature liquid such as sea water at 75°F. will result in the same charge-air temperature (127.5°F.) as an air-to-air heat exchanger but the air-to-liquid type will be much smaller and will not require a fan to circulate the cooling medium.

A drag racer or a Bonneville-type car can carry enough low-temperature liquid to cool the charge in much the same way that a tank of liquid is used to cool the engine. The tank could contain ice-water or acetone or alcohol with chunks of dry ice. Caution should be used with cooling media below 32°F. because the charge side might become clogged with ice on a humid day. Tom Keosababian used a Freon spray on one of his intercooler installations.

Let us start with a 300 CID engine turbocharged to 30 in. Hg gage boost at sea level with a 30 in. Hg Barometer and 80°F. ambient. The engine is run on a dynamometer and produces 350 HP at some speed. Assuming a compressor efficiency of 70%, the compressor-discharge temperature can be calculated. The

"Turbo Honker" Dodge with 7:1 compression ratio hemi engine assembled by Bud Faubel and George Weiler in 1966. Two ice-water-cooled intercoolers, one in each front fender and two T18 free-floating AiResearch turbos were used. Car turned 160 MPH in the quarter mile. Alex Walordy photo.

compressor pressure ratio is:

Comp. Out Absolute Press.

Comp. In Absolute Press.

$$= \frac{30 + 30}{30} = \frac{2}{1}$$

Refer to Table 1.
When r = 2.   Y = .217
  Ideal Temp. Rise = (80 + 460) x .217
                   ≅ 540 x .217 = 117°F.

Actual Temp. Rise = $\dfrac{\text{Ideal Temp. Rise}}{\text{Comp. Eff.}}$

$$= \frac{117°}{.7} = 167°F.$$

Compressor Discharge Temp.
         = 80° + 167°
         = 247°F.

Now if a 70% effective air-to-air heat exchanger is placed between the compressor discharge and the intake manifold, it will lower the charge temperature.

$$(247° - 80°) \times .7 = 167 \times 7° = 117°F.$$

The temperature entering the engine will now be 247° - 117° = 130°F.

Because the heat exchanger is not ideal, there will be a loss of pressure through it. To be conservative, assume a 2-inch Hg loss. Using these figures, the increase in density with the heat exchanger will be

$$\frac{247 + 460}{117 + 460} \times \frac{30 + 28}{30 + 30} = \frac{707}{577} \times \frac{58}{60} = 1.18$$

Jim Kinsler installed a 327 CID Chevrolet in a Maserati chassis in 1965. Large plenum with modified Rochester fuel injection used Chevrolet heater core as an intercooler. Liquid silicone cooled with dry ice circulated through the intercooler. Small photo shows intercooler and plenum details. Carbureted installation with two Quadrajets was used for street operation. Turbos are E-flow Rajays.

Bill Edwards' 327 CID Chevrolet equipped with AiResearch turbos in a free-floating configuration. Bosch fuel injection is used. Intercoolers mount in housings fabricated by Edwards. Engine is used for Bonneville Salt Flats high-speed attempts.

As a result, the intercooled engine can put out 18% more power at the same speed with 2 inches less manifold pressure. There is, however, a catch to this. In some cases, the exhaust temperature and pressure will drop in proportion to the intake-manifold conditions. When this happens, the turbocharger will slow down, further reducing the intake-manifold pressure. When this occurs, it is necessary to use a smaller turbine housing to maintain the same boost pressure.

Engines which run on gasoline are sensitive to charge temperature because of both pre-ignition and detonation limits. The octane requirement for a given engine output can be reduced substantially by intercooling. The tendency for a combustion chamber to develop a hot spot and ignite the charge before the plug fires is also reduced by intercooling.

It is possible to cool the charge below the temperature of the cooling medium by compressing it further with a secondary compressor, cooling it and expanding it through a turbine used to drive the secondary compressor, Figure 111. This method is used on some large stationary diesels with good success but it is rather complicated for a small engine.

Things aren't quite so bad as they were a few years ago when it comes to buying a heat exchanger. Gale Banks and Tom Scahill make liquid-to-air heat exchangers available for use as bolt-ons for popular automotive engines. These are designed for marine use but they will work well on a drag racer or Bonneville car with an ice-water reservoir and a circulating pump.

It is possible to connect turbochargers in series and obtain intake manifold pressures of over 100 psig if heat exchangers are used between the compressors as well as between the second compressor and the engine. This method is discussed in detail in Chapter 15, Tractor Pulling.

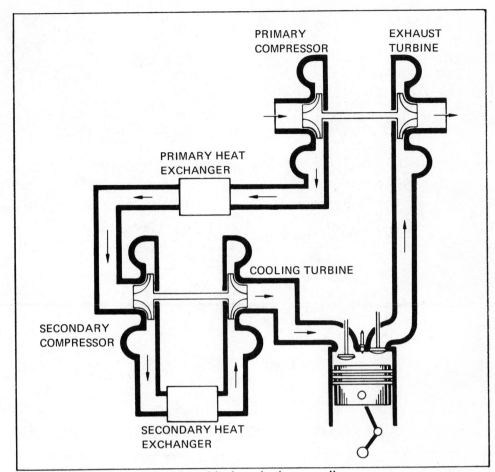

Figure 111—Turbocharged engine with air-cycle charge cooling

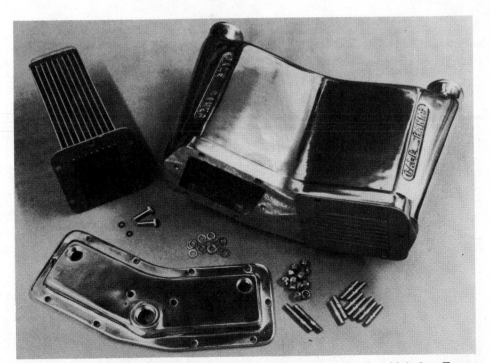

Gale Banks Stage III Venturi-Flow intercooler used dual elements in a V design. Two kinds are available: one for standard Holley four-barrel-carburetor manifolds; the other bolts to manifolds for Holley 4500 Series Dominator carburetors. End cover uses single water inlet. Dual outlets at top of housing eliminate air entrapment. Special O-ring-sealed bolts support tank ends to prevent vibration cracking of the element flangers.

Roy Woods underway in his turbocharged Dekon Monza at Willow Springs Raceway, California. Car went 5 seconds faster on its first turbocharged trial than in naturally aspirated form. Left headlight opening contains duct to radiator for intercooler fluid. Lower photo shows initial mockup of small-block Chevrolet engine. Turbocharger engineering and installation by Gale Banks Engineering includes TO4B turbos, Roto-Master wastegates and Banks dual intercooler assembly.

In some ways, marine engines are a lot easier to turbocharge than automobile engines and in other ways, they pose problems not encountered in automobile engines. In an automobile engine, even those equipped with a torque converter, engine speed at full throttle is limited by the instantaneous automobile speed and the gear ratio. An engine mounted in a boat driving a propeller can be accelerated until it is near its maximum speed long before the hull of the boat reached its maximum speed. In the case of a jet boat, the engine can be revved up to peak speed while the boat is still tied to the dock. For this reason, power available from the engine can only be fully utilized when it coincides with the power required by the hull. Figure 112 illustrates this for a non-planing hull. The shape of these curves will differ for each hull but the situation is about the same.

Except in the case of a drag boat, it is obvious that the extra power available at low hull speeds is of little use as long as the engine can approach full speed regardless of hull speed. As an example, supposing a boat is cruising at 20 knots and 2200 RPM and the throttle is opened fully. If the engine then accelerates to 4400 RPM immediately and remains there when the boat reaches 30 knots, then the extra torque available at 2200 RPM is of no value.

Turbocharging a marine engine makes it possible to produce a power curve which matches the engine closer to the hull requirement. Looking at Figure 113, the power available from the engine comes closer to the hull requirement and results in a more efficient system.

In Figure 114, available power curves are plotted for both naturally-aspirated and turbocharged engines in the same hull. Propellers are matched to the engines to make each power curve cross the hull-

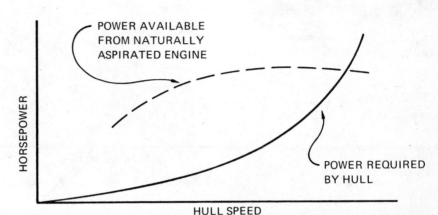

Figure 112—Engine power available compared to hull requirement with a naturally-aspirated engine

Figure 113—Engine power available compared to hull requirement with a turbocharged engine

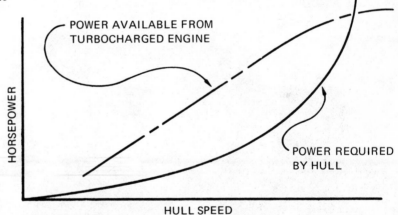

Figure 114—Naturally-aspirated and turbocharged engines matched to same hull with same maximum engine speed

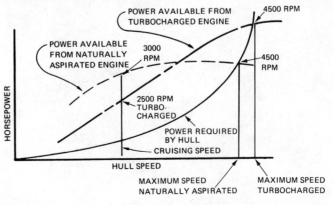

M & W turbo kit mounted crosswise on a four-cylinder 181 CID Chris Craft engine.

M & W turbo kit on six-cylinder Mercruiser (Chevrolet engine).

M & W Gear's MT-24 kit installs dual turbos on a Ford 460 CID engine with NICSON products. 420 HP is produced with regular fuel. This kit is used by Indmar, Holman-Moody and Hardin, among others.

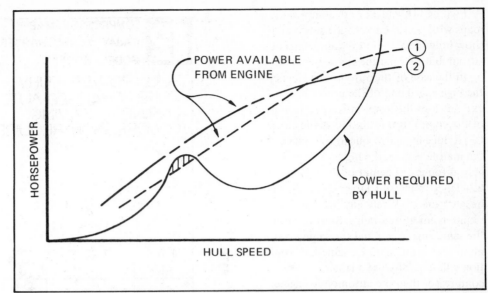

Figure 115—Turbocharged engine incorrectly and correctly matched to hull with special power requirements

requirement curve at the same engine speed. This is done by using a higher-pitched propeller on the turbocharged engine. When the boat is slowed down to cruising speed, the turbocharged engine will be running slower than the naturally-aspirated engine, resulting in better fuel consumption and longer engine life. Where high boat speed is required, the turbo-charged engine will drive the hull considerably faster than the naturally-aspirated engine without resorting to a higher maximum engine speed.

This has been demonstrated many times in long ocean races where the turbocharged engines running at somewhere around 4500 RPM were able to outlast the naturally-aspirated engines which had to run up to 7000 RPM to achieve the same power. A few years ago, turbocharged Daytona Engines so dominated the ocean racing scene that turbochargers were banned as being unfair. In 1978, the Pacific Offshore Powerboat Racing Association reinstated turbochargers in the open classes with no cubic-inch displacement penalty.

Because of the difference in torque requirements, matching a turbocharger to a marine engine is somewhat different than on an automobile engine. Instead of trying to get a broad torque curve, the turbocharger is sized to obtain maximum compressor efficiency at maximum engine speed and the turbine housing sized accordingly. Except on rare occasions where the hull requirement has a hump in it, supercharging will only be required at high speed. When this occurs, Figure 115, the turbocharger must be sized to allow the engine to produce enough power to accelerate the hull through the hump. The turbocharged engine in Figure 115 Curve 1, has plenty of power at the top end but it will never be used because the hull will never reach planing speed. Curve 2 shows the turbocharger matched to give a little more power at the low end to get the hull over the hump. If this becomes critical

Want 450 HP from regular 89-octane gas? Or how about 550 HP from premium gas? Gale Banks offers this budget-priced LS-5 Chevrolet 454 CID engine either way. Note twin turbos and intercooler. For more money you can get up to 850 HP at 5800 RPM.

and maximum speed is most important, it may be necessary to employ a waste-gate to permit the use of a smaller turbine housing for more boost at low speed without overboosting at maximum speed.

Tom Scahill has solved this problem in a different manner. He has modified an automatic transmission and placed it between the engine and Vee drive. The torque converter has been replaced with a solid coupling and he only uses two forward speeds and reverse. Tom says, "A lot of heads turn when they hear me shift!"

Figures 116 and 117 are compressor maps with power curves superimposed to show how the different requirements of automobile and marine engines are met.

In the case of the automobile engine, the high-speed end of the power line extends into the lower efficiency region of the compressor. This allows the engine to produce higher torque at mid-range. On the marine engine, the high-speed end goes through the center of the highest efficiency island of a larger compressor because there is rarely any high-torque requirement at mid-range. Starting with the same engine size and the same maximum speed, the marine-engine application will normally use a larger compressor than the automobile engine.

On a racing boat with dry exhaust manifolds, the correct turbine-housing size can be predicted without difficulty because the exhaust energy available will be similar to an automobile engine. This is not true of a pleasure boat with a water-cooled exhaust system. To begin with, the water jacket around the exhaust manifold will reduce the exhaust-gas temperature at least 200°F., thereby reducing the volume flow available to the turbine. These engines usually have a water trap after the turbine to prevent sea water from backing into the turbocharger when the engine is not running. This causes back pressure on the turbine. In addition, engine-cooling water dumped into the exhaust pipe after the trap adds still more back pressure to the turbine. To compensate for this, a smaller turbine housing is used, depending on the conditions encountered for the particular installation.

Because of the availability of water, intercooling is very practical on marine engines. In some cases, engines have been set up to run turbocharged on regular-grade gasoline. This might appear silly at first but premium gas is not always available at marinas. Intercooling, discussed in Chapter 10, reduces the octane requirement of a turbocharged engine and with 70° to 80°F. water available, intercooler size is small enough not to increase the overall envelope of the engine.

Now that Gale Banks and Tom Scahill have made intercoolers available, they should become less of a curiosity and more of a useful tool in getting the most out of an engine. Intercoolers, however,

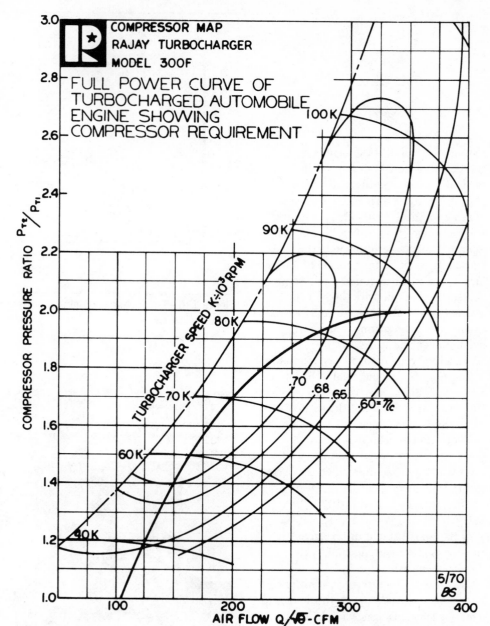

Figure 116—Full-power curve of turbocharged automobile engine showing compressor requirement

are not without problems of their own, particularly on a marine engine. One of the largest uses of turbocharged marine engines in the past has been sport-fishing boats. The fellows who own these boats like to get out to the fishing grounds fast, do their fishing at leisure, and get back home fast. The out and back are no problem, but it is the leisurely fishing which gives the trouble. Suppose the engine is idled down to trolling speed for

a half hour or so where the manifold vacuum will be very high and obviously no supercharging takes place. The air-fuel mixture will already be quite cool when it reaches the intercooler, which in turn will cool it still further with nice 70° or 80°F water. This will cause some fuel condensation in the intake manifold and after a while, a puddle of fuel will actually collect underneath the heat exchanger.

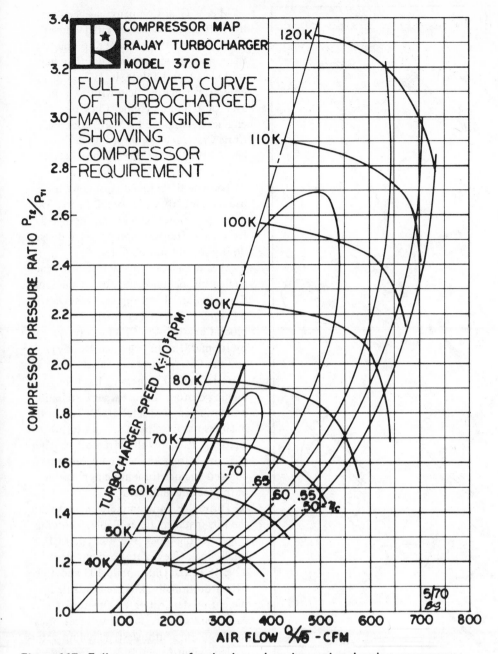

Figure 117—Full-power curve of turbocharged marine engine showing compressor requirement

Single Rajay turbo is used to add HP to this 180 CID Chevrolet four-cylinder engine in a Mercury outdrive installation. Intake duct from carburetor to the turbo is much larger than necessary.

All of a sudden, one of the fishermen gets a strike and hollers for full power. When the throttles are opened, the engine does not respond for several seconds. This can be very annoying, particularly if you lose a big fish as a result. Ted Naftzger had this problem and solved it by making two changes. First he added a water jacket to the bottom of the carburetor box and allowed engine-jacket water to warm the carburetor—much the same as is done on an automobile engine. And, he added a bypass valve around the inter-cooler so he could shut off the cold water and prevent fuel from condensing in the intake manifold. Ted used a manual valve on his installation but it would be possible to have a diaphragm-operated valve to allow water to flow through the inter-cooler only when the manifold pressure was above ambient.

Water-heated carburetor adapters are available from Ak Miller, Tom Scahill, Roto-Master, Shelby-Spearco and Gale Banks Engineering.

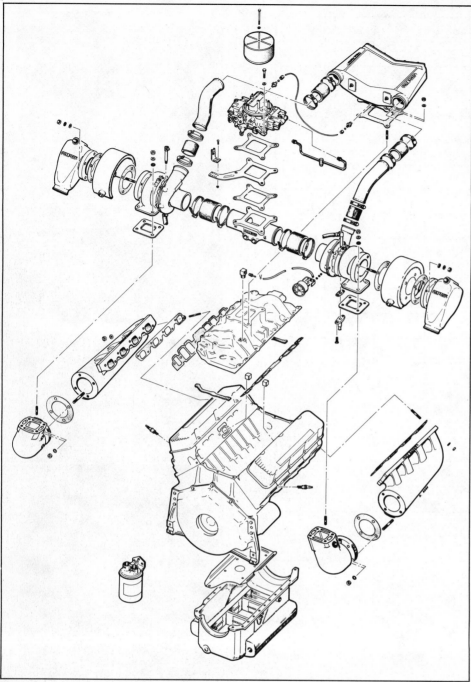

Exploded view of Gale Banks Stage III turbo kit for the 454 CID Chevrolet big-block engine. Fuel, oil and water plumbing is supplied with the kit, but has been omitted from this drawing for clarity. Drawing courtesy Gale Banks Engineering.

M & W Gear Company has been making bolt-on turbocharger kits for farm tractors since 1962. There's no doubt they make good ones because they have sold over 100,000 kits. In 1974, they entered the marine field with bolt-on kits for 4- and 6-cylinder Chevrolet engines as supplied by MerCruiser and Chris Craft. Jack Bradford did a thorough engineering job on these, as well as on their high-quality diesel kits.

Because these kits do not contain intercoolers, they are for a 20% to 25% increase in power and are not designed for racing. They are honest-to-goodness do-it-yourself bolt-on units.

M & W Gear Company makes marine-engine turbocharger kits for all MerCruiser Chevrolet and Ford applications, OMC 6-cylinder (Chevrolet), small- and big-block Chrysler, 460 CID Ford (as supplied by Indmar, Hardin, Holman-Moody) and the Caterpillar 3208 diesel.

Gale Banks Engineering has been making custom turbocharger installations on marine engines since 1970. This entire business has developed around turbocharging. It is now the foremost supplier of turbocharger kits and complete turbocharged engines for marine applications—both pleasure and racing.

Turbo kits and complete engines with the kits installed are available, including Chevrolet big-block 396, 427, 454 CID. small-block Chevrolet; Ford big-block 429, 460 CID; Oldsmobile 403 and 455 CID. Additionally, kits are available for the entire MerCruiser V8 engine line. Also, Banks offers numerous accessories for the marine enthusiast, including water-cooled exhaust manifolds, intercoolers, watercooled turbo housings and shields, oil pans with turbo drains, oil pumps and oil coolers.

Turbocharged marine engines are now widely used in closed-course and drag racing and in offshore racing. Turbochargers have now almost completely replaced superchargers on engines used for unlimited hydroplane racing. Typical output of 4000 HP at 4000 RPM is seen on the Allison V1710 engines.

"Hurry Round Hondo" jet boat is Gale Banks Engineering's racing test bed. Engine in hull is the one on the cover of this book. Boat won 1975 Jet Boat Nationals, holds APBA K Class (unlimited) Jet Boat 1600-meter course record: 112.5 MPH for 5 miles. Stock bore and stroke 454 CID Chevrolet big-block produces 1,067 lbs. ft. torque at 8,300 RPM; 1,687 HP at 28 lbs. boost with straight alcohol. Engine equipment includes Carillo rods, forged pistons with 1.094 in. Chrysler NASCAR pins, Iskenderian roller-tappet camshaft and rocker arms. O-ringed block and heads, polished combustion chambers, stock ports. TEO-691 turbochargers and the 2-3/8 in. wastegate are AiResearch units. Banks' shop did the blueprinting and assembly and supplied the stainless-steel exhaust system featuring cast stainless header flanges and expansion bellows to prevent stress cracking. No intercooler was used in this configuration. Boat photo by Al Bond.

Tom Scahill installation on a 454 CID Chevrolet includes his own aftercooling equipment which he sells to other marine enthusiasts. Kits include carburetor box, intercooler, Rajay turbochargers and AiResearch waste gate.

John DeMaio of Stonybrook, Long Island decided his 36 foot Bertram Off-shore Cruiser didn't have enough go. So he turboed the two 350 CID Chevys with 375F Rajays and his boat runs 60 MPH at 5500 RPM and 12 psi boost.

Don Markland installed this M & W kit on his 302 CID Ford and had to buy a new speedo for his boat because the old one only went to 50 MPH.

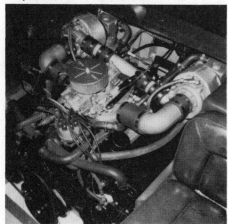

Performance First Marine converted 460 CID Ford for jet ski boat use. Two Rajay 370E10 turbochargers provide 7 psi boost. Air box on intake manifold is a water-cooled fabricated-aluminum unit. 780 CFM Holley with an electric choke is mounted on a heated box supplied with water from the water-cooled exhaust elbows. Water-cooled exhaust system features 4-inch wet pipes to provide quiet operation and avoid burning ski ropes. Performance First Marine also has Chevrolet kits.

18-foot jet ski boat is Performance First Marine's test bed. Stock 455 CID Oldsmobile engine and stock jet pump provide baseline references for Rick Mack's turbo testing.

12 TWO-STROKE ENGINES

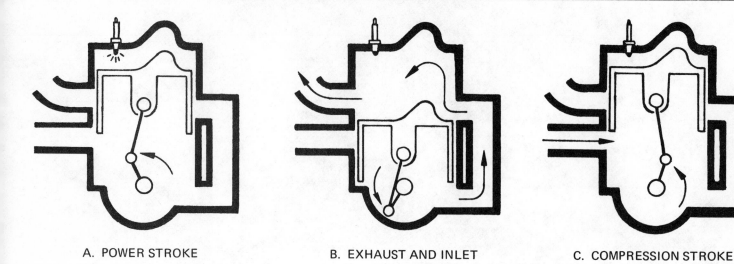

A. POWER STROKE   B. EXHAUST AND INLET   C. COMPRESSION STROKE

Figure 119—Simple two-stroke-cycle engine

When discussing the hows and whys of turbocharging, we normally think of the standard passenger-car engine, racing engine, marine engine or even an aircraft engine but two-stroke engines cannot be ignored because they are used in motorcycles, snowmobiles, all-terrain vehicles, boats and recently even in airplanes. Two-stroke engines can and have been successfully turbocharged although the conditions are quite different than on a four-stroke engine. Therefore, many of the problems have to be attacked in a different way. Except for the Wankel Engine, all four-stroke engines are about the same when it comes to valve location and combustion-chamber shape. Two-stroke engines are manufactured with many different types of porting and scavenging. These various methods must be treated differently when it comes to turbocharging.

Figure 119 shows the simplest of the two-stroke engines, often referred to as a *cross-flow crankcase-scavenged* type because the fresh charge enters one side of the cylinder from the crankcase while the exhaust leaves the other.

In Figure 119A the engine has just started its power stroke and both the inlet and exhaust ports are covered by the piston. The crankcase port is open. In Figure 119B the engine has completed

its power stroke and the exhaust port which is slightly higher than the inlet port has allowed cylinder pressure to drop to atmospheric. When the inlet port becomes uncovered, the pressure in the sealed crankcase forces the air-fuel mixture into the cylinder. The crankcase port is covered, preventing the charge from escaping back to the carburetor. In Figure 119C the piston is near the end of its compression stroke. The crankcase port has just been uncovered and the partial vacuum in the crankcase causes air-fuel mixture to be drawn into the crankcase through the crankcase port.

The baffle on the top of the piston prevents most of the charge from being blown out through the exhaust port.

Many variations of this design include reed or flapper-type check valves on the crankcase instead of the crankcase port. Another variation is to have the crankcase port mated to a rotary valve in or on the crankshaft.

None of these variations has much effect on the problems associated with turbocharging this type of engine, Figure 120. The main problem is the exhaust port which opens before the inlet port, closes after it. This means supercharge pressure will be determimed by the back pressure from the turbine and it is possible for some burned exhaust gases to re-enter

the cylinder after the inlet port has closed.

Both of these problems can have a substantial effect on the volumetric efficiency of the engine and actual results are often quite different than those calculated.

A similar type two-stroke engine is the loop-scavenged type, Figure 121. In this engine, both ports are on the same side of the cylinder and no baffle is required on the top of the piston. It still has the problem of the exhaust port closing after the inlet port.

Figure 122 is a schematic of a uniflow-scavenged engine. Here the exhaust port is replaced by a poppet valve of the same type used on four-stroke engines. This valve is opened and closed by a camshaft and can be timed to open before the intake port and close before it. This prevents the air-fuel mixture from being blown out through the exhaust port or exhaust gas from re-entering the cylinder. There are many other types including opposed-piston engines but the three described here will cover most cases.

It is not necessary to use the crankcase for a scavenge pump but on small engines it is convenient and inexpensive. Using the crankcase for this purpose means that a separate crankcase must be provided for each cylinder except where two cylinders are 180° apart and can fire at the same time. The efficiency of the crankcase as a scavenge pump is an inverse function of the volume of the crankcase when the piston is at bottom center. This means the smaller the crankcase volume, the better it will be as a scavenge pump. One of the problems with this design is the air-fuel mixture must lubricate the connecting-rod and crankshaft bearings. Because gasoline is not a very good lubricant, it is necessary to add oil to the mixture. This is fine except that oil has a detrimental effect on the octane rating of the fuel. If oil causes a problem normally aspirated, it is twice as bad turbocharged where octane rating is critical.

One way around the problem is to use mist lubrication in the crankcase, fuel injection, and hope the oil vapor is not carried into the cylinder with the air charge. A more positive answer is not to use crankcase scavenging. On large two-stroke engines it can be accomplished by driving the turbocharger mechanically until the engine develops enough energy to self-sustain. This method is not practical on small engines so a scavenge pump must be provided. Going back to Chapter 1, several types of mechanically driven compressors are discussed. All of these have been used at one time or another for scavenging two-stroke engines, Figure 123. In addition, the re-entry compressor sometimes referred to as a drag pump, has also been used for this purpose.

Right away the question arises, "If I have a high-pressure mechanically-driven scavenge pump, why can't it be used to supercharge my engine?" Except in the uniflow engine, much of the charge will blow right out the exhaust port and no supercharging will take place. If a turbocharger is added to the system, back pressure caused by the turbine will retain most of the high-pressure charge in the combustion chamber. When such a setup is used, the turbocharger compressor discharge is usually fed directly into the scavenge-pump inlet, Figure 124.

Remember when calculating through-flow for compressor matching, the two-stroke engine has a power stroke every revolution and uses twice as much air as a four-stroke engine of the same displacement at the same speed. Another thing to remember is most two-stroke engines have no oil pump and therefore a separate lubrication system—oil pump, reservoir, filter and cooler—must be provided when a turbo is installed.

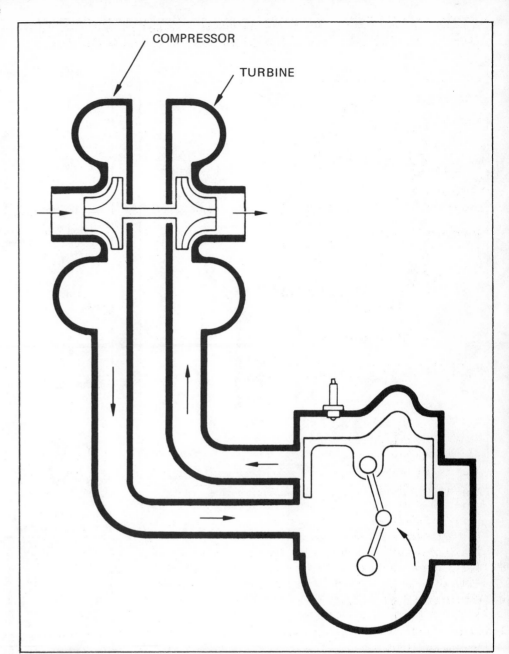

Figure 120—Simple two-stroke engine with a turbocharger

Two-stroke engines have been supercharged successfully to produce more than twice their normally-aspirated output and the potential should be as high as for a four-stroke engine.

97

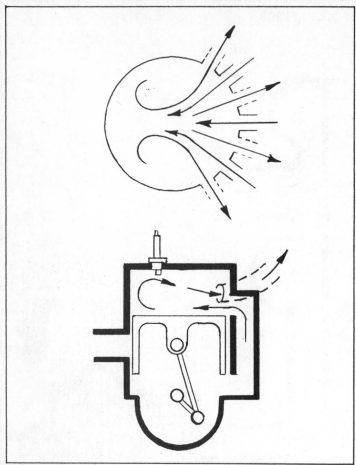

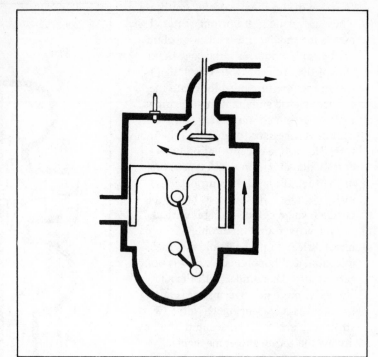

Figure 122—Uniflow-scavenged two-stroke-cycle engine

Figure 121—Loop-scavenged two-stroke-cycle engine

Figure 124—Two-stroke engine with turbocharger added to scavenge pump

Figure 123—Two-cycle engine with engine-driven scavenge pump

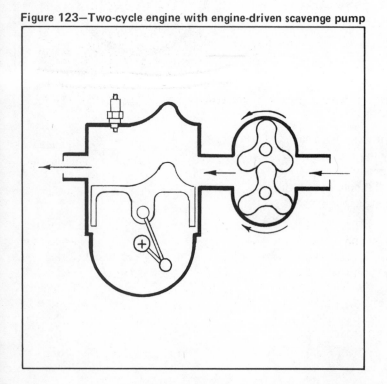

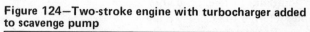

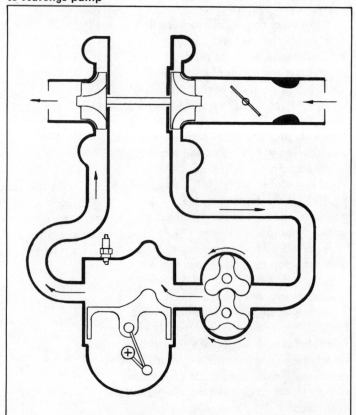

Piper Seneca is a light twin. This version has Rajay aftermarket kits on Lycoming Engines. Factory-turbocharged Continental engines on later versions are also Rajay turbocharged.

Turbocharging aircraft engines is a very specialized science, not only because of the unique problems involved but also from a safety viewpoint. A turbocharger or engine failure in a ground vehicle can be annoying but usually is not catastrophic. Because such a failure in an airplane, particularly a single-engine airplane, will normally cause the airplane to come down, every effort is made by the Federal Aviation Authority to be sure the turbocharger-engine system is not overstressed and any controls which might be used are fail-safe. Fail-safe in this case means they will not cause the turbocharger to overspeed and destroy itself or the engine.

Because of these very special requirements, I don't recommend airplane owners try to turbocharge their own engines. Certified kits are available for most of the popular light planes and if one is not available for a certain airplane, it will probably be less expensive to trade the plane in on one which does have a kit available, rather than going through the routine of getting a supplementary type certificate from the FAA. For someone who does not have previous test information to fall back on, the cost of building a dynamometer cell with high-altitude capabilities and running the tests will probably run upwards of $250,000. If this is not a deterrent, go to it.

Turbochargers used on aircraft installations may look identical to those used on farm tractors or automobiles but the quality control of raw material and machining operations are quite different. Manufacturers must be able to prove that the correct materials were used, any heat treatment was done under controlled conditions and the machining operations checked with regularly calibrated measuring instruments. Besides this, special operations such as Zyglo or Magnaflux must be performed on all critical parts. These are the reasons why aircraft turbochargers are so much more expensive than industrial units. This is also why repair and overhaul of aircraft turbochargers should only be done by licensed mechanics using parts from authorized manufacturers.

After this discouraging introduction, the reader might wonder why I include a chapter on high-altitude turbocharging. The reason is many engines must be operated at relatively high altitudes although they never leave the ground. Turbocharged engines have done very well in the past in the Pike's Peak Hill Climb and marine engines operating on Lake Tahoe, for instance, suffer a considerable loss of horsepower unless turbocharged.

This chapter is intended to cover regaining horsepower for engines which operate only at high altitude, maintaining horsepower on engines which operate from sea level to high altitude and the problems associated with an engine already turbocharged at sea level when it is operated at high altitude.

A naturally-aspirated engine will produce power in direct proportion to the density of the intake air. At sea level, air has a density of .0765 lb./ft.^{3} At 10,000 feet altitude, the density drops to 0.0565 lb./ft.^{3}

This means an engine which delivered 100 HP at sea level will deliver

$$100 \times \frac{.0565}{.0765} = 73.9 \text{ HP}$$

at 10,000 feet.

Airplane engines equipped with turbochargers to regain power loss due to altitude are referred to as *normalized* engines. A normalized engine usually will have a wastegate valve to pass all of the exhaust gas at sea level so no turbocharging will take place, Figure 125. As the engine starts to lose power at altitude, the wastegate is gradually closed, either manually or by an automatic control, and the turbocharger compresses the inlet air to sea-level pressure. This allows the engine to deliver essentially sea-level horsepower up to an altitude where the wastegate is completely closed and all the exhaust gases pass through the turbine.

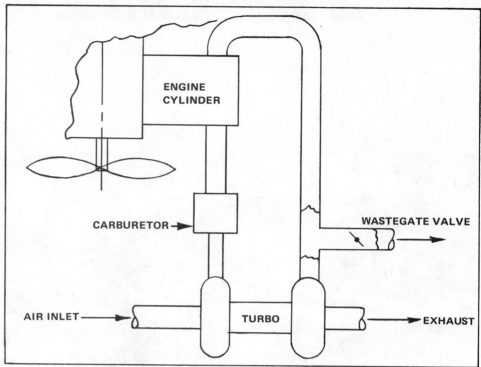

Figure 125—Schematic of aircraft engine with simple waste-gated turbocharger system

Piper Apache uses single Rajay turbocharger on each Avco-Lycoming 0-360 engine to maintain sea-level power at altitude.

When the airplane continues to climb above this altitude (critical altitude), the engine will start to lose power because the turbocharger can no longer deliver air at sea-level pressure. This critical altitude will vary with the engine and the turbocharger used. It is easy to attain a critical altitude of 15,000 feet and turbocharged engines with correct intercooling have been able to deliver sea-level naturally aspirated power at 40,000 feet.

If a vehicle is to be used only at a certain altitude, and sea-level power is to be maintained, then the turbocharger should be matched to deliver 30 inches Abs. If the engine must operate over a broad range of speed maintaining 30 inches intake-manifold pressure, then a boost control should be used, see Chapter 9. If the engine is to be operated at several different altitudes, an aneroid-type control should be used to prevent overboosting at lower altitudes. These are special cases where no more than sea-level naturally-aspirated power is desired.

In most cases, it is desired to supercharge the engine at sea level with as little loss as possible at high altitude. To accomplish this, several different approaches may be taken depending on the importance of maintaining full power at altitude.

Figure 126 shows how naturally-aspirated engine output is reduced as the altitude is increased. The output is a function of air density and decreases directly with it. If an engine is turbocharged at sea level with a free-floating turbocharger, it will also lose power as altitude is increased— but not so fast as a naturally aspirated engine, Figure 127. At wide-open throttle, the intake-manifold gage pressure will remain almost constant regardless of altitude. As an example, if the engine is turbocharged to 10 lbs. gage pressure at sea level, it will still be turbocharged at 10 lbs. gage at 10,000 ft. altitude. The ambient air pressure, however, will have been reduced from 14.7 lb./in.^{2} to 10.15 lb./in.^{2} At sea level, the absolute intake pressure was 24.7 lb./in.^{2} while at 10,000 ft. altitude it is only 20.15 lb./in.^{2} The naturally-aspirated engine will put out only 73% of sea-level power at 10,000 feet while the free-floating turbocharged engine will

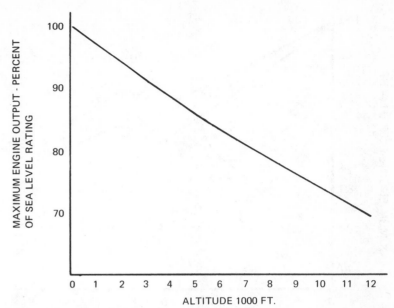

ALTITUDE 1000 FT.

Figure 126—Naturally-aspirated engine output at various altitudes

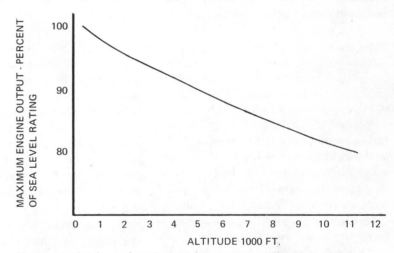

ALTITUDE 1000 FT.

Figure 127—Free-floating turbocharged-engine output at various altitudes

Piper Lance aftermarket kit uses two Rajay 315F10-2 turbochargers on Avco-Lycoming IO-540 engine. Separate wastegate for each turbo is operated by a single hydraulic controller.

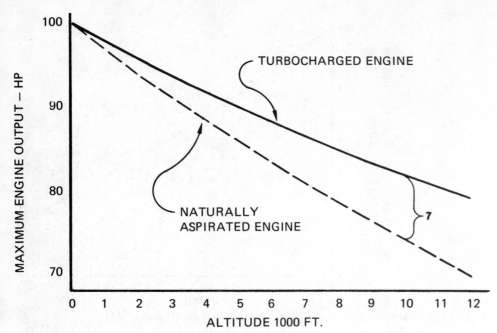

Figure 128—Comparison of naturally aspirated and free-floating turbocharged engine output at various altitudes

Jacobs 757 CID engine is rated at 350 HP for take-off with only 2 psi boost, provides sea-level cruise 275 HP performance at 19,500 feet altitude. Single AiResearch turbo is used.

be producing

$$\frac{20.15}{24.7} = 81.5\%$$

of sea-level power, see Figure 128.

Because of the ability of a free-floating turbocharged engine to compensate for at least part of the power loss due to altitude, a turbocharged engine with the same sea-level power as a naturally-aspirated engine will perform substantially better at altitude. Figure 128 shows the comparative performance of a naturally-aspirated engine and a free-floating turbocharged engine. If both of these engines are rated at 100 HP at sea level, the turbocharged engine will deliver horsepower at 10,000 feet 9.5% better than the naturally-aspirated engine. As a rule of thumb, the turbo speed will increase approximately 2% per 1,000 feet of altitude.

There may be applications where no loss of output can be tolerated and the free-floating turbocharger is not acceptable in the manner shown above. If the engine is to be used strictly at a given altitude, the turbine housing may be replaced by one with a smaller A/R to increase the rotor speed and boost pressure. I don't know of an exact method of determining the new A/R to retain sea-level performance, so the trial-and-error method is useful until the user has established enough "feel" to predict the exact size in advance.

Depending on the engine and the amount of supercharge at sea level, the engine should be able to produce sea-level power up to at least 16,000-ft. altitude even if the boost pressure is 15 psig at sea level. In this case, at sea level, the compressor will be producing 2:1 pressure ratio and the intake manifold pressure will be 30 psia. To maintain this manifold pressure at 16,000-ft. altitude where the ambient pressure is 7.95 psia, the compressor must put out 3.78 pressure ratio which does not seem possible with a compressor such as shown on Figure 117. This map, however, is based on 60°F. and the average ambient temperature at 16,000 feet is about 0°F. Centrifugal compressors produce pressure ratio at a lower speed as the inlet temperature goes down in the ratio of

$$\sqrt{\frac{\text{Standard temperature Abs}}{\text{Inlet temperature Abs}}}$$

which in this instance is

$$= \sqrt{\frac{520}{460}}$$

$$= 1.06$$

Figure 117 indicates a turbocharger speed of about 125,000 RPM to produce this pressure ratio but at 0°F. the actual speed will be only

$$\frac{125,000}{1.06} = 117,900 \text{ RPM, approximately,}$$

which is still possible to achieve without overspeeding the turbocharger. There may be other problems which will occur at this altitude to prevent the engine from delivering sea-level power. The small turbine housing size required to produce the necessary pressure ratio may cause excessive pressure which might reduce the output of the engine even though intake-manifold pressure is available. The high intake-manifold air temperature may cause detonation and valve burning. The higher combustion temperatures and pressures may cause a general deterioration of the engine. This is a nice way of saying the engine may come apart at the seams.

Some engines must be operated at several altitudes and still be capable of turning out sea-level power. It is neither convenient nor practical to change the turbine housing each time the engine is moved to a different altitude. The problem can be solved the same as on an airplane by using a turbine housing small enough for high altitudes and opening a wastegate to prevent overboosting at low altitudes. This type control may be operated either manually or by a servo motor and is covered in Chapter 9 on Controls.

When an engine is equipped with a wastegate, either manually or automatically operated, it is possible to maintain sea-level output up to some altitude where the wastegate is completely closed. Above this altitude, the engine will act the same as the free-floating turbocharged engine. Figure 129 shows engine output in percent of sea-level rating vs. altitude for an engine where the wastegate is fully closed at 15,000 feet. Assuming this engine is supercharged to 10 lbs. boost at sea level, the absolute intake manifold pressure is 25 psi. To maintain this at 15,000 feet where the ambient pressure is 8.3 psi, it will be necessary to increase boost to 25 - 8.3 = 16.7 psig. Above this altitude, the boost pressure will remain the same because the wastegate is fully closed and at 20,000 feet the absolute intake-manifold pressure will be 6.75 + 16.70 = 23.45 psia. This will reduce the engine output to

$$\frac{23.45}{25} = .94$$

or 94% of sea-level power. Here, as in the case of the free-floating turbocharger, the engine will have other limits which will determine the maximum altitude at which it can be operated.

The altitude at which the engine will no longer produce 100% of sea-level power is called the *critical altitude* of the engine.

An engine can be turbocharged to produce maximum sea-level output at high altitude, limited only by the mechanical integrity of the engine.

The critical altitude of a turbocharged engine which is already supercharged at sea-level will be lower than one which is naturally aspirated at sea-level and turbocharged only to maintain this output.

Turbocharging at high altitude can benefit greatly from the use of an intercooler and the higher the altitude the more the benefit. A turbocharged engine with 10 lbs. boost at sea-level will have an intake-manifold temperature of about 175°F. If this same engine is to produce about the same power at 15,000 feet, the boost pressure will have to increase to 16.7 lbs. and the pressure ratio will increase from 1.67 to 3.00. This pressure ratio will result in an intake-manifold temperature of 246°F. unless an intercooler is used. Because the standard temperature at 15,000 feet is 5.5°F., an intercooler with only 50% effectiveness will reduce the intake manifold temperature to 126°F.

Airplanes are frequently operated with a manually-controlled wastegate or with a manually-controlled throttle to limit the intake-manifold pressure because an airplane engine essentially is operated as a steady-state application. It would not

Helio Super Courier uses two Rajay turbos on an Avco-Lycoming GO-480 engine.

Figure 129—Altitude performance of waste-gated turbocharged engine

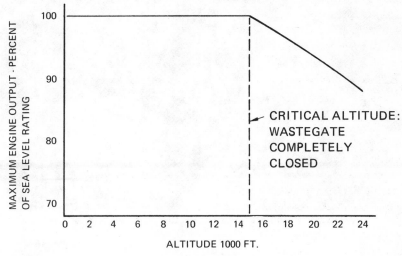

be practical to put a manually-controlled wastegate on a vehicle which must be driven up and down hills at various power settings and altitudes.

To summarize, a naturally-aspirated engine to be operated only at a specific high altitude, can be turbocharged without the use of a control, just as at sea-level. An engine turbocharged at sea-level can be operated between sea-level and some high altitude without a control if some

loss in horsepower can be tolerated at the higher altitude. The percentage loss of power at altitude will be less than if the engine were naturally aspirated. An engine which is either naturally aspirated or turbocharged at sea-level and is to be operated at many different altitudes where maximum horsepower must be maintained requires the use of a control—usually an aneroid-operated wastegate.

14 INSTALLATION DO'S, DON'TS & MAYBE'S

Anyone who needs lessons on making sanitary turbo installations should study this Renault in a Lotus Europa by Rick Mack of Performance First Marine.

Each of the chapters of this book covers certain points relating to the installation of turbochargers but it seemed like a good idea to put answers to the most often asked questions in one chapter, making it easier for the reader to have a ready reference. Many more people are involved in turbocharging now than a few years ago and I have requested several of those who have had considerable experience to pass this information along so that a new enthusiast will not lose his enthusiasm by making too many mistakes

before his first turbocharged automobile is completed.

People who have been successful in this field such as Doug Roe, Paul Uitti, Chuck McInerney, Don Hubbard, George Spears, Gale Banks, Chuck Sarson, Bob Keller and Ted Trevor have been kind enough to pass along information which, if used correctly, will save many hours and heartbreaks. I have included hints from many other experts as well, but the above-mentioned have given me written suggestions for this purpose.

If the reader has any specific problems such as inter-cooling or lubrication, the proper chapter should be referred to and reread if necessary to refresh his memory. When I work on a particular item such as a carburetor, I have found it to be extremely helpful to have a book describing that particular carburetor opened to the page covering the item on which I am working. The items covered in this chapter are based on the experiences of these experts and may, in some cases, tend to contradict each other. This is natural

Ak Miller uses jacket water to heat long crossover pipe on 2-liter Pinto installation. Special exhaust manifold mounts turbocharger.

because things which are good for one engine are not necessarily good for another. This is particularly true in the case of an air-cooled versus a liquid-cooled engine or an in-line engine versus a V or opposed engine.

To begin with, some basic suggestions from Doug Roe. "If it's necessary to buy a used turbo, follow a few suggestions or that $25 to $100 investment may cost you the entire effort.

Shop around to find a turbo for your engine that was designed for one of similar displacement and use. There is some latitude but too big a turbo dampens power response, while one too small may be short-lived and restrict mid-range and top-end performance. Keep in mind that automotive-type units turn approximately 80,000 RPM during high output. Using too small a turbo will cause it to exceed these revs and failure may result.

Before making a purchase, inspect the unit carefully. With the carburetor and

exhaust removed, you can reach the impeller and turbine with your finger or a pencil eraser. With mild effort, try to turn them from either end. They are joined by a common shaft so both should turn together. If each side turns independently there are internal problems. Do not put any hard object such as a screw driver against either impeller or turbine to try to turn it. One scratch or nick can cause failure at high revs. For this reason, never scrape carbon off. Use a carbon-dissolving solvent that does not attack aluminum because most impellers are made of that metal. I use carburetor cleaner. Many high-mileage turbos are heavily encrusted with carbon and will not turn as described above. This means a disassembly must be made to remove the carbon. Parts are very costly so at this point, add up the possible costs. A Corvair exhaust turbine is over $75.00—the compressor impeller on the boost side is over $20.00. A gasket, bearing and seal-overhaul kit is over $40.00. The latter two items will usually be needed.

If you are out to learn and decide to do the overhaul yourself, get a manual. Turbos are precision made and some caution must be exercised in working on them, but they are not complicated.

A used turbo relatively free of carbon will turn with mild effort. The exhaust seal affords a little drag so do not expect them to free wheel. Hopefully you can find one that appears good.

Now that you have a new or good used unit, it is time to plan the installation. Holding the turbo by hand, try it in various positions and you will soon narrow down the place for it by logic. Keep in mind the following:

1. Hood or body clearance
2. Routing of the exhaust to the unit
3. Routing of the exhaust from the unit
4. Plumbing of the compressor outlet to the carburetor or manifold depending on type chosen, and plumbing of oil-pressure and oil-drain lines

Item No. 4 requires further explanation. The only critical part of the entire plumbing job is how you direct the charge of fuel and air from the turbo to the manifold on in-line and V8 engines or to the cross-over pipe on opposed engines such as Corvair and VW types.

A. It is best to have the turbo slightly higher than the manifold or cross-over tube. This rule can be broken without big losses of power if need be.
B. Regardless of where the turbo is mounted, never plumb to the manifold or cross-over pipe so the charge is directed in on an angle.

The same applies when plumbing to a manifold setup on in-line or V8 engines. You must provide a means of shooting the fuel/air straight in so it is directed evenly to all cylinders.

When aimed wrong, Figure 130-1, heavy fuel particles will tend to continue along the easiest path and in this case richen the right-side cylinders. Because air is lighter, it can change direction faster, so it will make the sharp turn to the left and cause those cylinders to run lean.

In short, straighten the path of the fuel-air and let the cylinders have an equal chance at it.

A study of any turbo installation will reveal an exhaust pipe from all cylinders plumbed to the turbo. Plan your exhaust

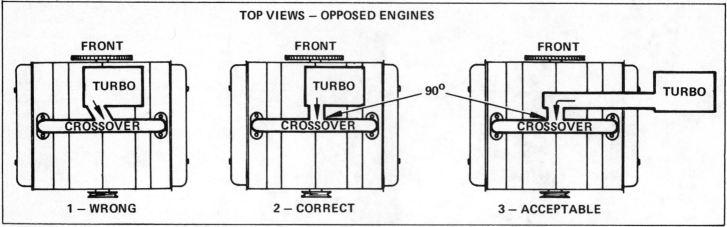

Figure 130—Intake-manifold plumbing for turbocharged opposed engines

to be as short as possible without causing tight bends. Use good sized pipe for your assurance of free flow."

Doug suggests wrapping the exhaust pipe with insulating material to keep from losing any heat in the exhaust system and also to lower the temperature of the engine compartment. This is considered standard practice for racing application where fractions of a second mean the difference between winning or losing. On street applications, the installation may cause more trouble than it cures. George Spears suggests the following: "In regard to the controversial subject of wrapping the hot pipe, we have experimented both on the V6 Capri and the V6 Mustang, and found very little or no gain in wrapping the piping. What we have found is a tremendous deterioration of the piping material beneath the wrapping. It rapidly oxidizes and, in some cases, we have found that the bends will distort, the cross-over pipe warps and when removed, it cannot be refitted. In our opinion, for most automotive applications, wrapping is unnecessary, costly, seriously affects exhaust pipe life, and generally is not attractive appearance-wise." In both cases, George was referring to a V6 engine which like any V or opposed engine is particularly hard on the cross-over pipe. The engine itself is water-cooled and will not get much over 220°F. Therefore, the distance between the exhaust ports on the two banks will not vary much. The cross-over pipe, on the other hand, which joins these two sets of exhaust ports may reach a temperature of 1400 or 1500°F. At this temperature, it will want to grow about

1/3 inch more if made from 300 series stainless steel. When this occurs, something has to give and because the engine block is usually far stronger than the cross-over pipe, the cross-over pipe will give. When Rajay first produced their Volkswagen Turbocharger Kit, the pipe which joined the four exhaust ports to the turbine inlet was wrapped with a very efficient heat blanket. A few months later, one of these pipes was returned as being defective when several pieces flaked out of the corners nearest the exhaust ports. This was thought to be a piece of bad tubing until several more headers were returned with the same problem. The kit was redesigned and the header was chrome-plated rather than insulated. No appreciable performance difference could be measured between the two types and the chrome-plated exhaust headers had a much better appearance.

Don Hubbard has this to say on the subject. "Some people say that the turbo is operated by the waste exhaust heat of the engine and they are tempted to insulate the exhaust tubes between the engine and the turbo to get more heat to the turbo. This usually causes overheating of the exhaust tubing and then premature failure. The exhaust gases actually have a velocity and pressure along with the heat that drives the turbo. Usually, the insulation used around the exhaust system is to keep radiant heat off the other engine parts. In some Indy Cars, insulation has been used to keep the high-speed air stream from cooling the tubes excessively because the state of tune of the engine requires every little bit from the turbo for response and

power and the balance is critical.

Connections between the compressor outlet and the intake manifold should not be overlooked because a leak at this location will not only cause a loss of power and rough idling but can be a fire hazard as well on those engines where the turbocharger is mounted between the carburetor and the engine."

Doug Roe suggests the following: "When connecting the turbo and your newly fabricated intake stack or cross-over pipe, use a good grade, fuel-proof hose and clamps. If a modest bend is required, use wire-lined flex hose with a relatively smooth interior. Hopefully, the pipe size in your intake system has been kept similar to the outlet size of the compressor so as to get best connection with least irregularity."

George Spears has found that the red or green silicone hose works very well for the connection between the compressor discharge and whatever piping may be used. Conventional radiator hose is quickly attacked by gasoline. He has found the silicone hose manufactured by Flexaust or Flex-u-sil to be excellent. Paul Uitti has had good results with that manufactured by Arrowhead.

When firing up a newly rebuilt engine with a turbocharger, it is not necessary to take any more lubrication precautions than those taken on a naturally-aspirated engine. Because the turbocharger barely rotates at engine idle, oil used to lubricate the turbocharger bearing during assembly will be adequate until the oil passages of the engine become filled. Because there is always the possibility of hooking up the

1979 Ford 2.3-liter uses AiResearch T-3 turbocharger with built-in wastegate. Compression ratio is 9:1, with detonation controlled by two-step electronic ignition retard: 6° at 1 psi and an additional 6° at 3—4 psi boost.

oil lines incorrectly, it is a good idea to disconnect the oil-drain line from the turbocharger and observe oil flowing from the turbocharger drain after the engine has started. This should occur within 30 seconds after the engine has started if the correct oil viscosity and line sizes are used.

Doug Roe has some advice about the Corvair which might help prevent a turbocharger failure. "Hook up the oil-pressure line from the engine block to the turbo. This should be 1/4-inch steel tubing or a good flexible pressure line with equivalent oil-flow capacity and capable of handling hot oil.

As a precaution to possible turbo-bearing damage, oil should be pumped through the turbo before firing the engine. This can be accomplished by turning the oil pump with an electric drill and light engine oil. On the Corvair I used a distributor with its drive gear removed. Determine how your system functions and devise a way. Turning the oil pump without running the engine also guarantees immediate oil pressure when you fire a newly-built engine. This is a very good practice. Run your oil system long enough to observe a good flow of oil out the drain hose. This will be a small steady stream with low pressure and room-temperature oil. When the oil gets hot and has full engine oil pressure against it, the drain will flow a larger amount of oil. Now you should double check everything and run the engine for leak checks."

Impressive "hardware collection" shows some of the trophies won by Doug Roe with his turbocharged Corvair. In photo above he displays two turbos he used on his competition engines. Bracket on AiResearch turbo supports weight of a four-barrel Holley carb. Engine is shown equipped with a stock Corvair Rajay (TRW) turbo and Carter YH side-draft carburetor. Until 1972, Doug Roe was a carburetor and emissions engineer with General Motors. He is now an automotive consultant handling special research and development projects and vehicle testing in Phoenix, Arizona.

Another Arizonan, Art Nolte of Scottsdale Automotive Specialists, turbocharged this 350 CID Chevrolet V8 in a Datsun 4 X 4 pickup. AiResearch turbos were used with Weber side-draft carburetors to keep a low profile.

Compressor-inlet provides an excellent clue to flow capacity. Left is original Corvair B-flow; right is Corvair E-flow kit by Crown Manufacturing. Three-inch-diameter inlet of E-flow requires adapter to mount carburetor. 1962-64 Corvair turbos bear part numbers: 3817254, 3830651, 3831691 or 3840830. 1965-66 units have P/N 3856709.

Don Hubbard as well as the others knows the importance of the turbocharger oil drain. He suggests the following: "The turbo needs a good direct drain to the engine. The drain tube should remain full size—approximately 3/4 to one inch inside diameter—to the engine. If the drain goes to the oil sump, it should never be covered with oil. It should terminate in a position above the oil level and be protected from oil throw-off from the crankshaft and rods. The engine crankcase should be well vented to prevent high crankcase pressures due to blowby. Most oil-leakage problems in the turbo can be traced to poor oil drains. The drains should always slope down and have no low spot to trap oil in the drain tube."

This item is discussed in the lubrication chapter but no matter how often it is talked about, some people still seem to think that oil can be made to flow uphill.

People who have run turbocharged engines frequently say they get valve float at a lower RPM than they did on the same engine when it was naturally aspirated. Some attribute this to the supercharge pressure on the under side of the valve causing it to open but this force is insignificant compared to the spring closing force and Doug Roe offers a few reasons which seem more reasonable. "If stock valve springs at stock installation heights are used in a turbocharged engine, valve float may occur at lower RPM than was the case with the naturally aspirated engine. The reasons for this are not completely clear, but can probably be attributed to the following possible causes:

1. There is a tendency to use the full rev limit capabilities of a turbocharged engine. The exhilarating experience tends to generate driver enthusiasm which may not be accompanied by tach watching to insure the critical RPM is not exceeded.

2. The valve springs in used engines may already be "tired out" and not giving specified seating pressure. Installing a turbo on such an engine—and then attempting to use full performance and RPM potential will often bring about valve float.

Continued use of high RPM weakens the valve springs in a hurry, requiring the use of stronger springs or a lesser installation height—either of which increases valve spring pressure so valve float does not occur prematurely.

If the springs are shimmed, it is important to observe the usual precautions to maintain adequate clearance between the spring coils with the valve at full lift. Also, be sure there is adequate clearance between the valve-spring retainer and the top of the valve guide at full lift.

An engine does not have to be very old to have 'tired springs' syndrone. If such an engine is turbocharged, consider changing the valve springs when the turbo is installed. Even a new engine, if it has been allowed to sit with the heads assembled, can have tired springs.

If excessive valve guide wear is encountered on a turbocharged engine—and this is not usually a problem—the guide bores can be knurled and then honed for correct fit. Bronzewall Guide rebuilding by the Winona Method can also be helpful as the aluminum bronze wire which is wound into the guides has more lubricity than guides made from Detroit Wonder Metal—cast iron.

Also, the valve-stem seals can be left off the exhaust valves/guides to insure that the exhaust valves get slightly more lubrication to offset any effects of higher exhaust gas temperature and increased back pressure.

On some engines, head-gasket problems may occur, especially as boosts get into the 13 to 15 psi region. If problems occur, they can be cured by 'O-ringing' the cylinder head. This requires cutting a groove in the gasket surface of the head around the outside of each combustion chamber. Soft-copper wire is installed in the groove so a portion of the wire extends above the surface. This applies additional clamping

HKS Turbo of Japan has this kit to pump the twin-cam Toyota 18 RG engine to 195 HP. Hasegawa is the designer. Photo courtesy Luckey Dodge.

pressure and a pressure seal which usually eliminates any tendency to blow gaskets.

Such problems are rare on air-cooled engines which spigot the cylinders into the heads. In these cases, gaskets are retained around their edges by the head design so there is little tendency for failure to occur, even at high boost pressures. VW and Porsche cylinders seal directly against the aluminum heads to provide a very effective seal if the cylinder lengths, spigot depths in the heads, and cylinder bases on the crankcase halves are correctly machined. Correct torque on the head bolts/nuts is essential and the usual practice of running the engine until it is well warmed up and retorquing after cooling is highly recommended.

Better quality exhaust valves are used by some builders when turbocharging. Turbocharged Corvairs, for instance, had Nimonic exhaust valves as standard parts. As valve diameter is increased and/or boost pressure is raised, the need for better quality exhaust valves increases.

It is very important to make sure that the turbo does not hit anything when the engine moves on its mounts or the chassis flexes during acceleration or braking or on rough roads, as in off road racing. Several turbo failures on a single car were finally traced to the fact that the turbo could hit a rollbar brace under certain circumstances, even though it appeared to have plenty of clearance with the engine and car at rest.

Remember that the turbo needs no expensive aftermarket type intake manifolds or exhaust headers. Eliminating these items alone can often offset the cost—even for a pair of turbochargers. Obviously, if you are intent on 'buzzing' the engine to higher RPM, it should be treated to a detailed blueprinting job."

George Spears suggests the following with respect to fabricating exhaust pieces: "We have experimented with various thicknesses of plate for the flame-cut flanges, and find 3/8 inch is a happy compromise. 1/4-inch has a tendency to warp during the fabrication and welding process, whereas 3/8 inch will not. In regard to tubing thickness, we have found that .083 inch, a standard gage tubing, is adequate and certainly anything thicker would be even better."

George has some other good suggestions when it comes to protecting engine components from hot exhaust pipes. "I think a question that could come up in some peoples' minds with regard to how close they can get the hot exhaust piping to heat-sensitive objects is one of the most frequently asked. Presently, we are operating our Mustang II Kit with a turbine discharge approximately 3/4 inch away from a 14-gauge metal heat shield. Electrical wiring is immediately behind this heat shield and in some cases, it is actually touching it. We have not experienced any problem with the wiring. We have placed thermocouples against the front side of the heat shield and generally can only measure about 200°F. Based on this experience, I think we can say that a 14-gauge steel shield placed one inch away from any of the hot metal parts, with at least one inch air space behind it, before any critical parts such as electrical wiring, master cylinders, etc. would give adequate protection from the heat. This might be useful information to an individual who has absolutely no idea of what the heat problems can be."

1975 National Tractor Pullers Association points champion in the 9,000-lb. class is this International 1066 driven by Danny Dean of South Charleston, Ohio.   Photo courtesy National Tractor Pullers Association.

Tractor Pulling is becoming a spectator sport in the United States and Canada in spite of the fact that most people on the west coast have never heard of it. The National Tractor Pullers Association (NTPA) had more than a million persons at sanctioned meets during 1973 with total purses of over $400,000. This increased to over $600,000 in 1974.

Because some readers are probably saying, "What is a tractor-pulling chapter doing in a turbocharger book?" some explanation is necessary. Information supplied by the NTPA states that the first recorded tractor pulls were in the year 1929 in Bowling Green, Missouri, and Monsville, Ohio. The tractor started out pulling a sled loaded with stones. As the sled was pulled along the course, a man climbed on it every 10 feet, so if he pulled the sled 100 feet he had the weight of the sled and stones plus the additional weight of the ten men. This continued until the tractor stalled, and in the early days, it was just that. As the the years went on, tractors became heavier and more powerful so it was necessary to divide them into classes. At most tractor-pulling contests, there are two classes, modified and super-stock. A modified tractor has any combination of engines, transmissions and final drive. They must have rubber tires and only two-wheel drive. Super-stock tractors are farm tractors with a standard block and crankcase of the make and model being entered.

These two classes are further divided into weight divisions of 5,000, 7,000,

9,000, 12,000 and 15,000 pounds gross. Many other rules are pertinent to safety, such as SEMA-Approved Scatterblankets. Rules may be obtained from the National Tractor Pullers Association, 104 East Wyandot Street, Upper Sandusky, Ohio 43351.

Tractors in the modified class, as can be seen from the various photographs, are low-speed dragsters. Of the top 15 point winners in the 12,000-pound modified class in 1973, six of the tractors had Allison V-12 Engines, three had tank engines while the rest had an assortment of Ford, Chrysler and Diesels—frequently in multiples.

Super-stocks are almost exclusively turbocharged diesels although propane conversions are sometimes used. This brings us to the reason for having a Tractor-Pulling Chapter in a Turbocharger Book.

The old method of pulling a sled with men climbing aboard every ten feet is no longer used for several reasons including safety. The method normally used today is to pull a trailer which has a skid on the front end and wheels on the back end, Figure 131. The trailer starts out with a fixed load on the skid end and a movable load on the wheel end depending on the track conditions and the tractor weight division. As the trailer is pulled along the course, the movable weight which starts out resting over the rear wheels is gradually moved forward, transferring the major part of the load from the wheels to the skid. The load eventually becomes so great, the tractor bogs down and the distance from the starting line to the trailer hitch is measured accurately to determine which tractor pulled the load the farthest. Because engine size is unlimited in any class as long as the tractor conforms to the other rules, it is uncommon for a tractor to stall or power-out. The usual way to end a run is for the tractor to come to a complete stop with the wheels still turning.

Turbochargers were first introduced to tractor pulling in the early 60's—long before they were common at such places as Indianapolis or on the CanAm Racing Circuit. Many of these first applications were pretty crude but it wasn't long before the pullers learned which turbochargers worked best on which engines

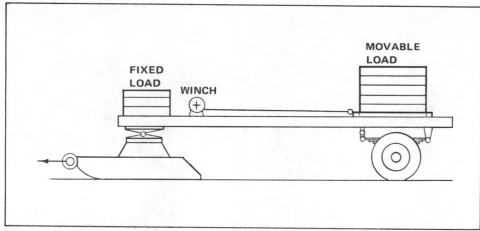

Figure 131—Dynamometer sled used in tractor-pulling contests

AiResearch T18A on top of T04B with aftercooling. John Deere engine.

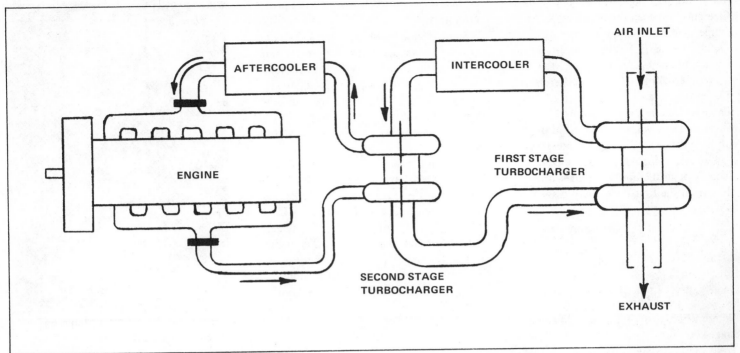

Figure 132—Schematic of tandem turbocharger system

and how much manifold pressure they could stand before the engine gave up. Originally, 10 to 15 pounds manifold pressure felt pretty good because it gave the puller such a big advantage over the naturally-aspirated engines. However, when the majority of pullers were using turbochargered engines, it was necessary to up the boost pressure to win. Forty psig was about the limit from a single-stage turbocharger and the engines still didn't give up. This is about the maximum pressure run on championship-type race cars.

The next step was to mount the turbochargers in tandem, Figure 132. By using this method, it is possible to get ridiculous manifold pressures without overstressing the turbocharger. It was necessary, however, to intercool between the two compressor stages or the intake-manifold temperature would go out of sight. Because each run only takes a couple of minutes, intercooling can be done rather easily with ice water as the cooling medium. If each compressor is matched to produce 2.7:1 Pressure Ratio, the interstage absolute pressure will be 2.7 x 15 = 40.5 psia. Intake-manifold pressure will then be 109 psia or 94 psig. Some of the tractor pullers have actually reported intake-manifold pressures as high as 105 psig.

In Dr. Alfred J. Büchi's *Monograph on Turbocharging* published in 1953, he dis-

cusses the power increase of a diesel engine as a function of the charging-pressure ratio. He determined the output of a given turbocharged engine when properly scavenged and intercooled continued to increase at pressure ratios as high as 4:1 without any increase in engine-exhaust temperature. Extrapolating these curves, it appears the output will continue to increase probably up to a charging-pressure ratio of 10:1. What this points out is a diesel engine properly turbocharged and intercooled will continue to increase in power at manifold pressures beyond the capabilities of today's engines. He also pointed out that these higher outputs are not necessarily accompanied by higher combustion temperatures. Dr. Büchi was running intake-manifold pressure of 71 psig in 1909. He would probably have run higher pressures even in those days if he had the materials to stand the added stress.

As a result of this high-pressure turbocharging with intercooling, tractor pullers are starting with 400 CID diesel engines designed to produce somewhere around 175 brake horsepower at 2,500 RPM and are obtaining up to 800 horsepower at 4,000 RPM. Two horsepower per cubic inch from a gasoline engine is considered pretty good at about 8,000 RPM. These fellows are doing it at half that speed and with a diesel no less.

When two turbochargers are used in tandem, it is necessary to match the output of the first-stage compressor with the input of the second-stage compressor after the charge has been intercooled. This must be done backwards just as a building is designed from the top floor rather than from the basement. As an example, a 400 CID engine running at 4,000 RPM at 80% volumetric efficiency will use 375 CFM, see Figure 40. Assuming 65% compressor efficiency and 2.7 pressure ratio, the density ratio will be 1.8.

$$1.8 \times 375 = 675 \text{ CFM}$$

This means a turbocharger with a compressor capable of producing 675 CFM at 2.7 pressure ratio must be used for the second stage. Either an AiResearch T04B V-1 Trim, Rajay 370E, or a Schwitzer 4LE-354 will handle this. Choosing the first-stage compressor is a little harder because an intercooler will be used between the two compressors. Assuming an effectiveness of the intercooler of 75%, the temperature of the air coming from the first-stage compressor will be reduced 75% of the difference of this temperature and that of the medium which, in the case of ice water, will be 32°F. Using Don Hubbard's Chart, Figure 19, and again assuming 65% compressor efficiency, discharge temperature of the first stage at 2.7 pressure ratio will be

360°F. Subtracting 32° from 360°, the difference between the compressor discharge temperature and the cooling medium is 328°F. Multiplying this by .75, the temperature drop across the intercooler will be 246°F and therefore the temperature of the air entering the second stage compressor will be 114°F. This means we will have 675 CFM of air entering the second-stage compressor at 114°F. Assuming a negligible pressure drop through the heat exchanger, the flow from the first-stage compressor will be:

$$CFM_2 \times \frac{T_1}{T_2} = 675 \times \frac{360 + 460}{114 + 460}$$
$$= 675 \times \frac{820}{574}$$
$$= 964 \, CFM_1$$

Where CFM_2 is the flow into the second-stage compressor and CFM_1 is the flow from the first-stage compressor into the intercooler. The 460 must be added to each of the temperatures because all ratio calculations must be done in degrees Rankine. The 964 CFM will be the output from the first-stage compressor. Because it is desirable to keep the pressure ratios of the two compressors about the same, the density ratio will also be the same or 1.8. Multiplying 964 x 1.8 = 1735 CFM, the required capacity of the first-stage compressor. This is where things start to get a little hairy because we are now talking about a fairly good size turbocharger. The turbocharger used for the first stage must be capable of supplying air to an 800 horsepower engine. The first-stage compressor doesn't know it is blowing the air into another compressor raising the pressure to a point where it can be forced into a 400 CID engine. The horsepower obtained from these engines is still a function of the amount of air which can be pumped through them. AiResearch T-18 Turbochargers have been used successfully but because there are so many versions of this, be sure to pick the right one. Model T18A40 with a 1.50 A/R turbine housing has worked out pretty well.

A little luck will be required in picking the correct turbine housing sizes the first time. It will be necessary to have two pressure gages, one on the intake manifold and one between the stages to determine if each turbocharger is running at the same pressure ratio. Remember in each case it is necessary to add atmospheric pressure to the gage pressure when working out pressure ratios.

Some engine builders use an aftercooler between the second-stage compressor and the engine in addition to the intercooler between stages. When this is done, it is necessary to calculate the increase in flow through the second-stage compressor in the same manner as it was done above for the first stage.

Dyed-in-the wool drag-race fans may laugh at the thought of a tractor pulling contest but there are many similarities between them, such as the super-stock class, the tractor version of the funny car. The pulling contest, however, has one big advantage; you can cheer your hero on for two minutes instead of six seconds. And, you can see the participants from start to finish!

A birds-eye view of the installation shown in the photo below.

International Harvester tractor with AiResearch T18A40 on top of an AiResearch TH08 with intercooling and aftercooling. 1HC DT-436 engine produces 800-1000 HP @ 4500–5000 RPM. Kolb photo.

Now that turbochargers have come of age, users are not quite as ready to blame engine failures on them as they were a few years ago. In spite of this, far too many turbocharger and engine failures occur from lack of maintenance which would have only taken a little time and saved the user many dollars and heartaches.

Over the years I have looked at enough failed turbocharger parts to be able to determine, in most cases, whether the failure was due to manufacturing problems or some reason outside of the turbocharger. In the vast majority of cases, the failures were caused by either lack of maintenance or misuse. If the information supplied by this chapter is heeded and used during an installation and afterwards when operating an engine with a turbocharger, it could very well prevent a premature failure which is not only discouraging but expensive.

Chapter 2 described the design and operation of a turbocharger. Chapter 4 went through the procedure of sizing and matching the turbocharger to the engine. Assuming this was done correctly, the turbocharger will run at least as long as the engine unless it is mistreated. The next few pages cover typical turbocharger failures and why they occur.

Jack Lufkin used to run this 300 CID turbocharged big-block Chevrolet in the gasoline-burning sportscar class at the Bonneville National Speed Trials. Car was third-fastest at 1971 meet with a 265 MPH run. Engine used AiResearch turbos, intercoolers and waste gates. Injection is a Bosch timed unit. Lufkin works with Ak Miller.

Journal-bearing failures are about as common as any other type. They are frequently caused by lack of lubrication which is easy to spot since the shaft journals will be discolored from the heat generated at high speed with no lubrication, Figure 133. This could be caused by a broken oil supply line, lack of oil in the engine or too heavy oil viscosity for the ambient temperature conditions. It could also be caused by placing an orifice in the oil-supply line to reduce oil pressure to the turbocharger bearings. One speck of dirt can clog a small orifice and cause a failure similar to that shown in the photograph in a matter of seconds.

Journal bearings will also fail when dirt gets into the lubricating oil. This type of failure, shown in Figure 134, will not necessarily have discolored journals but will usually have several grooves in the journals where dirt has become embedded in the radial bearings.

Another symptom of this type of failure is bearing material welded to the shaft journals. The cause could be one of several reasons. If dirt is allowed to enter the turbocharger from dirty working conditions during installation, such a failure could occur. Running an engine without a filter is another cause. Not changing a bypass type oil filter will result in oil flowing around the filter element without being cleansed and then into the turbocharger journals where the failure occurs.

There has been much controversy as to whether an oil filter should be installed in the turbocharger oil-inlet line. Many failures have occurred when a filter element became clogged and prevented oil from flowing to the turbocharger. Many failures have also occurred as stated above when the filter became clogged and oil flowed through the bypass. In either case these failures would not have occurred if the user changed the oil-filter elements at regular intervals. This is one place where it certainly is not economical to save a couple of dollars. As the man used to say in the TV oil-filter ads, "Pay me now or pay me later."

Anyone who builds a racing engine is usually very careful to put covers over all the inlets to the carburetor or fuel-injection system whenever the engine is not running. This is certainly a good practice because dirt or foreign objects are very

Figure 133—Journal and bearing failure caused by lack of lubrication. Dark areas are actually straw to dark blue in color. Bearing material has welded to the journal.

Figure 134—Journal and bearing failure caused by dirty oil. Both journals have been grooved by particles in the oil.

Figure 135—Compressor impeller failure caused by foreign object

Figure 136—Turbine wheel failure caused by foreign object

Figure 137A—Turbine wheel failure caused by over temperature and/or overspeed. This is a mild case because only one of the blades flew off. When the hub bursts it is much more damaging.

Figure 137B—Compressor impeller hub burst caused by overspeed. This type failure usually results in the impeller passing completely through the compressor housing.

destructive to any kind of engine. In spite of this, one of the major causes of turbocharger failure is a foreign object in the compressor impeller. If a nut or bolt enters the compressor housing when the turbocharger is running at high speed, it is like putting something in a meat grinder except that, in this case, the meat is tougher than the grinder. See Figure 135. To make things worse, pieces chewed off the impeller will enter the engine along with the original object, whatever it might be. This type of failure is about as bad as they come, because it may mean a new engine as well as a new turbocharger. For this reason, an air cleaner is always recommended on a turbocharged engine and if matched correctly should not cause any horsepower loss.

When building up a naturally-aspirated engine, little concern is shown for dirt in the exhaust manifold. If a few nuts or bolts happen to be left in there, they will be blown out and no harm done. Not so with a turbocharged engine. Several years ago, it was established that a turbocharger is an excellent spark arrester for engines which must operate in hazardous locations such as dry forests. The reason the turbocharger is a good spark arrester is that particles which are much heavier than air hit the tips of the turbine blades and are knocked back into the turbine housing until they are so small they are no longer considered a spark. The same thing happens with a nut or bolt or a small piece of exhuast valve or piston ring. Whenever one of these gets into the exhaust system of a turbocharged engine, it will hit against the tips of the turbine blades until it looks like a mouse has been chewing on them, Figure 136. This frequently occurs without loss of balance of the rotating group and the turbocharger may run for many thousand of hours without further damage. Most of the time, however, one of the blades will finally break off and the imbalance will cause immediate failure of the journal bearings.

Some users of turbochargers brag about how they get 50 psi out of their compressor when the compressor map for this particular unit only goes to 30 psi. They may be lucky for a while but eventually they will end up with a turbine or compressor wheel that looks something like Figure 137. When this occurs, it is like a hand grenade going off in the turbine housing and the higher the speed at which the burst occurs, the more dangerous it will be.

The most frequent complaint about turbochargers is that they leak oil. This condition is usually an installation or engine problem although it always gets blamed on the turbocharger. Many turbochargers are designed with a simple labyrinth seal at the turbine end and this design does not seem to leak oil any more or less than those with a piston-ring seal on the turbine end.

As mentioned before, lubricating oil enters the turbocharger from the engine system and *at engine pressure.* After the oil passes through the bearing it must flow *by gravity* out of the bearing housing and back to the engine. Anything which restricts the oil drain line will cause the level of oil in the bearing housing to rise above that of the oil seals and in the case of a labyrinth or piston ring seal, the oil will leak into the end housings. This is probably the main cause of oil leakage, although other things will contribute as well.

Starting at the compressor end, if the air cleaner is allowed to get so dirty it has a sizable pressure drop through it, it is possible, particularly at idle conditions where the turbocharger is blowing through the carburetor, to have a slight vacuum behind the compressor impeller. If the turbocharger has a piston-ring seal on the compressor end, oil will actually be sucked into the compressor housing and lots of blue smoke will come out of the exhaust. Because the piston-ring type seal on the compressor end is capable of preventing oil leakage against only a very small vacuum, it is not recommended to use this type seal when sucking through the carburetor because vacuums as high as 29 in. Hg abs will be imposed on the compressor housing. If the mechanical-face-type seal as used on Rajay and certain models of AiResearch T04 Turbochargers leaks, it has probably become gummed up with varnish and is not able to float freely. When this occurs, the seal should be cleaned or replaced immediately or dirt will enter the space between the carbon-seal face and mating ring and cause rapid seal failure. Other oil-drainage prob-

lems which can frequently cause oil leakage are discussed in detail in Chapter 8 on Lubrication.

Table IX shows a list of problems which occur on turbocharged engines and the probable cause of these problems. Whenever possible, try to find a remedy which does not include disassembly of the turbocharger because *it probably is not the culprit.*

NOTE: See Appendix for a thorough discussion of analyzing turbocharger failures.

Jack Lufkin has been running turbocharged cars at Bonneville for many years and is still using the same turbocharger he put in service back in the sixties. This isn't just luck and yours can last that long too if it is correctly installed, supplied with clean oil and protected from swallowing solid objects.

TABLE IX

CARE AND MAINTENANCE

Typical problems causing turbocharged-engine malfunction

SYMPTOM	CAUSE	HOW TO CHECK	REMEDY
Lack of boost	Gasket leak or hole in exhaust system	Block off tailpipe with engine running. If engine continues running, leaks are present	Repair leaks, usually gasket surfaces
Lack of boost	Worn valves or rings	Compression check engine	Repair
Lack of boost	Carburetor too small or butterfly does not open completely	Check pressure drop through carburetor	Use larger carburetor or adjust linkage
Lack of boost	Restriction in turbine discharge system (muffler)	Check turbine discharge pressure	Use larger muffler
Lack of boost	Dirty air cleaner	Remove air cleaner	Service air cleaner
Gasoline odor during boost conditions	Small leak at compressor discharge or intake manifold	Look for fuel stains around joints	Tighten joints or replace gaskets
Poor throttle response (stumble)	Clogged circuit in carburetor	Try another carburetor or richen jet/s	Clean carburetor and check jet sizes
Plugs miss at high power	Gap too large	Measure gap	Clean and reset to 0.025"(2)
Plugs miss often(1)	Bad leads	Check lead resistance against specifications	Replace leads
Oil leak into turbine housing	Blocked oil drain	Remove drain line and check for plugged or crimped line	Clean or replace drain line
Poor idling	Air leak between carburetor and compressor	Listen for hissing around carburetor at engine idle	Repair leak

1. At boost of 15 pounds or more, use the best capacitor-discharge ignition system available, preferably with a high-output coil.

2. Smaller gaps may be required if misfiring continues.

A few years ago, turbocharger kits for passenger cars—particularly those of the bolt-on type—were such a novelty that automobile magazines were glad to give them space. Today there are so many on the market that it is difficult to tell whose kit is on an engine unless a nameplate is hung on it. This is true not only of automobile kits but also those for motorcycles. Motorcycle kits are discussed separately in Chapter 21 on Motorcycles. Bolt-on kits and complete marine engines are covered in Chapter 11 on Marine Engines. Companies which offer kits are listed with complete addresses and phone numbers in the back of this book.

B.A.E. DIVISION OF TURDYNE CORP., TORRANCE, CALIFORNIA

B.A.E. started in 1968 as Bob's Automotive in Lawndale, California. Beginning with custom installations of turbochargers on street and race cars and on marine engines, Bob McClure directed his efforts toward the creation of kits for marine and automotive applications.

In 1977 the name was changed to B.A.E., the firm moved to larger quarters and former Rajay engineer, Bill Wilbur, joined the firm to assist in engineering. By 1978 the firm offered over 40 separate kits for U.S. and foreign cars, trucks, motor homes and vans. These include BMW 2002tii, 320i, 530i and 630i; Capri 2.6 and 2.8; Chevrolet small block for cars, pickups and Blazers; Datsun 510, 520, 240Z, 260Z and 280Z; Dodge 440 CID motor home; Fiat X1/9; Ford trucks 360, 390 and 460 CID; Honda Civic, International diesel (Nissan); Mercedes diesels 220D, 240D and 300D; Porsche 914, 924 and 911CIS; Saab; Toyota T2-C, 20 R.C.; VW air-cooled Types I and II, Rabbit and Scirocco carbureted or injected.

BMW 530i/630i BAE turbo kit with APC valve for boost control.

BAE kit installed on Rabbit/Scirocco VW with APC control valve.

Each time I hear of a new company in the turbocharger-kit business, I contact them immediately so I can pass along the information. Many new kits are being produced and sold that I have not heard about, but I have included all those I knew about when we put this book to press.

Checkpoint America's Lotus Europa twin-cam kit uses Rajay 377B40 turbo with the stock 9.5 compression. Boost starts at 2800 RPM, is restricted to 11 psi. Front Stromberg CD carb is retained. Standard air filter and exhaust systems are used. Exhaust manifold is stainless-steel seamless tubing; incorporates support brace for turbo. Distributor has standard advance curve; is retarded 2°. 0–60 MPH time is 6.1 seconds; 1/4 mile elapsed time is 13.7 seconds. Fuel consumption is same as stock.

1972 Lotus Super 7 twin-cam with Checkpoint America turbo kit. Rajay 377B40 turbo pumps up to 21 psi. Single Stromberg CD 1-3/4 inch replaced dual twin-choke Webers. Boost starts at 1500 RPM and a rev limiter is set at 7000 RPM. Lucas distributor is used with a CD unit. Fuel consumption is 37 MPG.

GALE BANKS ENGINEERING, S. SAN GABRIEL, CALIFORNIA

Gale Banks is discussed in the chapter on marine engines. However, the company also offers turbos for passenger and race cars, primarily for engines made in the United States.

BROADSPEED SOUTHAM, WARWICKSHIRE, ENGLAND

The ability of Ralph Broad's firm to produce results is known the world over. They have been responsible for winning many national and international saloon-car championships and very often are responsible for the preparation of works entered cars. It's hardly surprising that with all their attributes, they should turn their attention to turbocharging. At present they offer two turbocharged engines, the English V-6 in a turbo-charged form, and the turbocharged version of the 1.9-liter Opel Manta. Both turbocharger installations use the "blow-through-the-carb" method for installation reasons. A novel recirculating valve reduces throttle lag and serves as a boost limiter. Horsepower increase on the Opel is shown below:

1.9-liter Opel

RPM	Naturally Aspirated Horsepower		Turbocharged Horsepower
2000	35.5	X 1.26	45
3000	59	1.5	88.5
4000	77	1.72	133
5000	80	1.94	155
5500	80	1.96	157
6000	73	2.14	156

This performance is obtained with 9.5 psi boost.

CHECKPOINT AMERICA ST. LOUIS, MISSOURI

Checkpoint America of St. Louis, Missouri, has a turbocharger kit for the Lotus Europa equipped with a 1600cc twin-cam engine. Installation as shown in the photograph is quite simple but very effective. Robert Vandivort of Checkpoint

America has found it to be very responsive at low RPM, more tractable and easier to drive and if you desire, will out-accelerate a Daytona Ferrari from zero to 120 miles per hour. It will still cruise at better than 70 miles per hour at 33 miles to the gallon. If this isn't impressive enough, the rear-wheel horsepower on a chassis dynamometer showed the following before and after the turbocharger was installed:

RPM	Naturally Aspirated Horsepower		Turbocharged Horsepower
4000	39	x2	78
4500	46	2.4	110
5000	59	2.1	123
5500	72	1.8	132
6000	78	1.9	149
6500	81		

It is interesting to note the turbocharged version only goes to 6000 RPM rather than the 6500 of the naturally aspirated engine. This should impress the people who think a turbocharger only works at very high engine speed.

Their kit for the Lotus Super 7 is just as impressive. This model requires a little more work because the compression ratio must be lowered from 10.3:1 to 8.5:1 by using special forged J. E. Pistons. The 0-60 time runs around 5.0 seconds using 185/70-13 radial tires. The 1/4-mile time is 12.28 seconds. Vandivort uses it for daily transportation when weather permits.

Checkpoint America also has a kit for the MGB shown in the photograph. This particular installation not only produces a lot more horsepower but an emissions test showed it reduced all three pollutants.

CRANE CAMS INC., HALLANDALE, FLORIDA

Crane Cams sells Schwitzer Series 3LD Turbochargers. Don Hubbard wrote their manual on turbocharging engines using Schwitzer Turbochargers. It includes information on choosing the right turbocharger for the application and Don has actually picked the exact turbocharger to be used for many installations. The manual also contains cam information for turbocharged engines and service instructions for the turbochargers. Those wishing to use Schwitzer Turbochargers for their engines should obtain a copy of this manual—$1.00—and read it

Checkpoint America 1973-75 MGB prototype kit uses Rajay 377B40 turbo. Boost comes in at 1800 RPM, is restricted to 14 psi. SU carburetor uses a special air filter. Distributor is reworked to limit total advance. Exhaust HC and CO emissions reduced 50%, NO_x slightly lower than stock.

Offy 73 CID midget engine with wastegated Schwitzer 3LH-209 using double-flow turbine housing and divided exhaust manifold produced 250 HP at 9000 RPM.

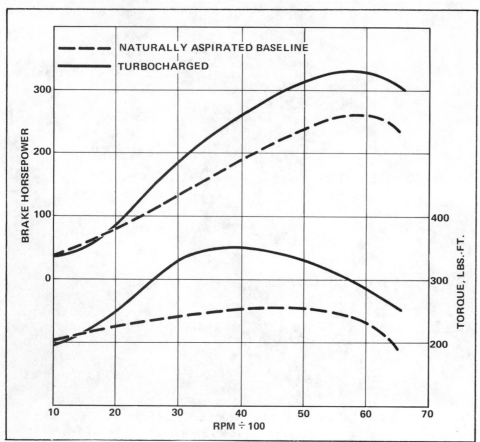

Figure 138—Power curve of Schwitzer 3MD-560 on Ford Boss 302 engine

Figure 139—Power curve of Schwitzer 3MD-560 on Ford 460 Cobra Jet engine

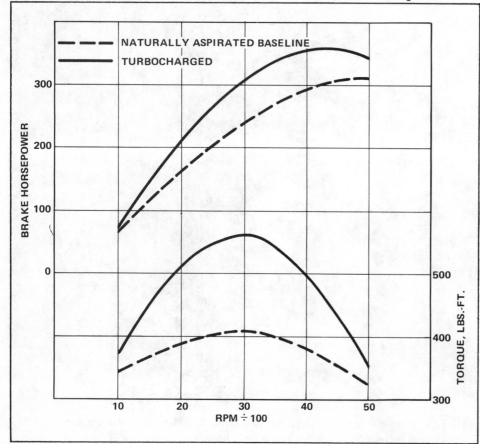

before starting on an installation. Most of the sizing and matching information from the Crane Manual is included in Chapter 4.

Compressor maps of the available Schwitzer Turbochargers are included in the appendix.

The Schwitzer 3MD-560 mounted on a Ford 302 Boss Mustang with a wastegate makes a neat package. The power curve is neat also as shown in Figure 138. The peak horsepower was increased from 262 to 330 while the peak torque not only increased about 40% but the speed for maximum torque decreased from around 4500 to 3800 RPM.

A similar installation including the wastegate was mounted on a Ford 460 Cobra Jet. The same turbo size (3MD-560) was used but the turbine nozzle increased from 3.0 in.^{2} to 3.4 in.^{2} because of the larger engine. Here the peak power was increased from 310 to 360 HP which is a modest increase but the peak torque jumped from 410 pounds feet to 560 which is a whopping increase, Figure 139.

Schwitzer on Ford 302.

Schwitzer on Ford 460.

CROWN MANUFACTURING CO.
NEWPORT BEACH, CALIFORNIA

Ted Trevor, the former owner of Crown Manufacturing, was one of the pioneers in turbocharging when he offered a smaller A/R turbine housing for the standard Corvair Turbocharger back in the 60's to obtain more boost pressure for racing purposes. Crown also offered adapters for the Corvair Compressor Inlet to allow the use of large Weber or SU-Type Carburetors. Back in 1972, the Crown Turbocharger Kit for the Datsun 240Z was one of the first of its kind offered and is now available for the 260Z and 280Z. Later the same year, Crown developed turbocharger kits for the 1600 and 1800cc Datsun Engines.

In 1973, Crown was sold to Derek Torley who, with the help of Rick Mack, continued to develop new turbocharger kits, including one for the Porsche 914. This kit was another first because the 914 has a fuel-injected engine and getting the right air/fuel ratio at the right time is a different story than with a carburetor. Figure 140 shows the improvement in performance when turbocharged.

Figure 141 compares the output of a stock 1600cc Datsun, one modified by BRE and the stock engine with the bolt-on turbocharger kit. Here again, it is interesting to note as in the case of engines turbocharged by Schwitzer, the horsepower increase was obtained without resorting to high engine RPM.

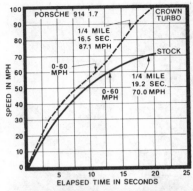

Figure 140—Performance of Porsche 914 with and without turbocharger. Photo below shows installation.

Crown 240Z and 260Z installation with cast manifold adapter.

Figure 141—Comparison of stock Datsun L-1600, one modified by BRE and stock engine with Crown turbocharger kit

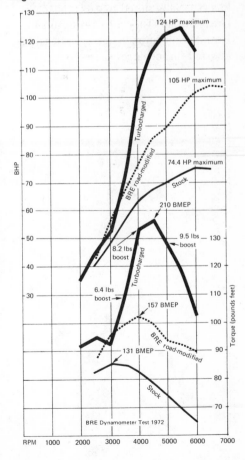

Crown Datsun 1600 installation with air cleaner removed.

Ak Miller's 1977 Pikes Peak hill climb Mustang was powered with a 250 CID Ford 6. An AiResearch TO4 turbo was used. Propane was the fuel.

JANSPEED ENGINEERING SALISBURY, WILTSHIRE ENGLAND

Janspeed has developed a number of kits especially suited to cars available in Great Britain. They are distributors for Roto-Master turbochargers, wastegates, kits and turbocharger accessories.

MATHWALL ENGINEERING THURSLEY, SURREY, ENGLAND

This firm has developed kits for the BMW 2002 and the Opel Manta. On a BMW installation, a large SU carburetor is used. It is sized in conjunction with exhaust restriction to prevent over-boosting. This makes for a very simple setup and with a careful matching of turbine housings, etc., has produced a useful power curve, plus a very good increase in top end HP. Mathwalls claim an increase from 100 to 175 HP; engines usually show between 180 and 185 HP on their dyno. The 0–100 time for the 2002 BMW is 17.8 seconds which compares very favorably with the 19 seconds for the works-turbo-ed 2002. A spot check on the chassis dyno produces 130 HP at the rear wheels at 5000, peak power being nearer 6000. On the Manta they use a similar system. 0–100 time is 19.2 seconds and the HP is up from 80 to a conservative 160.

AK MILLER ENTERPRISES PICO RIVERA, CALIFORNIA

Ak Miller and his cohorts Jack Lufkin, Burke LeSage and Bill Edwards have been in the hot-rod business since before they were called *hot rods*. These fellows, along with Duke Hallock (now retired) of AiResearch, have been using turbochargers to get added horsepower since the 50s. It is only natural that Ak should offer turbocharger kits. In some cases he has combined them with propane fuel for the cleanest turbocharger kits anywhere.

Ak has kits for the 2,000cc Ford (Pinto), Ford 6 170, 200, 240, 250 and 300 CID, Chevy 6, Capri V-6, fuel-injected Porsche 911 and 280Z Datsun. Truck kits are designed for Chevrolet, Dodge and Ford pickups, as well as for the Toyota and Courier mini-trucks. There is also a kit for the Ford 534 CID industrial engine. AiResearch turbo-chargers and other items such as carburetor adapters, manifolds and the IMPCO flow-control valve which prevents the engine from being overboosted are also available.

Ak has done considerable testing in the emission field, showing turbocharging an engine results in better overall emissions. This is discussed at length in Chapter 18, Exhaust Emissions.

AK Miller's open-wheel Pikes Peak entry for 1977 used dual AiResearch TO4 turbochargers, Impco propane carburetion and boost-limiting valves. Engine is 351 CID Ford.

Ak Miller turbocharged this 1978 Toyota Celica. It was the 1978 Long Beach Grand Prix pace car. Crossover pipe from compressor feeds carburetor through one of Ak's adapters which includes an IMPCO control valve.

Figure 142—Roto-Master TurboSonic kit for Chevrolet V8 uses the priority-valve Turbo-Module, BPR wastegate and Roto-Master turbocharger.

Pressure-retard/vacuum-advance mechanism retards ignition 1° per pound of boost to a maximum of 8° retard. This is one of many off-the-shelf items found in the accessory section of the Roto-Master catalog.

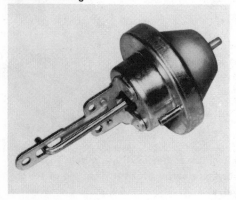

ROTO-MASTER TURBOSONIC SYSTEMS, NORTH HOLLYWOOD, CALIFORNIA

Several years ago, Bob Keller and a couple of other men started a company called Turbonics. It was a sideline while Bob was working at Grumman Aircraft. In 1973, Turbonics joined the Flagship Marine Engine Company as the Turbonics Division. In 1974 the Turbocharger portion of the business was sold to Accel Division of Western Automotive Controls, a part of Echlin Corporation. In 1975 Echlin acquired Roto-Master Inc. in North Hollywood, California. The Turbo-Sonic line is now manufactured and marketed by Roto-Master.

Bob Keller turbocharged his own car back in the 60s when nobody else was doing it. His slant-six Dodge installation was based on the AiResearch T-5 turbocharger used on the Oldsmobile Jetfire.

Turbonics made experimental installations for drag racers and offered a kit for the small-block Mustang in 1973.

Keller's approach was different from what others were doing. He designed a Turbo-Module to bolt between the standard carburetor and the inlet manifold. The module contains an automatic priority valve which allows the engine to operate in a naturally aspirated mode until the turbocharger is required. The priority valve passes fuel/air mixture directly into the intake manifold during non-turbocharged conditions, providing sharp-crisp throttle response and the smooth-idle characteristics of a stock engine. As the compressor provides boost, the priority valve closes so the fuel/air mixture passes through the compressor and then into the intake manifold.

Roto-Master offers a number of complete street and competition installation kits for popular engines, including small-block Chevrolet 262–350 CID, small-block Ford 260–351C, Chrysler 360 CID, Universal V-8 turbo kits to work with engines from 220–390 CID, and Universal In-Line 4 and 6-cylinder kits to work with engines from 50–310 CID. Competition kits are available for Dodge Colt, Ford Pinto and Chevrolet Vega engines.

Figure 142 shows a TurboSonic kit installed on a 350 CID Chevrolet. Performance results from this installation are shown in Figure 143.

Roto-Master's development group has spent considerable time and effort to offer desirable turbo-related accessories such as water-injection kits, ignition-retard kits, turbine adapters, inlet adapters, exhaust kits and wastegates. As anyone who has dabbled in the world of turbocharging knows, these items can prove to be extremely helpful in making an installation.

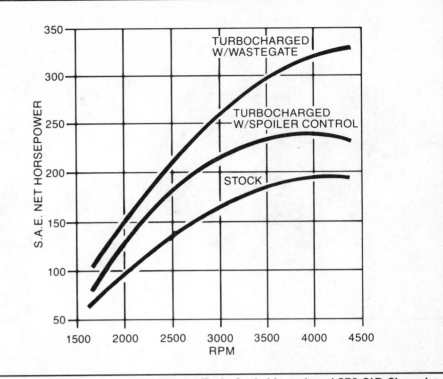

Figure 143—Roto-Master test results on a TurboSonic kit equipped 350 CID Chevrolet. This compares the horsepower available with their older spoiler-type variable-boost control and that available with the newer BPR Wastegate. Boost was 7.5 psi in these tests.

Roto-Master's irrigation and industrial conversion kits are used to normalize engines to provide full rated horsepower at any altitude. An example is this Caterpillar 3208 engine. Here, horsepower was increased 50% at 5,000 feet altitude with a significant torque increase. Smoke is eliminated. Exhaust temperatures are reduced, providing increased engine life.

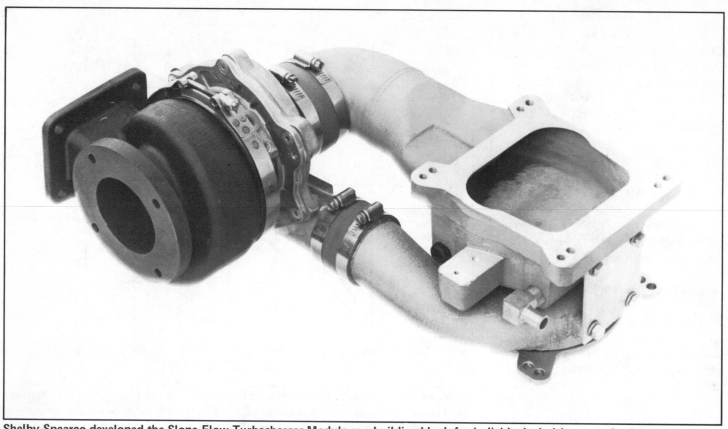

Shelby-Spearco developed the Slope-Flow Turbocharger Module as a building block for individuals desiring to turbocharge a passenger car, pickup truck or motor home. The module fits almost any V6 or V8 engine. The carburetor mounting pad and turbo swivel 360 degrees around the manifold connector pad. Passages are designed for optimum flow and heat is used to reduce fuel fallout and puddling. Drivability was the prime design goal in engineering the concept.

Honda Civic 1300cc with Rajay B-flow unit by Spearco Performance Products is boosted at 8 psi at around 5500 RPM.

Spearco 2000cc Ford kit puts turbocharger on left so Pinto factory air-conditioning can be retained. This eliminates relocating battery. Rajay 301B.4 turbo gives 10 psi boost.

SHELBY-SPEARCO DISTRIBUTING COMPANY INGLEWOOD, CALIFORNIA

Principal owners of this corporation are Carroll Shelby, widely known for his world-famous line of Cobra and Shelby Automobiles, and George Spears, well-known aftermarket parts engineer and turbocharger specialist. This team has put together an array of turbocharger kits for most popular vehicles including the small- and big-block Chevrolet and Ford vehicles. In addition to offering over 10 basic turbocharger kits, this company provides an interesting variety of accessories and special castings for custom installations. They have developed a universal downward-sloping Turbocharger Module for use on most V-8 engines.

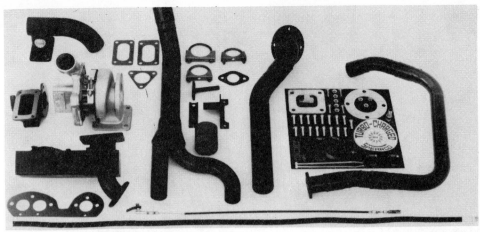

Figure 144—Shelby Spearco V-6 Mustang kit

SPEARCO PERFORMANCE PRODUCTS INGLEWOOD, CALIFORNIA

Spearco Performance Products specializes in turbocharger kits for small imported and domestic vehicles. They feature kits for Mustang II, Capri 2800 and 2600, Pinto 2000 and 2300 and several Toyota vehicles. The Pinto Kit designed for the street produces 7 psi boost to increase horsepower 45%. It operates on 91-octane unleaded fuel. An optional exhaust system and turbine housing ups maximum boost to 14 psi and output 100%. Water injection and O-ringing the head is recommended with this version.

The V-6 Mustang Kit in Figure 144 increases the output to 185 HP. It has excellent low-speed driveability, with boost pressure starting at 2,100 RPM. Spearco claims the kit improves fuel mileage.

They have designed and developed an electronically controlled water injection device which meters water in direct proportion to engine speed and boost pressure.

The popular Toyota 20R engine gets a fantastic improvement in acceleration when this Spearco kit is bolted on. All emission controls are retained.

Peugeot 504, 1974 diesel sedan turbo-ed by Turbocharger, Inc. Remote oil filter to supply turbo is at far left side of photo. This car was driven round trip from Los Angeles to Fairbanks, Alaska pulling a 3,000 lb. trailer all the way. Mileage averaged out at 24 MPG! Windshield washer reservoir and pump were relocated for exhaust clearance. Intake and exhaust manifolds are stock with a J-pipe making the exhaust-manifold-to-turbo connection. Stock air cleaner and factory air conditioning are retained with minor modifications.

Turbocharger, Inc. 300D Mercedes installation connects turbo directly to the air cleaner and intake manifold. Performance is about the same as 450SE.

TURBOCHARGER, INC. DOWNEY, CALIFORNIA

Many diesel kits have been offered for trucks, farm tractors and construction, but this one is for a passenger car. It is common knowledge the Mercedes diesel-powered cars are not very exciting when it comes to acceleration. This lack of performance is not due to the fact it is a diesel but rather because it is a *small* diesel. The largest four has a displacement of only 2.4 liters or 144 CID.

Turbocharging a diesel has all of the advantages of turbocharging a gasoline engine plus a few more. These are:

1. Lower exhaust temperature
2. Less smoke and odor problem
3. Lower noise level
4. Increase in fuel economy

The performance of this kit as measured by *Road and Track* (September 1973) is:

Time to Speed, Sec.	Stock 220D	Turbo 220D
0—30 MPH	7.0	6.5
0—40 MPH	12.3	9.4
0—50 MPH	18.0	13.2
0—60 MPH	27.5	17.9
0—70 MPH	44.2	24.3

The 0—60 MPH time was reduced by almost 10 seconds—not bad by any standards.

The kit fits all series 200, 220 and 240 diesels with either manual or automatic transmissions.

TURBO SYSTEMS, INC. AKRON, OHIO

Bill Laughlin of Turbo Systems decided a few years ago that turbochargers were the only way to go so he purchased the Pinto and Vega turbocharger kit lines from Car Corp. of Livonia, Michigan, and has since added a small-block Chevy kit of his own. This is a real performance kit using two turbochargers and will fit all of the small-block Chevy's from 265 up to 400 CID. Bill has cast new exhaust manifolds for the engine so the turbochargers can be mounted high on the front end. This kit is for the man looking for power rather than comfort because air conditioning cannot be used.

Turbo Systems has done quite a bit of work with diesel tractors used in tractor pulling contests.

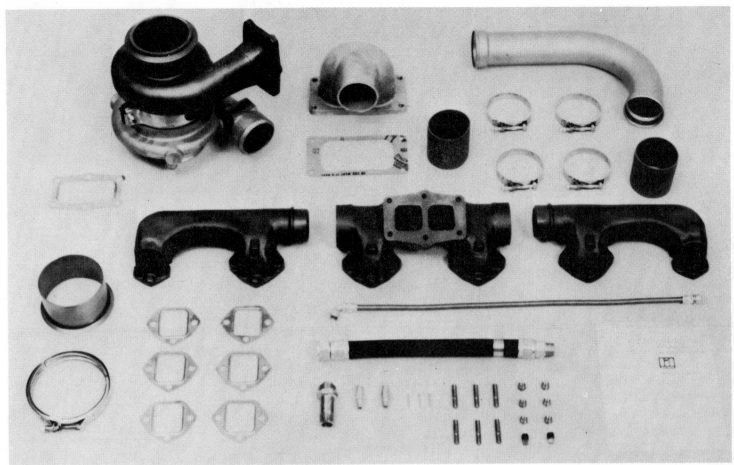

Roto-Master kit for the naturally aspirated Cummins 220 HP diesel is produced by the firm which author Hugh MacInnes serves as Vice President and Chief Engineer. Roto-Master is a division of Echlin Manufacturing Co., one of the largest automotive aftermarket suppliers.

Turbocharger, Inc. kits are available for Mercedes 200D, 220D, 240D, and 300D diesels. These kits allow use of factory air conditioning.

18 EXHAUST EMISSIONS

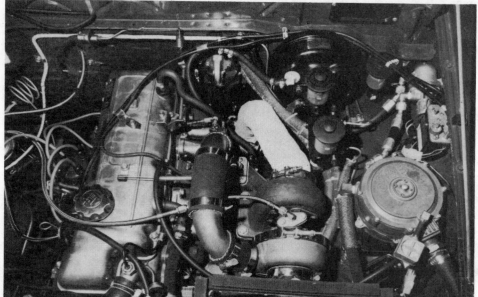

Northrop Institute of Technology entry in 1973 and 1974 Reduced Emission Rallies for college students was a turbocharged Toyota using propane fuel. One-third of the cars entered in 1974 had turbocharged engines.

NOTE: Tests have shown in nearly every case that turbochargers reduce emissions—or at least do not increase them. Even so, to add one to a non-turbocharged gasoline or diesel engine was illegal in California as of 1978. Propane use with an add-on turbocharger was apparently allowable.

One of the most frequently asked questions about turbochargers is "What will a turbocharger do for the exhaust emissions from my engine?" There is no simple answer to this question because a turbocharger is not a device designed to chop up exhaust emissions in little bits and spit them out as clean air. However, tests have shown that a turbocharger applied either to a diesel or a gasoline engine in good running condition will not significantly increase any of the measured exhaust emissions and in almost every case will decrease them. The nice part about this is it can be done while increasing the output of the engine by as much as 100%.

Looking at this from another viewpoint, the output of a standard U. S. gasoline engine, when equipped with all the devices to meet the 1975 and later exhaust-emissions requirements, has lost so much power the vehicle will no longer perform in a manner most of us have accepted as a way of life. A turbocharger applied directly to such an engine will allow it to produce the horsepower it had before all the emission devices were applied. The largest single disadvantage here is the fuel consumption will not be as good as the original high-compression naturally-aspirated engine.

With the diesel engine, it is a slightly different story. The diesel engines up until recently were not considered seriously for use in U. S. passenger cars for several reasons including a poor power-to-weight ratio and high initial cost. Even with the addition of all the emission-control devices, few people looked at the diesel engine seriously because the extra fuel burned in the gasoline engine wasn't all that expensive. The 1974 fuel shortage and subsequent price increase has altered our thinking considerably and it has suddenly become patriotic to try to reduce fuel consumption as well as exhaust emissions.

An engine such as the Nissan CN6-33 six-cylinder in-line diesel of 198 CID will run at 4,000 RPM—fast enough for any passenger car or pickup truck. This engine is almost competitive weight and power-wise with a small V-8 gasoline engine equipped with all the exhaust-emission devices including a catalytic converter. I say almost competitive because the simple addition of a free-floating turbocharger makes it more than competitive. The state of California has been conducting tests with this engine since January 1974 where fuel consumption is a consideration just as important as low exhaust emissions. The original test was run on two Dodge 3/4-ton pickups normally equipped with 360 CID gasoline engines. One of the trucks has a naturally-aspirated CN6-33 Nissan engine while the other has the same basic engine with a Rajay turbocharger. The naturally aspirated engine has a maximum output of 92 HP at 4,000 RPM while the turbocharged version of this engine produces approximately 130 HP. Both vehicles were tested for exhaust emissions and fuel consumption before the gasoline engines were removed. The emissions and fuel consumption tests were rerun after the diesel engines were installed and the comparative results are shown in Table X. The turbocharged diesel, when compared to the proposed California Requirements for 1976, was twice as good on HC, seven times as good on CO and only 7% too high on NO$_x$. The nicest thing about this is the engine contains no special devices which contribute to fuel consumption without producing power. Patricia Spears recently made a comment when looking at a 1974 car with the hood raised. She said, "The only people who make out from all these emission controls are the hose manufacturers."

Tony Capanna of Wilcap who made the installation for the State of California has been running several diesel-powered passenger cars including a Dodge Dart with a turbocharged diesel like one of the state pickups. Because of the light weight of this vehicle, he gets 40 miles to the gallon. He doesn't have to worry about passing through a town which may not have a diesel fuel pump. He might drive through an entire state without refueling.

Because most of us are concerned with gasoline rather than diesel engine vehicles, the effect of a turbocharger on exhaust emissions is of more importance

TABLE X

Fuel-Consumption & Exhaust-Emissions Comparison of a 1973 3/4-Ton Truck with Gasoline & Diesel Engines, both Air-Conditioned

| | | COLD START CVS TEST GRAMS/MILE | | | |
TRUCK	ENGINE	HC	CO	NO$_x$	MILES/GALLON
CHC 2747	Baseline Gasoline	3.72	53.82	4.93	11
CHC 2748	Baseline Gasoline	2.91	37.84	4.52	11
CHC 2747	Baseline Diesel	1.17	4.14	2.52	20
CHC 2748	Turbocharged Diesel	0.47	2.54	2.13	20

ADDITIONAL HOT CVS – 1 TEST

		HC	CO	NO$_x$
CHC 2748	Emissions	0.26	2.10	1.85

	SPEED (MPH)			
	30	40	50	60
Dynamometer Fuel Consumption	29.4	26.2	23.8	20.3

TABLE XI

Comparison of Exhaust Emissions of Naturally Aspirated and AK Miller Turbocharged Engines

EMISSIONS RESULTS

TURBOCHARGED VEHICLES

DATE	VEHICLE	CID	TRANS	FUEL	LAB	TEST	HC	CO	NO$_x$
9/4/73	Pinto Pangra (T)	120	4-spd	Gas	Scott	CVS 1-2	1.84	20	3.01
9/72	Pinto 2000 (T)	120	Auto	Gas	AESI	CVS 1-2	1.51	27.04	1.72
4/8/71	Pinto 2000 (T)	120	4-spd	Propane	Auto Club	7-mode	0.7	10.9	1.3
2/73	Maverick (NA)	250	Auto	Gas-EGR	AESI	CVS 1-2	1.70	24.07	1.92
9/72	Maverick (T)	250	Auto	Gas No EGR	AESI	CVS 1-2	1.23	19.73	3.2
3/7/72	Maverick (T)	250	Auto	Propane	Auto Club	7-mode	0.55	1.83	1.007
10/20/71	Dodge 440 (NA)	440	Auto	Gas	Auto Club	7-mode	1.15	19.05	5.13
4/5/72	Dodge 440 (NA)	440	Auto	Propane	Auto Club	7-mode	0.25	2.07	0.58
5/73	Dodge 440 (T)	440	Auto	Propane	Auto Club	7-mode	0.23	2.38	0.63
7/73	Aston Martin (NA)	327	4-spd	Gas	Auto Club	7-mode	0.32	8.17	1.30
8/73	Aston Martin (T)	327	4-spd	Gas	AESI	CVS 1-2	1.72	34.3	2.70

T - Turbocharged
NA - Naturally Aspirated

1972 Monte Carlo 350 CID Chevrolet turbocharged by Schwitzer for high power and low emissions. This system pressurizes the carburetor.

TABLE XII

Exhaust Emissions of Naturally-Aspirated
vs.
Turbocharged Datsun 240Z

		1973 California Standards	Test 1 Stock 240Z	Test 2 Turbocharged 240Z
1972 Weighted Test	HC	3.2	2.085	1.476
	CO	39.2	22.306	16.270
	NO$_x$	3.0	2.073	1.409
	MPG		18.83	19.398
	MPG (steady state 50 MPH)		31.74	31.99
Cold Start Test	HC	3.2	2.9*	2.9
	CO	39.0	29.0*	38.9
	NO$_x$	3.0	1.8*	1.1

*Baseline Data From Nissan Motor Car Co.

TABLE XIII

COMPRESSION PRESSURE OF VARIOUS
ENGINES CALCULATED FROM FIGURE 152

	Naturally Aspirated		Turbocharged	
Compression Ratio	10.5/1		7.0/1	7.0/1
Intake Manifold Pressure PSIA	14.7	P_b	29.4	25
Inducted Charge Temperature °R	600	T_b	750	700
Inducted Charge Density Ft³/Lb.	15.05	V_b	9.41	10.5
Entropy	.085	S	.095	.09
Charge Density at end of Compression Stroke — Ft³/Lb.	1.43	V_c	1.345	1.53
Compression Pressure PSIA	340	P_c	360	320

to us. Two companies, in particular Ak Miller Enterprises and Crown Manufacturing, have gone out of their way to show the results obtained by applying a turbocharger to a standard gasoline engine without disturbing the emission equipment. Ak Miller, in addition, has made many installations where the fuel system was converted to use propane and here, even better results were obtained. Table XI compiles these results and shows dates for the runs. Crown Manufacturing has concentrated on kits for the Datsun 240Z and 260Z. Emission tests were run before and after the turbocharger was installed. The results of these tests are shown on Table XII. Here again we see where an engine equipped with devices to meet the 1973 California Standards actually improved somewhat on exhaust emission when equipped with a turbocharger and at the same time nearly doubled its output.

Now that it is established that a turbocharger on either a diesel or gasoline engine will not hurt exhaust emissions and usually will improve them it is only fair to ask why? In the case of the diesel engine, the answer is relatively simple. Air flow through a naturally-aspirated diesel is strictly a function of engine speed and not power because the engine does not normally contain a butterfly in the air intake. Output is governed by the amount of fuel injected with each power stroke. Maximum output of a naturally-aspirated diesel is limited by the exhaust smoke. When a turbocharger is applied to a diesel engine, a manifold pressure of 10 psig—which is easy to obtain—will increase the air flow through the engine by about 67%. If the fuel setting is left the same as when naturally aspirated, the extra air will lower the combustion temperature and therefore the amount of NO$_x$ in the exhaust. The extra air will also do a better job of reducing hydrocarbons and carbon monoxide merely by having excess oxygen present to produce a more complete combustion. Even when the engine output is increased by burning more fuel per stroke, exhaust emissions will be reduced as long as the fuel/air ratio is kept considerably leaner than when naturally aspirated.

The gasoline engine is a different story. Here, regardless of output or operating condition, the fuel/air ratio must be kept close to a stoichiometric mixture or it will

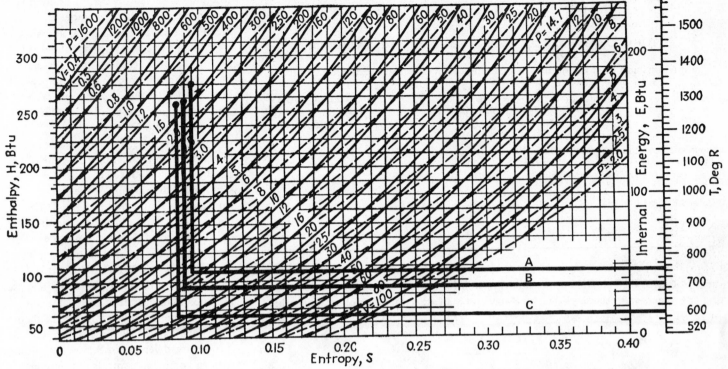

Figure 152—Compression chart for a chemically-correct octane-air mixture plus an average amount of clearance gases.
Line A is naturally aspirated, 10.5:1 compression ratio.
Line B is supercharged at 2:1 pressure ratio, 7:1 compression ratio.
Line C is supercharged at 1.7:1 pressure ratio, 7:1 compression ratio.
Lb fuel/lb air = 0.0665; E of combustion = 1280 (1-f); H of combustion = 1278 (1-f).
(From Hershey, Eberhardt and Hottel, Transactions of the S.A.E., October 1936).

not burn. This means the fuel/air ratio of the turbocharged engine will have to be approximately the same as the naturally-aspirated engine. Because of this, any improvement in the exhaust emissions after the turbocharger is applied must come from some other cause than air/fuel ratio. When the carburetor is placed upstream of the compressor, it is necessary for all of the fuel to pass through the compressor impeller on its way to the combustion chamber. A centrifugal compressor is inherently a high-speed device and even at part load, the compressor can easily be rotating at somewhere between 20,000 and 30,000 RPM. This high speed not only makes it impossible for small droplets of gasoline to be carried into the intake system but also does a thorough mixing job on the gasoline which has already been vaporized.

A naturally-aspirated gasoline engine does not have a perfect intake manifold and the fuel/air ratio will vary somewhat from cylinder to cylinder. As a result, some of the cylinders will be slightly lean while others will be slightly rich. Those which are slightly lean will tend to increase the output of NO_x while those which are slightly rich will tend to increase the output of HC and CO_2. If the turbocharger compressor is installed correctly so that no stratification takes place in the intake manifold, see Chapter 14—Installation Hints, there will be a relatively even fuel/air mixture to all cylinders, promoting consistent combustion in each.

This is not too hard to sell on the part-load basis on which the emission tests are run, but the next question is what about when the engine is really pulling power. Won't the emissions be a lot worse than they were on a high-compression naturally-aspirated engine? Back in 1936, some gentlemen named Hershey, Eberhardt and Hottel published the curve shown in Figure 152, in the *SAE Transactions*. This curve when used properly is a means of determining compression pressure at the end of the compression stroke when using a chemically-correct mixture of gasoline and air. Using it as a basis, a naturally-aspirated engine with 10.5:1 c.r. can be compared to a turbo-charged engine of 7:1 c.r. to find out how high the compression pressure will be which will have a direct effect on the combustion temperature. In Table XIII we see that with 10 lbs. intake-manifold pressure (25 psia) the compression pressure of the turbocharged engine will actually be 20 lbs. less than the naturally aspirated engine. The turbocharged engine with approximately 50% more air and fuel available will put out over 50% more power than the naturally-aspirated engine. However, because of the added turbulence due to the compressor impeller, and because the combustion temperature will not be any higher, exhaust emissions will usually be about the same or a little less with the turbocharged engine. When running at wide-open throttle, intake-manifold pressure will usually be higher than the exhaust-manifold pressure. This will remove the clearance gases and reduce the combustion temperature of the turbocharged engine even further.

Gary Knudsen of McLaren Engines ran tests on a big-block Chevy engine

TABLE XIV

TURBOCHARGED TCCS ENGINE-POWERED M-151 VEHICLE

Emissions and Fuel Economy With Gasoline Fuel & Without Emission Controls

| | EMISSIONS, GPM | | | FUEL ECONOMY MPG (Liters/100km) |
	HC	CO	NO$_x$	WEIGHT
Full emission controls	0.35	1.41	0.35	16.2 (14.5)
No emission controls	3.13	7.00	1.46	24.3 (9.7)
Carbureted L-141 engine	4.50	73.18	3.22	15.3 (15.4)
Proposed Federal Limit (1976)	.40	3.4	.41	

*Fuel: gasoline

Chevy 350 CID Z-28 engine on test at AiResearch for low emissions development. Similar projects were accomplished by Rajay and Schwitzer for Chevrolet Engineering.

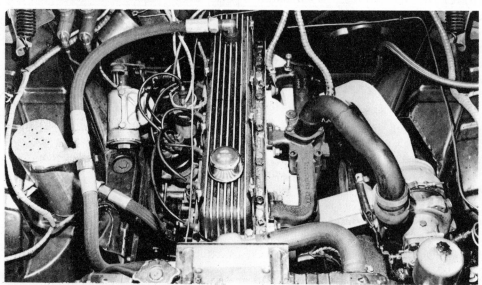

Australian Holden 186 CID in-line six-cylinder turbocharged with a Rajay unit. Carb is an SU.

where he observed the compression pressure in the combustion chamber by means of a pressure transducer and an oscilloscope. He was surprised to learn that the turbocharger did not appreciably increase the compression-pressure peak but fattened up the curve considerably. The fatter curve increased the BMEP and therefore the horsepower.

For many years, Texaco has been experimenting with a different type of combustion chamber known as the stratified-charge engine or the Texaco Controlled Combustion System, TCCS. Many S.A.E. papers have been published on this subject. I do not intend to go into detail on the design of this combustion system but would like to point out the addition of a turbocharger greatly increased the maximum output of the engine, improved fuel economy and reduced exhaust emissions. Table XIV shows where the turbocharged version of this engine equipped with full emission controls not only met the then-proposed 1976 Federal Limitations but did it at better fuel economy than the original engine with practically no emission-control devices. This engine which might be considered halfway between a diesel and a spark-ignition engine has cylinder injection which actually sprays the fuel on the spark plug. The word *fuel* is used because it will run on almost anything which will burn.

Turbocharging definitely has a place in the engine of the fututre, not just because it can improve the power-to-weight ratio but also because it can help reduce exhaust emissions without hurting the fuel consumption.

Most bolt-on kits for street use will produce a maximum intake-manifold boost pressure of somewhere between 5 and 10 psig. This amount of boost normally will not require any modification of the engine and it will not detonate on premium fuel when the fuel/air mixture and the ignition are set correctly. If modifications are made to the engine to allow the boost pressure to go above 10 psig, it is not always possible to prevent detonation, even with a retarded spark.

In Chapter 5 on Carburetion, I discussed enriching the fuel/air ratio as a method of preventing detonation when the engine is in the supercharged condition. This method will work up to a certain limit and beyond that the engine will detonate regardless of how rich the mixture is. Beyond this point either water or water-alcohol injection are required to prevent detonation.

We all have a tendency when we discover such phenomenon and the solution to it, to think we have "invented the wheel." This problem, for one, has been around a long time and Ricardo not only faced it but ran a series of tests in the early 1930's, plotted in Figure 153. Reference: *The High-Speed Internal Combustion Engine* by H. Ricardo. To quote Mr. Ricardo, "In this case, running throughout at a speed of 2,500 RPM and with a compression ratio of 7:1, the engine was run on an economical mixture, i.e. about 10% weak, and supercharge applied to the first incidence of detonation, which occurred when the BMEP had reached 168 pounds per square inch. The mixture strength was then increased, step by step, and more supercharge applied until the same intensity of detonation was recorded; this process was continued until a point was reached at which no further enrichment was effective. In fact, after about 60% excess fuel, not only did further enrichment have no effect but there was even some indication that it increased the tendency to detonate. A finely pulverized water spray was then delivered into the

Tom Keosababian combined ecology with engineering by running on propane to break the record for the class at Bonneville in August 1974. He ran over 170 MPH that year. He used two Rajay turbochargers and two propane carburetors. Water for injection comes from a valve on the firewall to each compressor inlet.

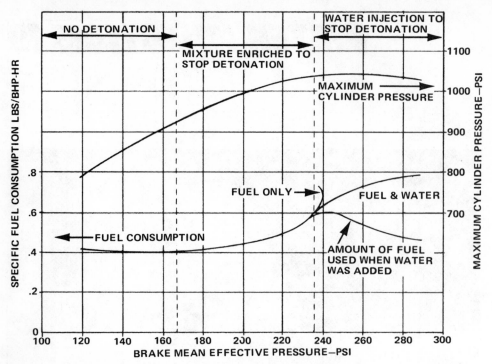

Figure 153—Variation in maximum BMEP without detonation by enriching mixture and with water injection. Fuel was 87-octane gasoline.

induction pipe which served to suppress detonation, in part by the inter-cooling it provided, and in part by the influence of steam as an anti-detonant, and so allow of further supercharging. This was continued progressively, admitting just sufficient water at each stage to ward off detonation until a BMEP of 290 pounds per square inch was reached, which was found to be the limit of the dynamometer. At the same time, it was noted that, with the addition of water, the influence of steam as an anti-knock allowed the fuel/air ratio being much reduced. From this curve, Figure 153, it will be seen that under these operating conditions a limiting BMEP that could be reached with 87 octane petrol alone at an economical mixture strength was 168 psi. By enriching the mixture to the limit of usefulness, the BMEP could be stepped up to 237 psi. By the introduction of water, it could be further stepped up 290 psi and probably more; at the same time the fuel/air ratio could be reduced once again; in fact with water injection, no appreciable advantage was found from the use of an overrich fuel/air mixture. It will be noted that the total specific consumption of liquid, i.e., fuel plus water, is not so very much greater than when running on a very rich mixture of fuel alone."

"The slope of the curve of maximum

cylinder pressure is interesting in that after the injection of water, *it no longer rose but even tended very slightly to fall,* and the same applied to the gross heat flow to the cooling water which reached a maximum at a BMEP of about 230 pounds per square inch, and thereafter fell off, until at a BMEP of 290 pounds per square inch it had fallen to the same level as that of 170 pounds without water injection."

The result of this kind of test will vary with engine speed, engine size, compression ratio, fuel octane etc. These variations are not important as far as the principle is concerned. The main thing the curve shows is detonation may be prevented up to a certain point by fuel enrichment, but after that point, water or water-alcohol injection must be used.

Water is usually combined with methanol (methyl-alcohol) in proportions up to 50-50 water-methanol to increase the volatility of the injected mixture—and therefore its cooling effect—to add part fuel instead of all water for further horsepower increase, and to eliminate the possibility of the water freezing on a cold day. Harry Ricardo, again quoting from his book, *The Higher Speed Internal Combustion Engine,* says "Higher percentages of methanol are not desirable because methanol, itself, is prone to pre-ignition."

Tests made in 1971 by Ted Trevor of Crown Manufacturing showed that mixtures containing more than 50% methanol provided no additional HP gains over a 50/50 mixture. Dick Griffin confirmed that 50/50 is practical in his tests which were made several years earlier.

Opinions vary as to the amount of boost pressure which makes water or water/alcohol injection mandatory. Some say any boost over 5 psi should be accompanied by injection. Others claim that 8 psi is where the "borderline" begins. And, we've talked with some racers who felt 15 psi boost was a good place to start using water injection. As the saying goes, "Circumstances alter cases." Obviously, a higher compression ratio or advanced spark will require such injection at a lower boost pressure than would a lower c.r. and lesser spark advance. If detonation is occurring at a particular boost pressure and RPM, then water injection should be started prior to the onset of detonation. Should detonation occur, it is essential to back off on the throttle instantly because sustained detonation will destroy the engine very quickly. In any case, water should not be injected at a manifold pressure much below where it is needed. If injection does not take place below 5 lbs. boost, there will usually not be any loss of power due to the cooling effect. It should be noted that engines which are equipped with water-injection will be unusually free from carbon when torn down for inspection or repair. Pistons, combustion chambers and valves all stay remarkably clean with water injection. As a side benefit, spark plugs last longer too.

At least three types of water-injection systems can be considered—and probably a lot more types that I did not think of as this chapter was put together. Two types apply manifold boost pressure to the anti-detonant liquid to push the water through a tube to the carburetor inlet, Crown Figure 154, or through a fitting in the carburetor base—Griffin Figure 155—when boost occurs.

Crown's system uses a vent at the carburetor air inlet, alongside the injector outlet jet. This vent bleeds off pressure applied to the tank so injection does not start until after boost pressure has reached several psi. The boost pressure at which injection begins is tailored by the size of the restrictor jet in the vent line.

A third type turns on a constant-pressure windshield-wiper pump when a pressure switch on the intake manifold sees 5 psi boost—Ak Miller, Figure 156. This system is probably the most economical because it can be made by modifying an electric-type windshield washer with the pump in the reservoir. All that is needed is a pressure switch and a tube to the carburetor. A modification of this type could use water stored under pressure and a solenoid valve actuated at 5 psi by a pressure switch on the intake manifold.

From these variations you can develop many other combinations depending on your imagination, pocketbook and inclination toward time and experimentation.

Doug Roe uses a slightly different approach to the problem by spraying water into the cooling-air stream of a Corvair engine. 3/16-inch V-type "shooter" or spray tubes with 0.040-inch orifices are located at the front and rear of the cooling-fan inlet and are supplied with water when boost pressure reaches 5 psi or more. Roe's system uses boost pressure to move the water, but a windshield-wiper pump actuated by a manifold-pressure switch could be used instead. Also, this type of system could be augmented by using water-injection into the manifold with the air/fuel mixture.

Tom Keosababian has clearly shown what can be done if water injection is used to its limit. His 1965 Corvair is a street machine with stock suspension. He used two stock Corvair Rajay F turbochargers. Water was injected into each compressor inlet from a valve mounted on the top of the firewall. Carburetion was two Impco CA425 Propane mixers.

This setup with a few other goodies such as a Mallory distributor and transistor ignition produced 450 HP @ 6,700 RPM and ran 176.125 MPH at Bonneville in 1974. He showed it is possible to break a record without spending a fortune.

Motor-driven water-injection systems are available from Ak Miller, Roto-Master and Shelby-Spearco distributors. If you use any one of these systems, make sure the motor is wired in series with both the pressure switch *and* the ignition switch. This will prevent any possibility of pumping water into the engine when it is not running.

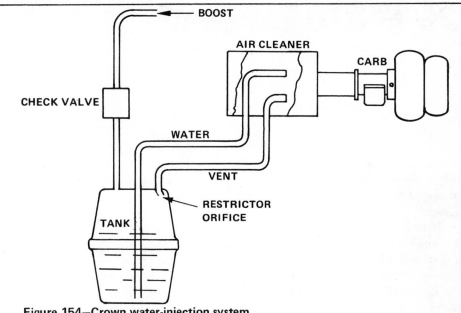

Figure 154—Crown water-injection system

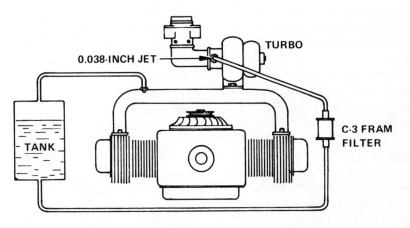

REAR VIEW · CORVAIR INSTALLATION

Figure 155—Dick Griffin water-injection system

Figure 156—Ak Miller water-injection system

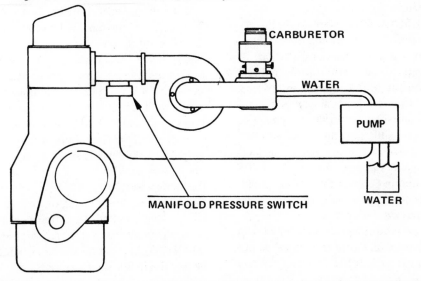

20 MOTORCYCLES

Turbocharging a motorcycle engine may involve all the same basic principles as any other engine but the problems associated with it are quite unique.

Starting with turbocharger size, even the smallest models manufactured by AiResearch, Rajay and Schwitzer are really too large even for the Harley Davidson Electra Glide but in spite of this many installations have been made which give outstanding results and several companies are now in the business of producing bolt-on kits for turbochargers. If Schwitzer would produce the prototype turbocharger shown in Figure 157 mounted on a Petter Diesel Engine, we could almost turbocharge a large-size lawn mower.

The amount of lubricating oil used by a turbocharger compared to a passenger-car engine, even a small one, is so insignificant that it is rarely necessary to add any capacity to the engine oil pump. This is not so on a motorcycle engine where the half gallon a minute used by a turbocharger may be enough to lower the oil pressure to the rest of the engine when it needs it the most. For this reason it is advisable to have a good oil-pressure gage on the bike and if there are signs of oil starvation, a larger oil pump should be installed.

In Chapter 8 on Lubrication, the increase in oil temperature due to the turbocharger bearings was discussed. This can also be a serious problem because the capacity of the oil sump in the motorcycle is limited. If possible, it is desirable to put an oil cooler on the system.

It is possible to turbocharge a two-stroke-cycle motorcycle but the lack of an oil pump makes it more difficult. This is covered in Chapter 12 on Two-Stroke Engines, and poses many more problems than a four-stroke engine.

Some motorcycles are equipped with distributors similar to those used on passenger cars while others have a very simple breaker device which fires at the top of the exhaust stroke as well as at the top of the compression stroke. This apparently does not give any problems on a naturally-aspirated engine. However, on a turbocharged engine there is the possibility, particularly at wide-open throttle and high engine speed, for the intake-manifold pressure to be greater than the exhaust-manifold pressure. Under these conditions when both the exhaust valve and intake valve are open at the top of the exhaust stroke, air/fuel mixture will be blown into the combustion chamber and ignited by the plug. This, of course, will cause severe back firing and loss of power. When this happens, it is necessary to install an automotive-type distributor in place of the breaker points.

A four-cylinder engine with an intake stroke every 180° will cause an almost uninterrupted flow from the compressor discharge and therefore not much volume is required between the compressor housing and the intake ports. A two-cylinder engine, on the other hand, does not necessarily have an intake stroke every 360° and even if it did, the intake stroke would last less than 180° and air in the pipe between the compressor discharge and the intake ports would be stagnant half the time. For this reason, it is advisable to have a plenum chamber on the intake manifold on a two-cylinder engine. The volume of all the pipes from the compressor discharge to the cylinder heads should be at least twice the volume of a single cylinder and preferably three times as great. If the volume is not great enough, intake-manifold pressure will drop off at high engine speed even though the flow is far below the capacity of the compressor.

We are so used to seeing one exhaust stack for each cylinder and one carburetor for each cylinder of a naturally-aspirated bike, it may be hard for the uninitiated to believe a simple exhaust system, where all the cylinders are connected into a single pipe and a simple intake system where a single carburetor is used, can give much better performance just because of a little gadget called a turbocharger. I can assure you this is the case. American Turbo Pak has been able to get street-bike performance which is scary to say the least. Figure 158 shows the BMW designers must have had turbocharging in mind because it fits in so neatly. Turbos are not obvious on most motorcycle installations. The only thing noticeable as it drives by is the lack of exhaust pipes.

If the performance of your stock Honda, Kawasaki, Suzuki or BMW with a turbocharger is not enough, American Turbo Pak offers racing turbo kits which will provide even more performance. Their alcohol-burning Kawasaki 903 has turned the quarter mile at 159 MPH in 8.81 seconds! A gasoline-burning Suzuki GS750 can turn the quarter at over 135 MPH in under 11 seconds, with experienced riders showing times in the 9.35-second area.

Figure 157—Schwitzer's smallest experimental turbo on a Petter 16 CID diesel

Figure 158—American Turbo Pak kit installed on 1977 BMW R100S.

Joe Haile, Sr. and Jr. have been turbocharging Harley-Davidson bikes since 1970. Unfortunately, there is no convenient place to hide the turbo as is the case on Hondas and Kawaskis. Joe is a strong advocate of lowering the compression ratio as a means of reducing detonation tendencies and to allow using higher boost.

Bill Schroeder, left, drives this turbo-ed 74 CID Harley for owner, Duane Nealen, of Northfield, Ohio. A torque converter buried in hub of rear wheel makes the bike easier to control on the starting line.

Figure 159—GS750 Suzuki gets a big power boost with the Blake Enterprises Kit shown installed on this bike. It knocks 2 seconds off the 1/4-mile time and increases top speed 2000 RPM. Kit includes Blake BPM wastegate for boost control.

Blake Enterprises of Muskogee, Oklahoma has a kit for the Suzuki as shown in Figure 159. Their kit for the stock Z-1 Kawasaki starts to get boost at 5000 RPM and reaches 18 psi at 8500 RPM. It easily pulls 10,000 RPM in fifth gear. Depending on fairing, gearing and tires it will run 150 to 190 MPH in street trim. This kit goes all the way with water-alcohol injection, pressure-retarded spark and a separate oil pump and filter. Any one for a Sunday drive int the country? Note that the turbocharger is not obvious in Figure 160.

Figure 161 shows Blake's Honda GL1000 kit which adds 50% torque and horsepower for improved street and touring performance.

One of the most annoying things to non-cyclists is the noise bikes make—particularly if you travel alongside of one for any length of time. The combination of joining the exhaust pipes together and running them through the turbocharger does an excellent job of quieting the exhaust. The turbocharged motorcycle without any muffler runs quieter than a naturally aspirated one with a muffler each exhaust pipe. This might not appeal to the purist, but it is pleasing to guy or gal who drives behind or alongside.

Figure 160—900 Kawasaki turbocharger kit by Blake Enterprises uses a 377B.25 Rajay turbocharger with a Blake BPM wastegate. Installation is capable of over 30 psi boost. Water injection is used.

Figure 161—Blake Enterprises kit for Honda GL-1000.

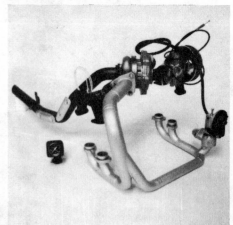

1975 Indianapolis winner was this Gurney Eagle. Powerplant was a Turbo-Drake (Offy) modified by John Miller of All-American Racers.

With the advent of the wing on championship-type race cars, peak horsepower has become the most important item to achieve maximum lap speeds. Acceleration or power below peak RPM is still important but with car speeds varying only 25% from straightaway to turns, rather than 33% or more without the wings, it is less significant.

There are several ways power in excess of 900 HP may be obtained with the aid of turbocharging. The method used will determine not only the acceleration and peak power obtainable but also the optimum RPM and have a definite effect on engine stress and life. Engine power is a function of speed, inlet-manifold pressure and inlet-manifold temperature. Exhaust back pressure will have some effect but it is not as direct as the other three. Let us look at these variables and try to determine the optimum operating conditions.

ENGINE SPEED

Air flow through the engine in CFM is a direct function of engine speed. For an engine of this type, assume a volumetric efficiency (η_{vol}) of 120%. This volumetric efficiency is extremely high and is the result of high valve overlap and intake-manifold pressures which run as much as 10 psi above exhaust-manifold pressures. It will vary from engine to engine depending on porting, valve timing and the turbocharger overall efficiency, but we will use the 120% figure so the calculations will be consistent.

$$\text{Air Flow} = \frac{\text{Displ (in.}^3\text{) x RPM x } \eta_{vol}}{1728 \text{ x } 2}$$

$$= \frac{160 \text{ x RPM x } 1.2}{1728 \text{ x } 2}$$

Air Flow = .0556 CFM x RPM
See Figure 163

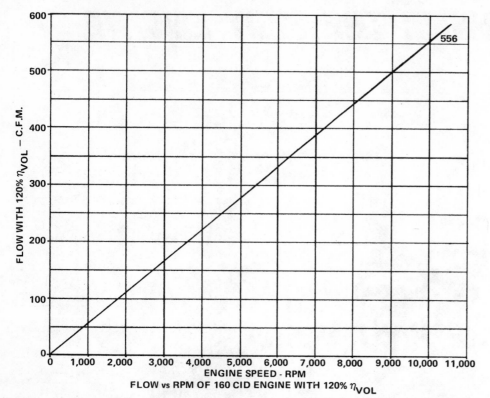

Figure 163—Flow versus RPM of 160 CID engine with 120% volumetric efficiency

This CFM air flow must be converted to lbs./hr. before we can determine how much power can be obtained. In a naturally-aspirated engine we can use a direct conversion factor because air density will remain relatively constant over the operating range. This is not the case with a turbocharged engine. Here we must take into account both the intake-manifold pressure *and* temperature to convert from cubic feet of air to pounds. The formula to convert air at standard conditions from CFM to lbs./min. is:

CFM x .0765
= lbs./min. (at 29.92 in. Hg bar. and 60°F.)

When the conditions are other than standard, corrections must be made for pressure and temperature. All units must be absolute (Rankine Temp.).

Lbs./min.

$$= \frac{\text{CFM x Man. Press in. Hg Abs x } 520° \text{x .0765}}{29.92 \text{ x Manifold Temp. } °R. (°F. + 460)}$$

For example, take a 160 CID engine running at 8,000 RPM with intake manifold pressure of 92 in. Hg Abs and 350°F.

Lbs./min.

$$= \frac{445 \text{ CFM (From Fig.158) x 92 x 520 x .0765}}{29.92 (350 + 460)}$$

$$= \frac{445 \text{ x 92 x 520 x .0765}}{29.92 \text{ x 810}}$$

Lbs./min. = 67.2
Lbs./hr. = 67.2 x 60 = 4,032

MANIFOLD PRESSURE

An increase in intake-manifold pressure will increase lb./hr. of air at a given engine speed while an increase in intake-manifold temperature will decrease lb./hr. Because of this, it is advantageous to achieve a combination of engine speed, intake-manifold pressure and temperature which will result in the maximum output with the least stress. Because different engines run best at different speeds, the effect of compressor efficiency was plotted for all engine speeds from 5,000 to 10,000 RPM: Figures 164, 165, and 166. In addition a plot was made of the 65% compressor with jacket-water intercooling, Figure 167.

To make use of the air-flow charts, we will assume a given amount of air is needed to produce a certain horsepower but with varying stress on the engine. Let us say that 4,000 lbs./hr. of air is needed for 800 HP. This flow may be obtained by several combinations of intake-manifold pressure and engine speed. In addition, the effect of compressor efficiency and an intercooler are plotted.

COMPRESSOR SIZES

Figures 168, 169 and 170 are three compressor maps with different flow capacities. The 4000 lbs./hr. conditions are plotted on each to show which engine speed falls in the optimum location and which size compressor is best suited for the application.

Starting with Figure 168 it is apparent that this compressor is too small to handle the flow. If the engine were driven 9,000 RPM, it would still need 4000 lbs./hr. of air to produce 800 HP. But because this point falls in the 50%-efficiency region of the map, the intake-manifold pressure will be 96 in. Abs and the intake-manifold temperature will be about 500°F. The intercooled condition is not plotted because it would fall off to the right of this compressor map in the choked condition.

If the compressor in Figure 169 is used the power may be obtained at several engine speeds with different intake-manifold pressures and temperatures, tabulated in Figure 171.

It is apparent the Figure 169 Compressor may be used to obtain the desired horsepower at different engine speeds both with and without intercooling. The user has the choice of setting up the engine to run at 8,000 RPM with high intake-manifold pressure and temperature or to run it a little faster at 9,000 RPM, with considerably less pressure and temperature. The choice will be governed by the comparative ability of the engine to run at high pressure or high speed. The best operating point will no doubt vary from engine to engine.

In either case, intercooling makes a vast difference by reducing both the intake-manifold temperature and pressure. In addition, for a given output, exhaust temperature will vary directly as the intake-manifold temperature. At 8,500 RPM intercooling can cool the exhaust temperature by 150°F. This lower exhaust temperature can mean

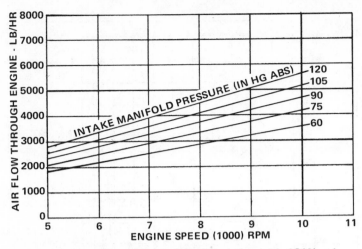

Figure 164—Air flow through 160 CID engine with 120% volumetric efficiency at various intake-manifold pressures. Compressor efficiency 65%, temperature 90°F (550°R)

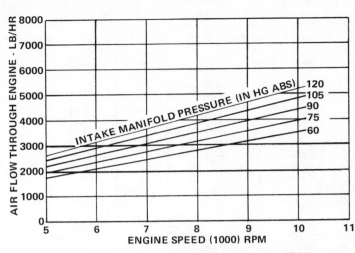

Figure 166—Air flow through 160 CID engine with 120% volumetric efficiency at various intake-manifold pressures. Compressor efficiency 55%, temperature 90°F (550°R)

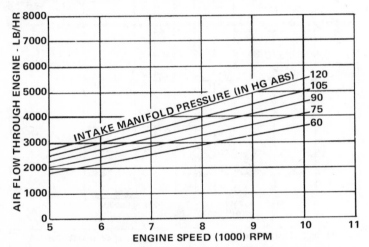

Figure 165—Air flow through 160 CID engine with 120% volumetric efficiency at various intake-manifold pressures. Compressor efficiency 60%, temperature 90°F (550°R)

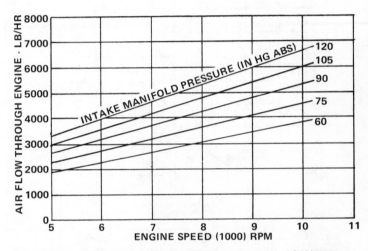

Figure 167—Air flow through 160 CID engine with 120% volumetric efficiency at various intake-manifold pressures. Compressor efficiency 50%, temperature 90°F (550°R) with 50%-effective intercooler using 200°F (660°R) jacket water

AiResearch turbo and wastegate installed on Cosworth V-8. Note how wastegate is supported from transaxle.

Typical AiResearch turbo installation on USAC championship race car with 4-cylinder Drake Offy engine.

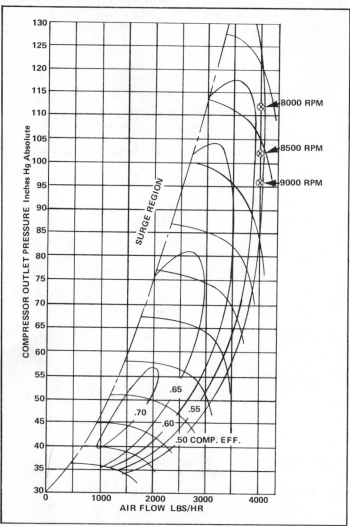

Figure 168—Compressor map of low-flow-capacity turbocharger

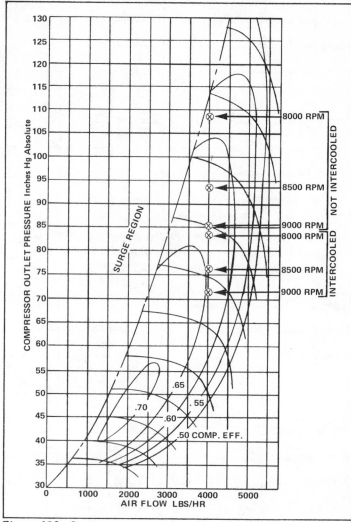

Figure 169—Compressor map of medium-flow-capacity turbocharger

Photo shows Al Unser's winning turbocharged Ford setup. Chief Mechanic George Bignotti chose a Schwitzer turbo and waste gate with Bendix fuel injection. Schematic drawing shows exhaust and intake routing.   Photo and drawing courtesy Schwitzer.

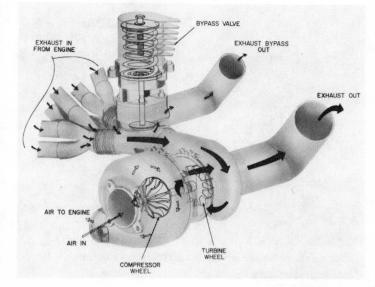

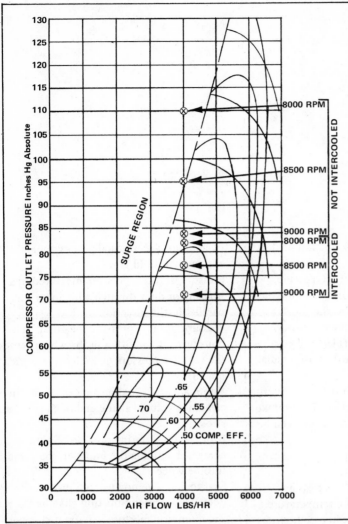

Figure 170—Compressor map of high-flow-capacity turbocharger

Engine Speed RPM	Intake Manifold Pressure in Hg Abs	Intake Manifold Temperature °F.	Intercooling
8000	109	510	No
8500	93	425	No
9000	85	389	No
8000	83	291	Yes
8500	77	275	Yes
9000	72	265	Yes

Figure 171—Intake-manifold temperature and pressure using compressor on Figure 169 with and without intercooling.

USAC car designers often mount the turbo and wastegate as a single easily removable unit to simplify servicing.

the difference between finishing or not finishing a race.

If the compressor is too large for the air requirement, a situation will occur as shown in Figure 170. Here, the requirement of 110 in. Hg at 8,000 RPM will put the compressor in the surge area. This could cause pulses in the intake system great enough to destroy both the engine and the turbocharger. *This would occur before the driver was aware that anything was wrong.*

The same compressor would be all right at higher engine speeds and with intercooling it would work at even lower engine speeds.

The purpose of making these illustrations is to show a compressor which is good for one set of operating conditions is not necessarily good if the conditions are changed. If the engine and turbocharger are set up for a certain horsepower

and speed on the dynamometer, it could be disastrous to make changes on the track. Moving into either the surge or choke regions can overstress both engine and turbocharger. Operating in the center of the map will allow the lowest intake-manifold temperature and pressures for a given horsepower output.

This survey is concerned only with the compressor but it is obvious the turbine and nozzle should also be matched for best performance, because most race cars use wastegates.

It is no problem to set it to provide the proper intake-manifold pressure; however, a poorly matched turbine or nozzle will cause unnecessarily high back pressure which will spoil everything gained by intercooling. On the other hand, it is possible that intercooling will drop the exhaust temperature to the point where the turbine will not produce enough power to

spin the compressor fast enough to open the wastegate. If this condition exists, it is necessary to reduce the nozzle size or perhaps even the turbine size.

All intercooling calculations were done using engine-cooling water as the cooling medium but the car builder is not limited to this. Back in the 20's, they used air-to-air coolers sticking out into the slip stream. Today's cars already have a wing or wings which could be finned and cored without any substantial increase in drag.

As I have mentioned earlier, they used to run the Indy 500 back in 1936 with a limit of 37.5 gallons of fuel for the whole race. Now the owners are complaining about being cut to below 300 gallons. If they used the fuel for power alone instead of as a cooling agent as well, they could run just as fast but with a lot less fuel and considerably less stress on the engines.

APPENDIX

Glossary

Adiabatic — ideal reversible compression of a gas; implies that there is no heat loss in the process.

Blower — term often applied to all types of superchargers, but usually to low-pressure-ratio units.

Blow-off valve — a spring-loaded valve in either intake or exhaust manifold to prevent over boosting.

Boost — difference in pressure between barometer and intake manifold on a supercharged engine.

Charge — air/fuel mixture to be burned in combustion chamber.

Clearance volume — the volume of a cylinder between the top of the piston and the cylinder head.

Combustion chamber — volume formed by cavity in cylinder head and top of piston when piston is at top of stroke.

Compression ratio — ratio of clearance volumes of a cylinder top and bottom dead center.

Compressor — that portion of the turbocharger which increases the pressure of the air or air/fuel mixture.

Compressor flow range — that area of the compressor map between the surge line and 60% efficiency (for centrifugal compressors only).

Compressor housing — the housing which encloses the compressor. Sometimes referred to as a scroll.

Compressor impeller — the rotating portion of the compressor.

Compressor pressure ratio — compressor outlet absolute pressure divided by compressor inlet absolute pressure.

Critical gas flow — maximum flow through an orifice or restriction for a given pressure upstream of the orifice or restriction.

Density — weight of air or charge per cubic foot of volume.

Diffuser — the stationary portion of the compressor which increases the static pressure of the air or air/fuel mixture.

Efficiency — actual performance of a piece of equipment compared to the ideal.

Enthalpy — internal energy of a working fluid. Usually stated in BTU/Lb.

Exducer —the gas-exit portion of a radial turbine wheel.

Exhaust gas recirculation (EGR) — ducting some engine exhaust back into the intake manifold to reduce oxides of nitrogen in the exhaust.

Inducer — the gas-entry portion of a centrifugal compressor rotor.

Intercooler (aftercooler) — a heat exchanger which reduces the temperature of the compressed charge before it enters the combustion chamber.

Micron — particle-size measurement used to indicate quality of air or oil filter. 1 micron = 0.00004 inch.

Naturally aspirated — an engine without a supercharger. Abbreviated N.A.

Normalize — supercharge an engine running at high altitude, but only to regain power lost because of lower air density.

Nozzle — the stationary portion of the turbine which increases the velocity of the exhaust gases and directs them to the turbine wheel. Most small turbochargers accomplish this with a scroll-shaped turbine housing.

Positive crankcase ventilation (PCV) — engine crankcase fumes ducted back to the intake manifold to reduce air pollution.

Pressure, absolute — pressure measured above a complete vacuum.

Pressure, boost — intake manifold gage pressure. 1 psi boost = 2 in. Hg boost (approximately).

Pressure, gage — pressure measured between two places, usually between ambient and manifold.

Pressure, static — pressure measured in a housing or duct through a hole in a wall parallel to the direction of flow.

Pressure, total — pressure measured in a housing or duct with a probe which senses the velocity pressure as well as the static pressure.

Residual gases — exhaust gases left in the clearance volume at the end of the exhaust stroke.

Rotor — the rotating portion of a turbocharger, including the impeller, shaft and turbine wheel.

Scavenging — removing combustion products from the combustion chamber.

Stoiciometric mixture — correct chemical mixture of fuel and air for complete combustion of both.

Stroke — distance travelled by piston between top and bottom dead center.

Supercharge — increase density of charge by compressing it before it enters the combustion chamber.

Surge line — a line on a centrifugal-compressor map representing minimum flow at each pressure ratio.

Turbine — that portion of the turbocharger which converts the energy of the engine exhaust gases to shaft power.

Turbine wheel — the rotating portion of the turbine.

Turbocharger — an engine supercharger driven by an exhaust-gas turbine.

Valve overlap — the number of crankshaft degrees expressing the time when both the intake and exhaust valves are open.

Vane — stationary guide of diffuser or nozzle.

Volute — A scroll or snail shaped housing.

Vortex — free-flowing inward spiral such as seen at the drain of a bathtub.

Symbols

Symbol	Name	Used For	Units
A		Acceleration	in./sec.^{2} or ft./sec.^{2}
A		Area	Sq. in.
ABDC	After BDC	Valve timing vs. piston position	Degrees ($^\circ$)
ABS	Absolute	Pressure or temperature above absolute zero	
A/R	Area Ratio	Turbine housing size	In.
ATDC	After TDC	Valve timing vs. piston position	Degrees ($^\circ$)
BDC	Bottom Dead Center	Piston position/valve timing	
BBDC	Before BDC	Valve timing vs. piston position	Degrees ($^\circ$)
BSFC	Brake Specific Fuel Consumption		Lb/BHP-Hr.
BTDC	Before TDC	Valve timing vs. piston position	Degrees ($^\circ$)
BTU	British Thermal Unit	Unit of energy	778 Ft. Lbs.
cc	Cubic Centimeters	Engine size	Cu. cm.
CFM		Volume flow	Cubic feet per minute
CID	Cubic Inch Displacement	Engine size	Cu. in.
$\triangle$	Delta	Differences	none
e.t.	Elapsed time	Timing	Sec.
h	Eta	Efficiency	none
F	Fahrenheit	Temperature	Degrees ($^\circ$)
F	Force	Calculating horsepower	Lb.
FPS		Speed	Feet per second
G		Acceleration of gravity	384 in./sec.^{2} or 32.2 ft./sec.^{2}
HP	Horsepower	Engine output	$\frac{550\ ft.\ lb.}{sec.}$
In. Hg	Inches mercury	Pressure	Inches
I		Moment of inertia	Lb. in. Sec.^{2}
K	Radius of gyration	Moment of inertia	In.
L	Liter	Displacement	Liters
M	Slug	Mass	$\frac{Lb.\ sec.^2}{ft.}$
M.E.P.	Mean Effective Pressure	Calculating torque	psi
MPH		Speed	Miles per hour
N	Rotational speed		RPM
N.A.	Naturally aspirated	Engine designation	
P		Pressure	Lb./in.^{2} or In. Hg (mercury)
PSIA		Absolute pressure	Lb./in.^{2} Absolute
PSIG		Gage pressure	Lb./in.^{2} gage
Q		Volume rate of flow	Ft^3/Min.
r		Pressure ratio	none
R		Radius	In.
R	Rankine	Temperature (absolute)	Degrees ($^\circ$)
T		Temperature	$^\circ$F or $^\circ$R
θ	THETA	Temperature ratio	$\frac{T^\circ R}{520}$
TDC	Top Dead Center	Piston position/valve timing	
T		Torque	Lb. ft.
TC	Turbocharged	Engine designation	
v		Volume	Cu. ft. or cu. in.
V		Velocity	Ft/Sec.
W		Weight	Lbs.
Y		Calculating compressor temperature rise	

Altitude chart

Altitude Ft.	Air Press. in.Hg	$^\circ$F	Standard Day $^\circ$R	$\sqrt{\theta}$
Sea Level	29.92	59.00	518.69	1.00
1000	28.86	55.43	515.12	.997
2000	27.82	51.87	511.56	.993
3000	26.81	48.30	507.99	.989
4000	25.84	44.74	504.42	.986
5000	24.90	41.17	500.86	.982
6000	23.98	37.61	497.30	.979
7000	23.09	34.05	493.73	.975
8000	22.23	30.48	490.17	.972
9000	21.39	26.92	486.61	.969
10000	20.58	23.36	483.04	.965
11000	19.80	19.79	479.48	.962
12000	19.03	16.23	475.92	.958
13000	18.30	12.67	472.36	.954
14000	17.58	9.11	468.80	.951
15000	16.89	5.55	465.23	.947
16000	16.22	1.99	461.67	.943
17000	15.58	− 1.58	458.11	.940
18000	14.95	− 5.14	454.55	.936
19000	14.35	− 8.69	450.99	.933
20000	13.76	−12.25	447.43	.929
21000	13.20	−15.81	443.87	.925
22000	12.65	−19.37	440.32	.921
23000	12.12	−22.93	436.76	.918
24000	11.61	−26.49	433.20	.914
25000	11.12	−30.05	429.64	.910
26000	10.64	−33.60	426.08	.906
27000	10.18	−37.16	422.53	.903
28000	9.741	−40.72	418.97	.899
29000	9.314	−44.28	415.41	.895
30000	8.903	−47.83	411.86	.891
31000	8.506	−51.38	408.30	.887
32000	8.124	−54.94	404.75	.883
33000	7.756	−58.50	401.19	.880
34000	7.401	−62.05	397.64	.876
35000	7.060	−65.61	394.08	.872
36000	6.732	−69.16	390.53	.868
37000	6.417	−69.70	389.98	.867
38000	6.117	−69.70	389.98	.867
39000	5.831	−69.70	389.98	.867
40000	5.558	−69.70	389.98	.867

Y tables

VALUES OF "Y" FOR NORMAL AIR AND PERFECT DIATOMIC GASES

$$Y = r^{.283} - 1 \qquad r = P_{T2}/P_{T1} \qquad K = 1.395$$

r		0	1	2	3	4	5	6	7	8	9
1.00	0.00	000	028	057	085	113	141	169	198	226	254
1.01		282	310	338	366	394	422	450	478	506	534
1.02		562	590	618	646	673	701	729	757	785	812
1.03		840	868	895	923	951	978	006	034	061	089
1.04	0.01	116	144	171	199	226	253	281	308	336	363
1.05		390	418	445	472	500	527	554	581	608	636
1.06		663	690	717	744	771	798	825	852	879	906
1.07		933	960	987	014	041	068	095	122	148	175
1.08	0.02	202	229	255	282	309	336	362	389	416	442
1.09		469	495	522	549	575	602	628	655	681	708
1.10		734	760	787	813	840	866	892	919	945	971
1.11		997	024	050	076	102	129	155	181	207	233
1.12	0.03	259	285	311	337	363	389	415	441	467	493
1.13		519	545	571	597	623	649	675	700	726	752
1.14		778	804	829	855	881	906	932	958	983	009
1.15	0.04	035	060	086	111	137	162	188	213	239	264
1.16		290	315	341	366	391	417	442	467	493	518
1.17		543	569	594	619	644	670	695	720	745	770
1.18		796	821	846	871	896	921	946	971	996	021
1.19	0.05	046	071	096	121	146	171	196	221	245	270
1.20		295	320	345	370	394	419	444	469	493	518
1.21		543	567	592	617	641	666	691	715	740	764
1.22		789	813	838	862	887	911	936	960	985	009
1.23	0.06	034	058	082	107	131	155	180	204	228	253
1.24		277	301	325	350	374	398	422	446	470	495
1.25		519	543	567	591	615	639	663	687	711	735
1.26		759	783	807	831	855	879	903	927	951	974
1.27		998	022	046	070	094	117	141	165	189	212
1.28	0.07	236	260	283	307	331	354	378	402	425	449
1.29		472	496	520	543	567	590	614	637	661	684
1.30		708	731	754	778	801	825	848	871	895	918
1.31		941	965	988	011	035	058	081	104	128	151
1.32	0.08	174	197	220	243	267	290	313	336	359	382
1.33		405	428	451	474	497	520	543	566	589	612
1.34		635	658	681	704	727	750	773	795	818	841
1.35		864	887	910	932	955	978	001	023	046	069
1.36	0.09	092	114	137	160	182	205	228	250	273	295
1.37		318	341	363	386	408	431	453	476	498	521
1.38		543	566	588	611	633	655	678	700	723	745
1.39		767	790	812	834	857	879	901	923	946	968
1.40		990	012	035	057	079	101	123	145	168	190
1.41	0.10	212	234	256	278	300	322	344	366	389	411
1.42		433	455	477	499	521	542	564	586	608	630
1.43		652	674	696	718	740	761	783	805	827	849
1.44		871	892	914	936	958	979	001	023	045	066
1.45	0.11	088	110	131	153	175	198	218	239	261	283
1.46		304	326	347	369	390	412	433	455	476	498
1.47		520	541	562	584	605	627	648	669	691	712
1.48		734	755	776	798	819	840	862	883	904	925
1.49		947	968	989	010	032	053	074	095	116	138
1.50	0.12	159	180	201	222	243	264	286	307	328	349
1.51		370	391	412	433	454	475	496	517	538	559
1.52		580	601	622	643	664	685	706	726	747	768
1.53		789	810	831	852	872	893	914	935	956	977
1.54		997	018	039	060	080	101	122	142	163	184
1.55	0.13	205	225	246	266	287	308	328	349	370	390
1.56		411	431	452	472	493	513	534	554	574	595
1.57		616	636	657	677	698	718	739	759	780	800
1.58		820	841	861	881	902	922	942	963	983	003
1.59	0.14	024	044	064	085	105	125	145	165	186	206
1.60		226	246	267	287	307	327	347	367	387	408
1.61		428	448	468	488	508	528	548	568	588	608
1.62		628	648	668	688	708	728	748	768	788	808
1.63		828	848	868	888	908	928	948	968	988	007
1.64	0.15	027	047	067	087	107	126	146	166	186	206
1.65		225	245	265	284	304	324	344	363	383	403
1.66		423	442	462	481	501	521	540	560	580	599
1.67		619	638	658	678	697	717	736	756	775	795
1.68		814	834	853	873	892	912	931	951	970	990

r		0	1	2	3	4	5	6	7	8	9
1.69	0.16	009	028	048	067	087	106	125	145	164	184
1.70		203	222	242	261	280	299	319	338	357	377
1.71		396	415	434	454	473	492	511	531	550	569
1.72		588	607	626	646	665	684	703	722	741	760
1.73		780	799	818	837	856	875	894	913	932	951
1.74		970	989	008	027	046	065	084	103	122	141
1.75	0.17	160	179	198	217	236	255	274	292	311	330
1.76		349	368	387	406	425	443	462	481	500	519
1.77		538	556	575	594	613	631	650	669	688	706
1.78		725	744	762	781	800	818	837	856	874	895
1.79		912	930	949	968	988	005	023	042	061	079
1.80	0.18	098	116	135	153	172	191	209	228	246	265
1.81		283	302	320	339	357	376	394	412	431	449
1.82		468	486	505	523	541	560	578	596	615	633
1.83		652	670	688	707	725	743	762	780	798	816
1.84		835	853	871	890	908	926	944	962	981	999
1.85	0.19	017	035	054	072	090	108	128	144	163	181
1.86		199	217	235	253	271	289	308	326	344	362
1.87		380	398	416	434	452	470	488	506	524	542
1.88		560	578	596	614	632	650	668	686	704	722
1.89		740	758	776	794	811	829	847	865	883	901
1.90		919	937	954	972	990	008	026	044	061	079
1.91	0.20	097	115	133	150	168	186	204	221	239	257
1.92		275	292	310	328	345	363	381	399	416	434
1.93		452	469	487	504	522	540	557	575	593	610
1.94		628	645	663	681	698	716	733	751	768	786
1.95		804	821	839	856	874	891	909	926	944	961
1.96		979	996	013	031	048	066	083	101	118	135
1.97	0.21	153	170	188	205	222	240	257	275	292	309
1.98		327	344	361	379	396	413	431	448	465	482
1.99		500	517	534	552	569	586	603	620	638	655
2.00		672	689	707	724	741	758	775	792	810	827
2.01		844	861	878	895	913	930	947	964	981	998
2.02	0.22	015	032	049	066	084	101	118	135	152	169
2.03		186	203	220	237	254	271	288	305	322	339
2.04		356	373	390	407	424	441	458	474	491	508
2.05		525	542	559	576	593	610	627	644	660	677
2.06		694	711	728	745	762	778	795	812	829	846
2.07		863	879	896	913	930	946	963	980	997	013
2.08	0.23	030	047	064	080	097	114	130	147	164	181
2.09		197	214	231	247	264	281	297	314	331	347
2.10		364	380	397	414	430	447	463	480	497	513
2.11		530	546	563	579	596	613	629	646	662	679
2.12		695	712	728	745	761	778	794	811	827	844
2.13		860	877	893	909	926	942	959	975	992	008
2.14	0.24	024	041	057	074	090	106	123	139	155	172
2.15		188	204	221	237	253	270	286	302	319	335
2.16		351	368	384	400	416	433	449	465	481	498
2.17		514	530	546	563	579	595	611	627	644	660
2.18		676	692	708	724	741	757	773	789	805	821
2.19		838	854	870	886	902	918	934	950	966	983
2.20		999	015	031	047	063	079	095	111	127	143
2.21	0.25	159	175	191	207	223	239	255	271	287	303
2.22		319	335	351	367	383	399	415	431	447	463
2.23		479	495	511	526	542	558	574	590	606	622
2.24		638	654	669	685	701	717	733	749	765	780
2.25		796	812	828	844	859	875	891	907	923	938
2.26		954	970	986	001	017	033	049	064	080	096
2.27	0.26	112	127	143	159	175	190	206	222	237	253
2.28		269	284	300	316	331	347	363	378	394	409
2.29		425	441	456	472	488	503	519	534	550	566
2.30		581	597	612	628	643	659	675	690	706	721
2.31		737	752	768	783	799	814	830	845	861	876
2.32		892	907	923	938	954	969	984	000	015	031
2.33	0.27	046	062	077	092	108	123	139	154	169	185
2.34		200	216	231	246	262	277	292	308	323	338
2.35		354	369	384	400	415	430	446	461	476	492
2.36		507	522	538	553	568	583	599	614	629	644
2.37		660	675	690	705	721	736	751	766	781	797
2.38		812	827	842	857	873	888	903	918	933	948
2.39		964	979	994	009	024	039	054	070	085	100
2.40	0.28	115	130	145	160	175	190	205	220	236	251
2.41		266	281	296	311	326	341	356	371	386	401
2.42		416	431	446	461	476	491	506	521	536	551
2.43		566	581	596	611	626	641	656	671	686	701
2.44		716	730	745	760	775	790	805	820	835	850
2.45		865	879	894	909	924	939	954	969	984	998
2.46	0.29	013	028	043	058	073	087	102	117	132	147
2.47		162	176	191	206	221	235	250	265	280	295
2.48		309	324	339	353	368	383	398	412	427	442

r		0	1	2	3	4	5	6	7	8	9
2.49		457	471	486	501	515	530	545	559	574	589
2.50		604	618	633	647	662	677	691	706	721	735
2.51		750	765	779	794	808	823	838	852	867	881
2.52		896	911	925	940	954	969	984	998	013	027
2.53	0.30	042	056	071	085	100	114	129	144	158	173
2.54		187	202	216	231	245	260	274	289	303	318
2.55		332	346	361	375	390	404	419	433	448	462
2.56		476	491	505	520	534	548	563	577	592	606
2.57		620	635	649	663	678	692	707	721	735	750
2.58		764	778	793	807	821	836	850	864	879	893
2.59		907	921	936	950	964	979	993	007	021	036
2.60	0.31	050	064	079	093	107	121	136	150	164	178
2.61		193	207	221	235	249	264	278	292	306	320
2.62		335	349	363	377	391	405	420	434	448	462
2.63		476	490	505	519	533	547	561	575	589	603
2.64		618	632	646	660	674	688	702	716	730	744
2.65		759	773	787	801	815	829	843	857	871	885
2.66		899	913	927	941	955	969	983	997	011	025
2.67	0.32	039	053	067	081	095	109	123	137	151	165
2.68		179	193	207	221	235	249	262	276	290	304
2.69		318	332	346	360	374	388	402	416	429	443
2.70		457	471·	485	499	513	527	540	554	568	582
2.71		596	610	624	637	651	665	679	693	707	720
2.72		734	748	762	776	789	803	817	831	845	858
2.73		872	886	900	913	927	941	955	968	982	996
2.74	0.33	010	023	037	051	065	078	092	106	119	133
2.75		147	161	174	188	202	215	229	243	256	270
2.76		284	297	311	325	338	352	366	379	393	407
2.77		420	434	448	461	475	488	502	516	529	543
2.78		556	570	584	597	611	624	638	651	665	679
2.79		692	706	719	733	746	760	773	787	801	814
2.80		828	841	855	868	882	895	909	922	936	949
2.81		963	976	990	003	017	030	044	057	070	084
2.82	0.34	097	111	124	138	151	165	178	191	205	218
2.83		232	245	259	272	285	299	312	326	339	352
2.84		366	379	393	406	419	433	446	459	473	486
2.85		500	513	526	540	553	566	580	593	606	620
2.86		633	646	660	673	686	700	713	726	739	753
2.87		766	779	793	806	819	832	846	859	872	886
2.88		899	912	925	939	952	965	978	991	005	018
2.89	0.35	031	044	058	071	084	097	110	124	137	150
2.90		163	176	190	203	216	229	242	255	269	282
2.91		295	308	321	334	347	361	374	387	400	413
2.92		426	439	452	466	479	492	505	518	531	544
2.93		557	570	584	597	610	623	636	649	662	675
2.94		688	701	714	727	740	753	767	780	793	806
2.95		819	832	845	858	871	884	897	910	923	936
2.96		949	962	975	988	001	014	027	040	053	066
2.97	0.36	079	092	105	118	131	144	157	169	182	195
2.98		208	221	234	247	260	273	286	299	312	324
2.99		337	350	363	376	389	402	415	428	440	453
3.0	0.3	647	659	672	685	698	711	723	736	749	761
3.1		774·	786	799	811	824	836	849	861	874	886
3.2		898	911	923	935	947	959	971	984	996	008
3.3	0.4	020	032	044	056	068	080	091	103	115	127
3.4		139	150	162	174	186	197	209	220	232	244
3.5		255	267	278	290	301	313	324	335	347	358
3.6		369	380	392	403	414	425	437	448	459	470
3.7		481	492	503	514	525	536	547	558	569	580
3.8		591	602	612	623	634	645	656	666	677	688
3.9		698	709	720	730	741	752	762	773	783	794
4.0		804	815	825	835	846	856	867	877	887	898
4.1		908	918	928	939	949	959	970	980	990	000
4.2	0.5	010	020	030	040	050	060	070	080	090	100
4.3		110	120	130	140	150	160	170	179	189	199
4.4		209	219	228	238	248	258	267	277	287	296
4.5		306	316	325	335	344	354	363	373	382	392
4.6		401	411	420	430	439	449	458	467	477	486
4.7		495	505	514	523	533	542	551	560	570	579
4.8		588	597	606	616	625	634	643	652	661	670
4.9		679	688	697	706	715	724	733	742	751	760
5.0		769	778	787	796	805	814	822	831	840	849
5.1		858	867	875	884	893	902	910	919	928	936
5.2		945	954	962	971	980	988	997	006	014	023
5.3	0.6	031	040	048	057	065	074	082	091	099	108
5.4		116	125	133	142	150	159	167	175	184	192
5.5		200	209	217	225	234	242	250	258	267	275
5.6		283	291	300	308	316	324	332	340	349	357
5.7		365	373	381	389	397	405	413	421	430	438
5.8		446	454	462	470	478	486	494	502	509	517
5.9		525	533	541	549	557	565	573	581	588	596

r		0	1	2	3	4	5	6	7	8	9
6.0		604	612	620	628	635	643	651	659	666	674
6.1		682	690	697	705	713	721	729	736	744	752
6.2		759	767	774	782	789	797	805	812	820	827
6.3		835	843	850	858	865	873	880	888	895	903
6.4		910	918	925	933	940	948	955	963	970	978
6.5		985	992	000	007	014	021	028	036	043	050
6.6	0.7	058	065	073	080	087	095	102	110	117	124
6.7		131	138	145	153	160	167	174	181	189	196
6.8		203	210	217	224	232	239	246	253	260	267
6.9		274	281	288	295	302	309	316	323	330	338
7.0		345	352	359	366	373	380	386	393	400	407
7.1		414	421	428	435	442	449	456	463	470	477
7.2		483	490	497	504	511	518	524	531	538	545
7.3		552	559	565	572	579	586	592	599	606	613
7.4		620	626	633	640	646	653	660	666	673	680
7.5		687	693	700	706	713	720	726	733	740	746
7.6		753	760	766	773	779	786	792	799	806	812
7.7		819	825	832	838	845	851	858	864	871	877
7.8		884	890	897	903	910	916	923	929	936	942
7.9		949	955	961	968	974	981	987	993	000	006
8.0	0.8	013	019	025	032	038	044	051	057	063	070
8.1		076	082	089	095	101	108	114	120	126	133
8.2		139	145	151	158	164	170	176	183	189	195
8.3		201	207	214	220	226	232	238	245	251	257
8.4		263	269	275	281	288	294	300	306	312	318
8.5		324	330	336	343	349	355	361	367	373	379
8.6		385	391	397	403	409	415	421	427	433	439
8.7		445	451	457	463	469	475	481	487	493	499
8.8		505	511	517	523	529	535	541	547	552	558
8.9		564	570	576	582	588	594	600	605	611	617
9.0		623	629	635	641	646	652	658	664	670	676
9.1		681	687	693	699	705	710	716	722	728	734
9.2		739	747	751	757	762	768	774	779	785	791
9.3		797	802	808	814	819	825	831	837	842	848
9.4		854	859	865	871	876	882	888	893	899	905
9.5		910	916	921	927	933	938	944	949	955	961
9.6		966	972	977	983	989	994	000	005	011	016
9.7	0.9	022	028	033	039	044	050	055	061	066	072
9.8		077	083	088	094	099	105	110	116	121	127
9.9		132	138	143	149	154	159	165	170	176	181
10.0		187	192	198	203	208	214	219	225	230	235

From: 'Engineering Computations for Air and Gases" by Moss and Smith, Transactions A.S.M.E., Vol. 52, 1930, Paper APM-52-8

EXAMPLE:

Assume: $P_{T2}/P_{T1} = r = 1.82$

Air Flow = 290 CFM

T_1 (inlet temperature = $92°F = (92 + 460)°R = 552°R$

h_c (from Figure 5) = 68%

Y (from table) = 0.18468

T_i (ideal temperature rise) = $T_1 \times Y = 552 \times .18468 = 102°$

ΔT_A (actual temperature rise) = $\frac{\Delta T_i}{h_c} = \frac{102}{.68} = 150°$

T_2 (compressor outlet temperature) = $T_1 + \Delta T_A = 92 + 150 = 242°F$

Turbocharger failure analysis

by Robert Elmendorf,
Service Engineer, Schwitzer

Despite the outward appearance of utter simplicity, the modern Diesel turbocharger is, in fact, the end product of a highly specialized technology, and though not readily apparent on first observation, the methods used in turbocharger manufacture have been brought to a high level of sophistication, particularly during the past two decades.

The greatest demands on this technology are made in the areas of metallurgy, dimensional tolerance control, and dynamic unbalance correction. The reasons for extreme emphasis in these areas are easy to appreciate, once the typical stresses acting on a turbocharger are known. In normal operation, then, gas introduction temperatures can easily exceed 1,000° F, rotative speeds can run above 70,000 RPM, and the internal power of the turbocharger can approach values equivalent to the flywheel horsepower of the engine.

It is known even to most neophytes that turbocharger failures are inherently expensive, and have a devastating effect on engine performance. It is a widespread misconception even among the seasoned "experts", however, that all turbocharger failures occur instantaneously of primarily internal causes, and are therefore unpreventable; on the contrary, the vast majority of failures are the direct result of faulty engine maintenance or operation, and many are progressive in nature.

It is the purpose of this bulletin to acquaint the owner or operator of a "turbo"-equipped engine with the several categories of common failure, to help him recognize the symptoms associated with each, and hopefully, to enable him to avoid the expense and aggravation of repetitive failures. However, to develop a complete and well-rounded turbocharger service program, it is suggested that the information contained herein be supplemented with the wealth of routine and preventive maintenance information available for both the complete engine and the turbocharger assembly alone.

FAILURES RELATED TO FAULTY LUBRICATION

Oil plays a vital role in the life of a turbocharger, because it serves the triple function of lubricating, cooling and cleansing many of the most critical and highly stressed parts in the assembly.

Even momentary interruptions in the supply of high quality lubrication can produce disastrous results, but particularly under conditions of high speed or heavy load.

There are several facets to proper turbocharger lubrication, and as a consequence, a deficiency of any one aspect usually produces a specific symptom.

Abrasive Contamination—The presence of sufficient abrasive material in the lubricating oil will result in wear of the various bearing surfaces, and is usually most prevalent on the thrust bearing and outside diameters of the shaft bearings. Occasionally, the abrasive particles are so small that they escape the centrifuge effect of the rapidly spinning bearings; in such a case, considerable scouring of the journal sections of the rotor shaft might be noted.

The depth of scratching and amount of wear can vary widely, and depend primarily on the degree and nature of the contaminant, the operating time accumulated with the contaminant present, and the severity of engine operation.

Insufficient Pressure or Flow—It is essential that a sufficient quantity of oil flow through the turbocharger at all times to ensure suspension and stabilization of the full floating/rotating bearing system, and to continually wash heat from the unit, thereby keeping internal temperatures within workable limits.

The most frequently seen damage that can be related to insufficient oil flow is the result of what might be termed the "oil lag syndrome." This involves a faulty operating habit, in which a cold turbocharged engine is started and immediately taken to a condition of high speed or heavy load. In such a case, the rotative speed of the turbocharger approaches the peak allowable value before an effective oil cushion is established to sustain the bearings. The result is rotor gyration (often called "shaft motion" or "whirl") with attendant distress of the bearings.

Marginal oil flow—that in which sufficient oil is circulating to prevent a sudden failure—can also produce detrimental effects, the most notable of which is the gradual accumulation of varnish on internal surfaces, which makes unit disassembly quite difficult.

Improper Oil Type or Lack of Change at Recommended Intervals—The principal condition noted when either of these conditions exist is generalized sludge or varnish formation on the internal surfaces of the turbocharger; these are usually found to be heaviest at the turbine end of the unit, because the higher prevailing temperature in that area results in accelerated loss of the volatile oil components.

In certain applications, this varnish formation causes eventual seal ring fouling and wear,

and can only be corrected by complete unit teardown and replacement of the turbine wheel-and-shaft assembly; this is a very expensive proposition, at best.

FAILURES RELATED TO FOREIGN MATERIAL INTAKE

The vulnerability of a turbocharger will become instantly apparent the first time a particle of significant size is inducted into either the compressor or turbine section with the unit at speed.

The sources and types of air-and exhaust-stream contamination are many and varied, but can range from atmospheric sand and dust (through the compressor) to engine valve fragments (through the turbine).

The point of foreign material entry usually becomes apparent as soon as the core has been separated from the compressor cover and turbine housing; though the damaging particle is seldom present or intact, some clue as to its size and type can usually be gained by close inspection of the involved wheel.

The secondary effects of high speed particle impact on either wheel are usually visible throughout the unit, but tend to focus on the bearings, which suffer from both the initial gyration and the running unbalance condition which follows.

FAILURES RELATED TO HIGH EXHAUST TEMPERATURES OR UNIT OVERSPEED

The procedure employed in the matching of a turbocharger to a particular engine is part of the specialized technology mentioned in the introduction to this bulletin, and always includes a live proofing session in the lab, using an actual engine under closely controllable conditions.

The reasons for this final precautionary measure are simple: As a free-wheeling device with intense and tremendous internal power, a mismatched turbocharger could easily "run away", damaging the engine and creating a threat to the well-being of the bystanders and attendants.

As seen in the field, mismatched engine/turbocharger combinations are most often the result of an attempt to boost power output by means of various "adjustments", such as fuel rate tampering, indiscriminate compressor or turbine nozzle changes, or even the application of complete turbochargers to engines arbitrarily. Any of these attempts can cause overspeed damage to the bearing system of a turbocharger, distortion, warpage or erosion of the turbine wheel casting, and heat damage to such other engine components as piston crowns, valves and exhaust manifolds.

ACKNOWLEDGEMENTS

If this book were about reciprocating engines or gas turbines, a good portion of the information could have been gleaned from existing literature because of the many books and papers on these subjects. Although a few technical papers have been published, modern books on turbocharging are almost nonexistent. Turbocharger development has progressed over the last 35 years mainly because of better materials. For this reason and because thermodynamic principles do not change, the work done by Büchi in the early 1900s and Ricardo in the 1920-1930s is still valid.

AiResearch, Rajay, Roto-Master and Schwitzer all contributed pictures and technical information. The performance outlets of these manufacturers also helped. Don Hubbard authored a manual for Crane Cams detailing how to turbocharge an engine with Schwitzer Turbochargers. I borrowed quite a few installation tips and illustrations from this manual. Ak Miller and cohorts Jack Lufkin, Burke LeSage, Bill Edwards and Jon Meyer were more than cooperative.

George Spears of Shelby-Spearco and Spearco Performance provided many excellent pictures and helped me get pictures of his customers' installations. Bob Keller added much useful information. Gale Banks has been diligent in making superbly engineered marine installations. He also spent several days working on the cover photo engine with Publisher Bill Fisher and Art Director Josh Young.

Crown Manufacturing has been one of the pioneers in turbocharging engines and producing kits. Derek Torley has the same enthusiasm toward turbochargers as did founder Ted Trevor. Derek gave me numerous pictures and a lot of data.

John Gaspari sold Rajay Turbochargers all over the world for TRW International. He faithfully sent pictures and other information for many countries.

M & W Gear is an important manufacturer in marine turbocharging. Jack Bradford, their Chief Engineer, has been turbocharging diesel and gasoline engines since about 1960 and really knows how to make complete bolt-on kits.

Tom Scahill became interested in turbocharging when he helped Howard Arneson install them on his off-shore racing boat. Since then Tom has established quite a reputation doing custom installations.

Vince Piggins, Bill Howell and John Pierce of Chevrolet Engineering sent us several excellent pictures of experimental installations.

Doug Roe's hints about installations will be helpful to the old timer as well as the novice.

Herb Fishel of Buick Engineering was especially helpful in supplying photos and technical information on their turbocharged V-6.

Last and certainly not least, my wife Betty Jane typed every word at least twice and put up with me in the process.

INSTALLATION DRAWINGS

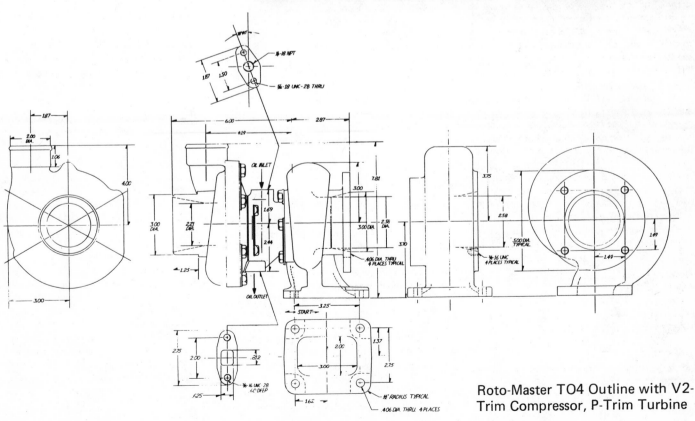

Roto-Master TO4 Outline with V2-Trim Compressor, P-Trim Turbine

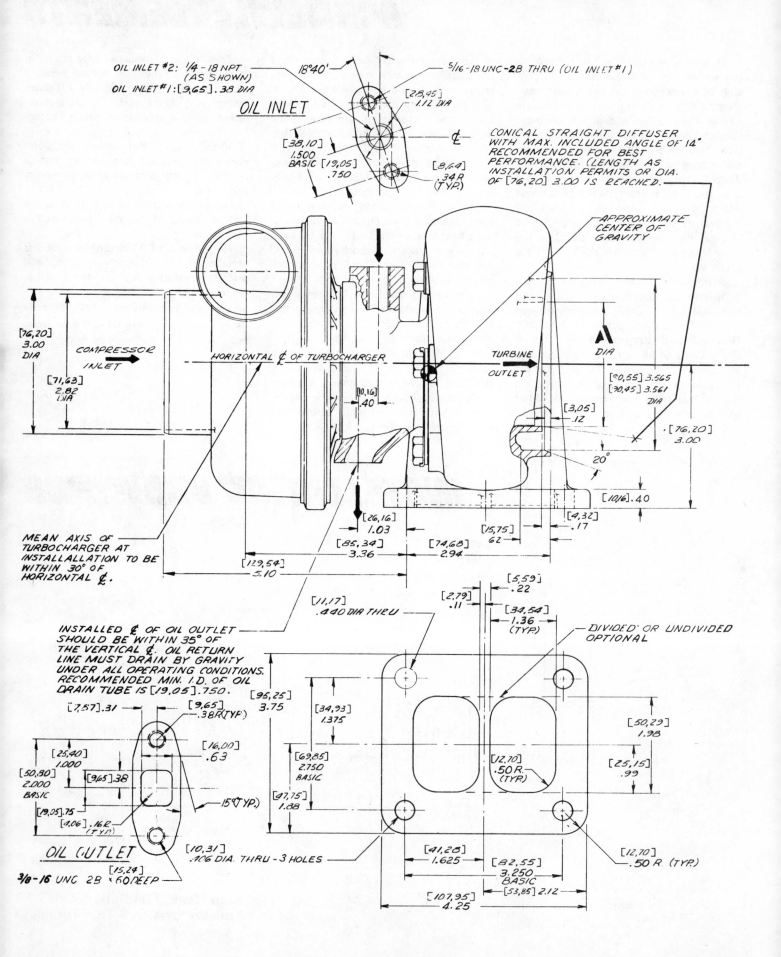

OIL INLET #2: 1/4 -18 NPT (AS SHOWN)
OIL INLET #1: [9,65] .38 DIA

18°40'

5/16-18 UNC-2B THRU (OIL INLET #1)

OIL INLET

[28,45] 1.12 DIA

[38,10] 1.500 BASIC [19,05] .750

[8,64] .34 R (TYP.)

CONICAL STRAIGHT DIFFUSER WITH MAX. INCLUDED ANGLE OF 14° RECOMMENDED FOR BEST PERFORMANCE. (LENGTH AS INSTALLATION PERMITS OR DIA. OF [76,20] 3.00 IS REACHED.

APPROXIMATE CENTER OF GRAVITY

[76,20] 3.00 DIA

COMPRESSOR INLET

[71,63] 2.82 DIA

HORIZONTAL ₵ OF TURBOCHARGER

TURBINE OUTLET

DIA

[90,55] 3.565
[90,45] 3.561 DIA

[76,20] 3.00

[10,16] .40

[3,05] .12

20°

[10,16] .40

[4,32] .17

[26,16] 1.03

[15,75] 62

[85,34] 3.36

[74,68] 2.94

[129,54] 5.10

MEAN AXIS OF TURBOCHARGER AT INSTALLATION TO BE WITHIN 30° OF HORIZONTAL ₵.

INSTALLED ₵ OF OIL OUTLET SHOULD BE WITHIN 35° OF THE VERTICAL ₵. OIL RETURN LINE MUST DRAIN BY GRAVITY UNDER ALL OPERATING CONDITIONS. RECOMMENDED MIN. I.D. OF OIL DRAIN TUBE IS [19,05] .750.

[11,17] .440 DIA THRU

[5,59] .22

[2,79] .11

[34,54] 1.36 (TYP.)

DIVIDED OR UNDIVIDED OPTIONAL

[7,57] .31

[9,65] .38 R (TYP.)

[25,40] 1.000

[16,00] .63

[50,80] 2.000 BASIC

[9,65] .38

[19,05] .75

[1,06] .16 R (TYP.)

15° TYP.)

OIL OUTLET

[10,31] .406 DIA. THRU - 3 HOLES

3/8-16 UNC 2B x 60 DEEP

[15,24]

[96,25] 3.75

[34,93] 1.375

[69,85] 2.750 BASIC

[47,75] 1.88

[12,70] .50 R. (TYP.)

[50,29] 1.98

[25,15] .99

[41,28] 1.625

[82,55] 3.250 BASIC

[53,85] 2.12

[12,70] .50 R. (TYP.)

[107,95] 4.25

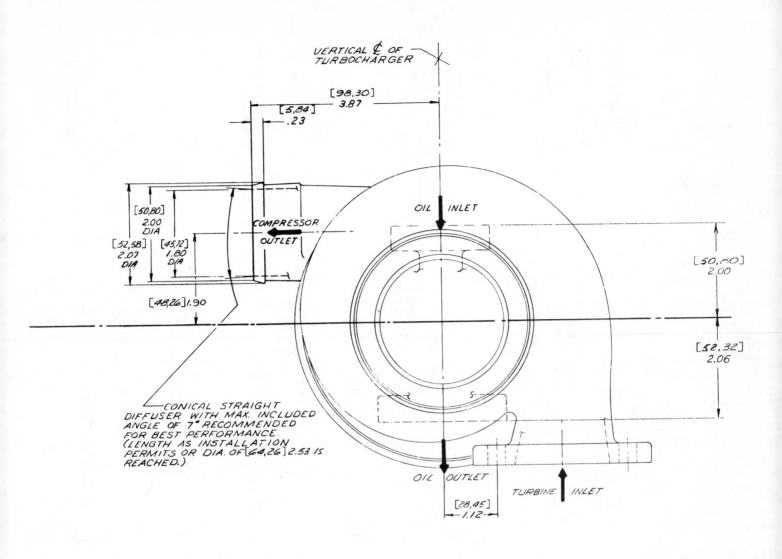

VERTICAL ₵ OF TURBOCHARGER

[98,30] 3.87

[5,84] .23

[50,80] 2.00 DIA

[52,58] 2.07 DIA

[45,12] 1.80 DIA

[48,26] 1.90

COMPRESSOR OUTLET

OIL INLET

[50,80] 2.00

[52,32] 2.06

CONICAL STRAIGHT DIFFUSER WITH MAX. INCLUDED ANGLE OF 7° RECOMMENDED FOR BEST PERFORMANCE. (LENGTH AS INSTALLATION PERMITS OR DIA. OF [64,26] 2.53 IS REACHED.)

OIL OUTLET

TURBINE INLET

[28,45] 1.12

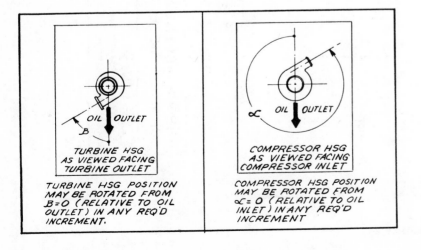

OIL OUTLET

B

TURBINE HSG AS VIEWED FACING TURBINE OUTLET

TURBINE HSG POSITION MAY BE ROTATED FROM B=0 (RELATIVE TO OIL OUTLET) IN ANY REQ'D INCREMENT.

OIL OUTLET

∝

COMPRESSOR HSG AS VIEWED FACING COMPRESSOR INLET

COMPRESSOR HSG POSITION MAY BE ROTATED FROM ∝=0 (RELATIVE TO OIL INLET) IN ANY REQ'D INCREMENT

STANDARD TURBINE
HOUSING SIZES

A/R

.68
.81
.96

AiResearch TO4 Turbocharger Outline

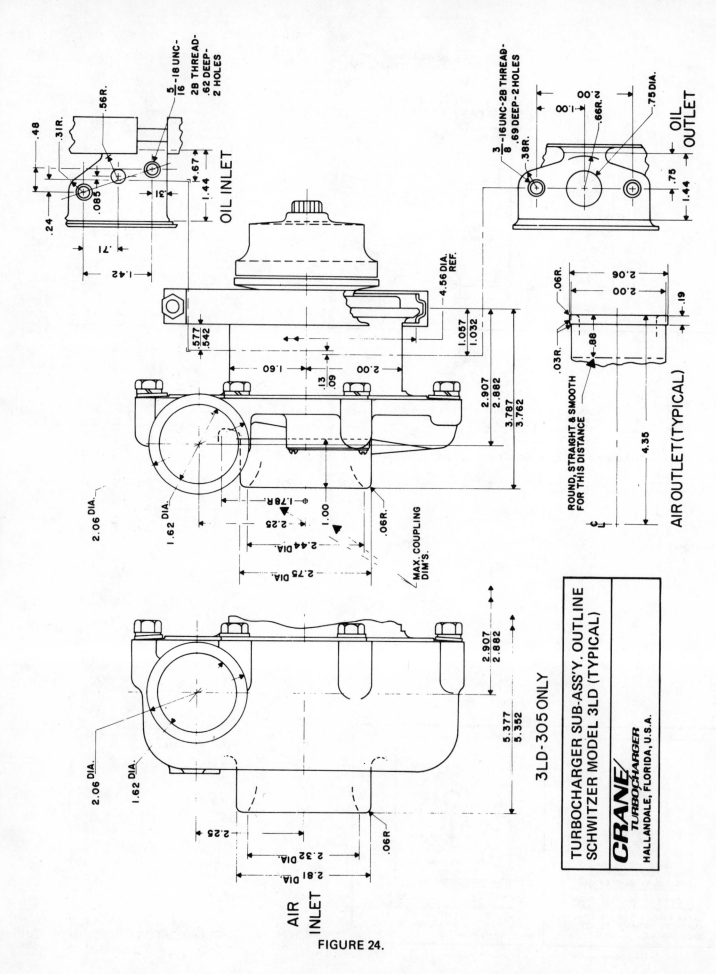

OIL INLET

OIL OUTLET

AIR OUTLET (TYPICAL)

ROUND, STRAIGHT & SMOOTH
FOR THIS DISTANCE

MAX. COUPLING
DIM'S.

3LD-305 ONLY

AIR INLET

FIGURE 24.

TURBOCHARGER SUB-ASS'Y. OUTLINE
SCHWITZER MODEL 3LD (TYPICAL)

CRANE
TURBOCHARGER
HALLANDALE, FLORIDA, U.S.A.

156

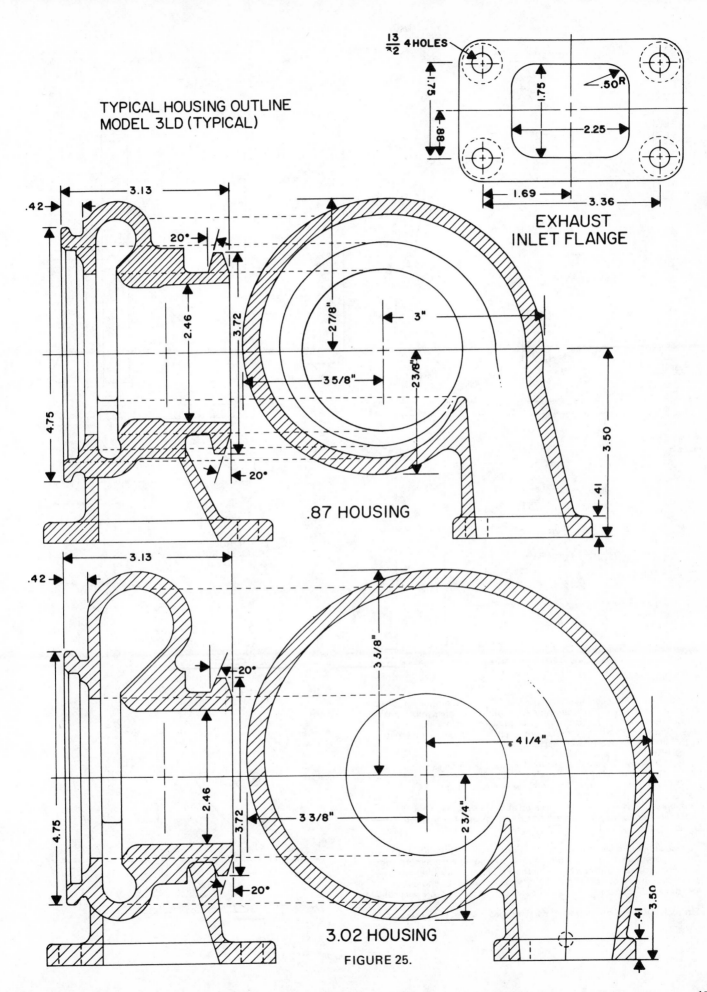

TYPICAL HOUSING OUTLINE
MODEL 3LD (TYPICAL)

EXHAUST
INLET FLANGE

.87 HOUSING

3.02 HOUSING

FIGURE 25.

157

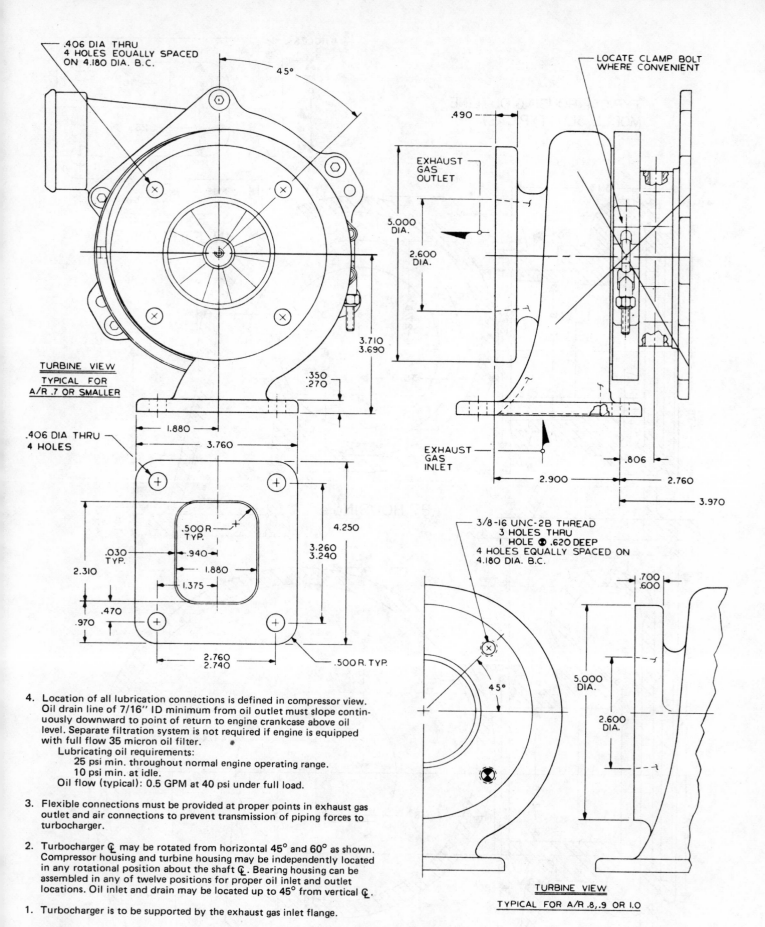

.406 DIA THRU
4 HOLES EQUALLY SPACED
ON 4.180 DIA. B.C.

45°

LOCATE CLAMP BOLT
WHERE CONVENIENT

TURBINE VIEW
TYPICAL FOR
A/R .7 OR SMALLER

.406 DIA THRU
4 HOLES

3.710
3.690

.350
.270

1.880

3.760

.500 R TYP.

.030 TYP.

.940

.500 R.
TYP.

1.880

1.375

2.310

4.250

3.260
3.240

.470

.970

2.760
2.740

.500 R. TYP.

.490

EXHAUST
GAS
OUTLET

5.000
DIA.

2.600
DIA.

EXHAUST
GAS
INLET

2.900

.806

2.760

3.970

3/8-16 UNC-2B THREAD
3 HOLES THRU
1 HOLE ⊕ .620 DEEP
4 HOLES EQUALLY SPACED ON
4.180 DIA. B.C.

45°

.700
.600

5.000
DIA.

2.600
DIA.

TURBINE VIEW
TYPICAL FOR A/R .8,.9 OR 1.0

4. Location of all lubrication connections is defined in compressor view.
Oil drain line of 7/16'' ID minimum from oil outlet must slope continuously downward to point of return to engine crankcase above oil
level. Separate filtration system is not required if engine is equipped
with full flow 35 micron oil filter.
  Lubricating oil requirements:
      25 psi min. throughout normal engine operating range.
      10 psi min. at idle.
  Oil flow (typical): 0.5 GPM at 40 psi under full load.

3. Flexible connections must be provided at proper points in exhaust gas
outlet and air connections to prevent transmission of piping forces to
turbocharger.

2. Turbocharger ₵ may be rotated from horizontal 45° and 60° as shown.
Compressor housing and turbine housing may be independently located
in any rotational position about the shaft ₵. Bearing housing can be
assembled in any of twelve positions for proper oil inlet and outlet
locations. Oil inlet and drain may be located up to 45° from vertical ₵.

1. Turbocharger is to be supported by the exhaust gas inlet flange.

158

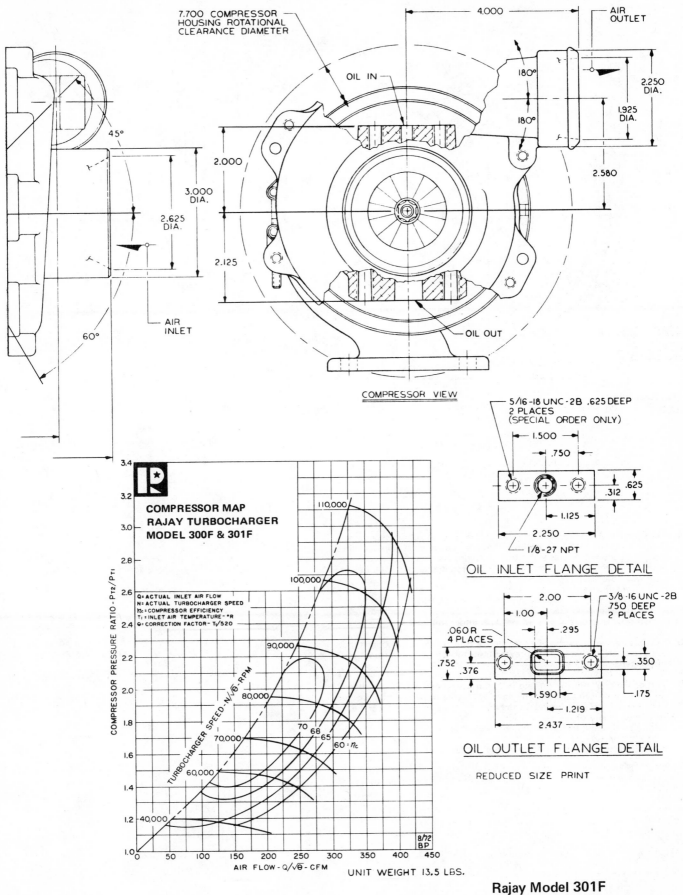

7.700 COMPRESSOR HOUSING ROTATIONAL CLEARANCE DIAMETER

4.000

AIR OUTLET

OIL IN

180°

180°

2.250 DIA.

1.925 DIA.

45°

2.000

2.580

3.000 DIA.

2.625 DIA.

2.125

AIR INLET

60°

OIL OUT

COMPRESSOR VIEW

5/16-18 UNC-2B .625 DEEP 2 PLACES (SPECIAL ORDER ONLY)

1.500

.750

.625

.312

1.125

2.250

1/8-27 NPT

OIL INLET FLANGE DETAIL

COMPRESSOR MAP RAJAY TURBOCHARGER MODEL 300F & 301F

Q= ACTUAL INLET AIR FLOW
N= ACTUAL TURBOCHARGER SPEED
η_c= COMPRESSOR EFFICIENCY
T_1= INLET AIR TEMPERATURE- °R
θ= CORRECTION FACTOR- $T_1/520$

COMPRESSOR PRESSURE RATIO - P_{T2}/P_{T1}

110,000

100,000

90,000

80,000

70,000

60,000

40,000

70
68
65
60 · η_c

TURBOCHARGER SPEED- N/√θ- RPM

AIR FLOW- Q/√θ- CFM

8/72 BP

UNIT WEIGHT 13.5 LBS.

3.4
3.2
3.0
2.8
2.6
2.4
2.2
2.0
1.8
1.6
1.4
1.2
1.0

0 50 100 150 200 250 300 350 400 450

2.00

1.00

.295

3/8-16 UNC-2B .750 DEEP 2 PLACES

.060 R 4 PLACES

.752

.376

.350

.175

.590

1.219

2.437

OIL OUTLET FLANGE DETAIL

REDUCED SIZE PRINT

**Rajay Model 301F
Turbocharger Installation Drawing**

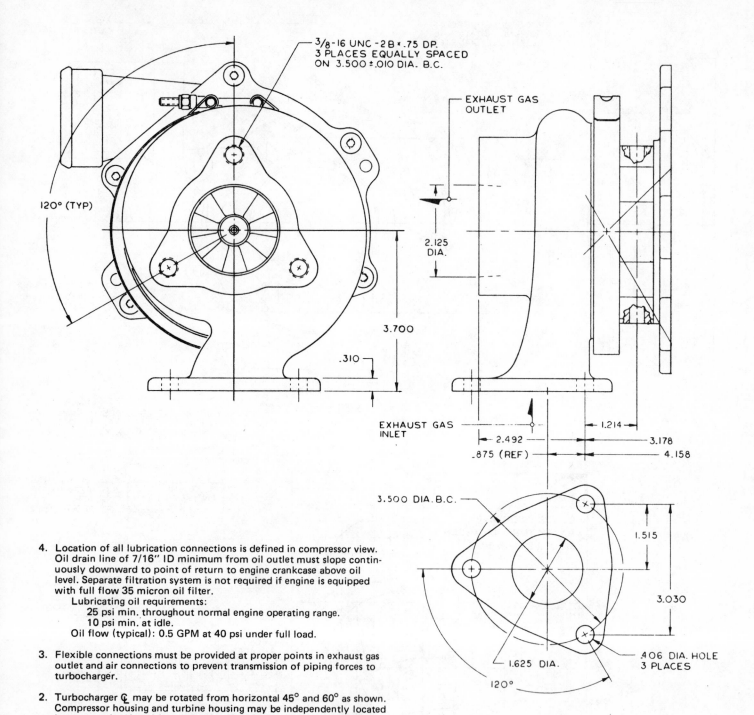

3/8-16 UNC-2B x .75 DP.
3 PLACES EQUALLY SPACED
ON 3.500 ±.010 DIA. B.C.

EXHAUST GAS
OUTLET

120° (TYP)

2.125
DIA.

3.700

.310

EXHAUST GAS
INLET

1.214

2.492

.875 (REF)

3.178

4.158

3.500 DIA. B.C.

1.515

3.030

.406 DIA. HOLE
3 PLACES

1.625 DIA.

120°

4. Location of all lubrication connections is defined in compressor view. Oil drain line of 7/16″ ID minimum from oil outlet must slope continuously downward to point of return to engine crankcase above oil level. Separate filtration system is not required if engine is equipped with full flow 35 micron oil filter.
    Lubricating oil requirements:
       25 psi min. throughout normal engine operating range.
       10 psi min. at idle.
    Oil flow (typical): 0.5 GPM at 40 psi under full load.

3. Flexible connections must be provided at proper points in exhaust gas outlet and air connections to prevent transmission of piping forces to turbocharger.

2. Turbocharger ℄ may be rotated from horizontal 45° and 60° as shown. Compressor housing and turbine housing may be independently located in any rotational position about the shaft ℄. Bearing housing can be assembled in any of twelve positions for proper oil inlet and outlet locations. Oil inlet and drain may be located up to 45° from vertical ℄.

1. Turbocharger is to be supported by the exhaust gas inlet flange.

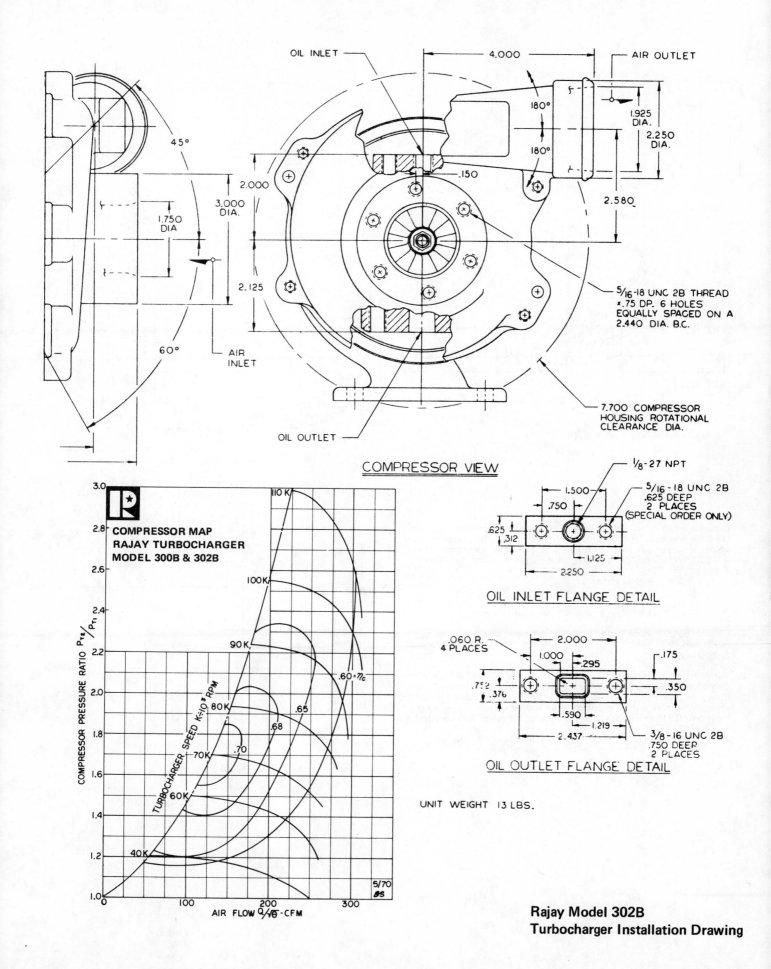

OIL INLET

AIR OUTLET

4.000

180°

180°

1.925 DIA.

2.250 DIA.

.150

2.000

3.000 DIA.

1.750 DIA

2.125

45°

60°

AIR INLET

2.580

5/16-18 UNC 2B THREAD x.75 DP. 6 HOLES EQUALLY SPACED ON A 2.440 DIA. B.C.

7.700 COMPRESSOR HOUSING ROTATIONAL CLEARANCE DIA.

OIL OUTLET

COMPRESSOR VIEW

**COMPRESSOR MAP
RAJAY TURBOCHARGER
MODEL 300B & 302B**

110 K

100K

90 K

.60 = η_c

.65

.68

.70

80K

70K

60K

40K

3.0

2.8

2.6

2.4

2.2

2.0

1.8

1.6

1.4

1.2

1.0

COMPRESSOR PRESSURE RATIO P_{T_2}/P_{T_1}

TURBOCHARGER SPEED K=10³ RPM

0   100   200   300

AIR FLOW $Q/\sqrt{\theta}$ - CFM

5/70

1/8-27 NPT

5/16-18 UNC 2B .625 DEEP 2 PLACES (SPECIAL ORDER ONLY)

1.500

.750

.625

.312

1.125

2.250

OIL INLET FLANGE DETAIL

.060 R. 4 PLACES

2.000

1.000

.295

.175

.752

.376

.350

.590

1.219

2.437

3/8-16 UNC 2B .750 DEEP 2 PLACES

OIL OUTLET FLANGE DETAIL

UNIT WEIGHT 13 LBS.

**Rajay Model 302B
Turbocharger Installation Drawing**

161

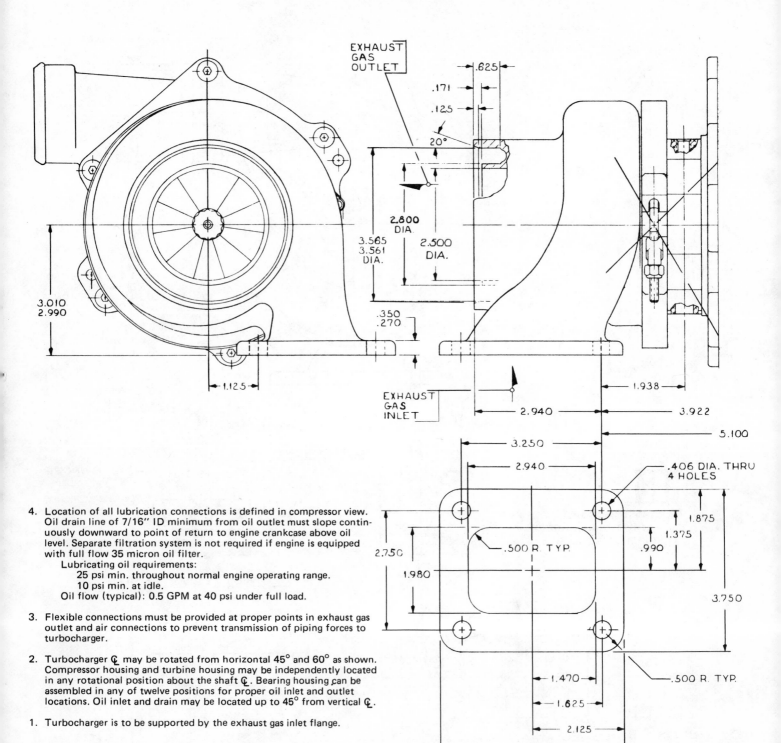

EXHAUST GAS OUTLET

EXHAUST GAS INLET

.625

.171

.125

20°

2.800 DIA.

3.565 3.561 DIA.

2.500 DIA.

.350 .270

3.010 2.990

1.125

1.938

2.940

3.922

5.100

3.250

2.940

.406 DIA. THRU 4 HOLES

1.875

1.375

.990

.500 R. TYP.

2.750

1.980

3.750

1.470

1.625

2.125

.500 R. TYP.

4.250

4. Location of all lubrication connections is defined in compressor view. Oil drain line of 7/16″ ID minimum from oil outlet must slope continuously downward to point of return to engine crankcase above oil level. Separate filtration system is not required if engine is equipped with full flow 35 micron oil filter.
    Lubricating oil requirements:
       25 psi min. throughout normal engine operating range.
       10 psi min. at idle.
    Oil flow (typical): 0.5 GPM at 40 psi under full load.

3. Flexible connections must be provided at proper points in exhaust gas outlet and air connections to prevent transmission of piping forces to turbocharger.

2. Turbocharger ℄ may be rotated from horizontal 45° and 60° as shown. Compressor housing and turbine housing may be independently located in any rotational position about the shaft ℄. Bearing housing can be assembled in any of twelve positions for proper oil inlet and outlet locations. Oil inlet and drain may be located up to 45° from vertical ℄.

1. Turbocharger is to be supported by the exhaust gas inlet flange.

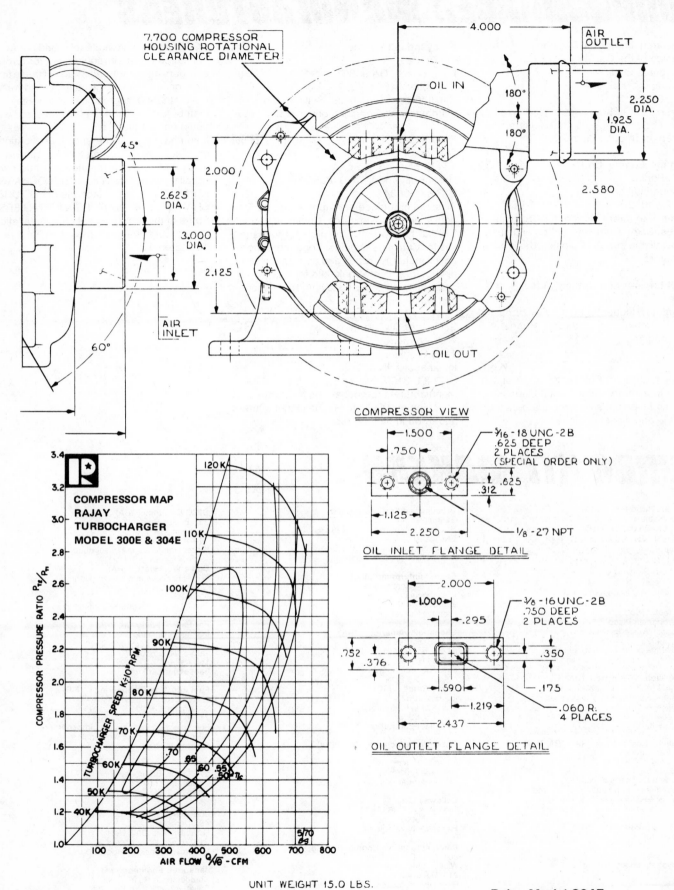

7.700 COMPRESSOR
HOUSING ROTATIONAL
CLEARANCE DIAMETER

4.000

AIR
OUTLET

OIL IN

180°

180°

2.250
DIA.

1.925
DIA.

2.580

4.5°

2.000

2.625
DIA.

3.000
DIA.

2.125

AIR
INLET

60°

OIL OUT

COMPRESSOR VIEW

1.500

.750

5/16 - 18 UNC - 2B
.625 DEEP
2 PLACES
(SPECIAL ORDER ONLY)

.625

.312

1.125

2.250

1/8 - 27 NPT

OIL INLET FLANGE DETAIL

2.000

1.000

.295

3/8 - 16 UNC - 2B
.750 DEEP
2 PLACES

.752

.376

.350

.590

.175

1.219

.060 R.
4 PLACES

2.437

OIL OUTLET FLANGE DETAIL

**COMPRESSOR MAP
RAJAY
TURBOCHARGER
MODEL 300E & 304E**

3.4
3.2
3.0
2.8
2.6
2.4
2.2
2.0
1.8
1.6
1.4
1.2
1.0

COMPRESSOR PRESSURE RATIO P_{T_2}/P_{T_1}

TURBOCHARGER SPEED K÷10³ RPM

120K
110K
100K
90K
80K
70K
60K
50K
40K

.70
.65
.60
.55
.50 ηk

5/70
BG

100 200 300 400 500 600 700 800

AIR FLOW $^0/\sqrt{\theta}$ - CFM

UNIT WEIGHT 15.0 LBS.

**Rajay Model 304E
Turbocharger Installation Drawing**

TURBOCHARGER MANUFACTURERS

AiResearch Industrial Division   **AiR**
A Division of the Garrett Corp.
3201 Lomita Blvd.
Torrance, CA 90505
213/530-1981
Many sizes of turbochargers used on all types of equipment. Sells to engine manufacturers or through distributors.

Cummins Engine Co.   **CU**
500 S. Poplar
Seymour, Indiana 47274
812/522-4052
Medium-size turbochargers for Cummins Engines (USA). Complete turbos and spare parts available through Cummins dealers and distributors.

Holset Engineering Comany, Ltd.   **HO**
PO Box A9
Turnbridge, Huddersfield HD1 GRD, England
Small and medium-size turbochargers for diesel engines.

KKK   **KKK**
Aktiengesellschaft Kühnle, Kopp & Kausch
D6710 Frankenthal/Pfalz, West Germany
Small and medium-size turbochargers for gasoline and diesel engines.

Rajay Industries, Inc.   **RA**
PO Box 207
Long Beach, CA 90801
213/426-0346
Small turbos for all uses. Sells through distributors and engine converters.

Roto-Master, Inc.   **R-M**
Division of Echlin
13402 Wyandotte St.
North Hollywood, CA 91605
213/875-0634
All sizes of replacement turbochargers equivalent to AiResearch, Cummins, Holset, KKK and Schwitzer. Complete turbocharger kits for Cummins engines. Conducts schools on turbocharger repair and application for its distributors. TurboSonic kits for passenger cars and trucks, plus installation accessories and wastegates.

Schwitzer-Division   **SC**
Wallace-Murray Corp.
1125 Brookside Ave.
Indianapolis, IN 46206
317/269-3100
Manufacturers turbochargers for many types of equipment. Sells to engine manufacturers and through distributors.

NOTE: If you have a diesel or industrial appliation or repair requirement for turbochargers manufactured by any of these firms, write or call them for the name and address of the distributor nearest you. Hundreds of distributors serve these few firms and we could not list them all.
If you have a gasoline-engine application or a requirement for custom automotive, truck, motorcycle or marine application, write or call the firms listed under TURBOCHARGER KIT MAKERS, or contact one of the TURBOCHARGER DISTRIBUTORS & INSTALLERS. Some of the firms may not offer installations, even though we have chosen to list them in this category.

TURBO KIT MAKERS

American Turbo-Pak   (RA)
2141 S. Hathaway
Santa Ana, CA 92705
Motorcycle kits

Arkay, Inc.   (RA)
14005-C S. Crenshaw Blvd.
Hawthorne, CA 90250
213/675-9161
Honda Accord & Triumph TR-7 kits

Aviaid Metal Products
7570 Woodman Place
Van Nuys, CA 91405
213/786-4025
Oil scavenge pumps for turbocharged engines, oil pans, dry-sump oiling systems.

BAE Division of Turdyne   (RA)
3032 Kashiwa
Torrance, CA 90505
213/530-4743
Passenger-car, truck and motor home turbo kits. Rajay turbos. Catalog $1.00

Gale Banks Engineering   (AiR, RA, R-M)
929 S. San Gabriel Blvd.
San Gabriel, CA 91776
213/285-3107
Complete turbocharged marine engines, auto and marine turbo kits, oil pans, intercoolers. AiResearch, Rajay & Roto-Master turbos. Catalog $2.00

Blake Enterprises, Inc.   (RA)
Rt. 1, Box 403
Muskogee, OK 74401
918/683-2967
Motorcycle turbo kits, wastegates

Broadspeed Engineering Ltd.
Banbury Road
Southam, Warwickshire CV33 OBJ
ENGLAND
Tel. Southam (092-681)3191
Automotive kits & installations

Castell Enterprises, Inc.
4943-L McConnell Ave.
Los Angeles CA 90066
213/822-7130
Prototype development, Porsche kits

Checkpoint America   (RA)
2555 S. Hanley
St. Louis, MO 63144
314/644-2440
Passenger-car kits

Crane Cams   (SC)
PO Box 160
Hallandale, FL 33009
305/457-8888
Schwitzer 3LD turbos

Crown Manufacturing Co.   (RA)
858 Production Place
Newport Beach, CA 92660
714/642-7391
Passenger-car kits. Catalog $1.00

Callaway Cars
Old Lyme, CT 06371
203/434-9002
Prototype development

Daigh Automotive Engineering Co.
201 West D Street
Wilmington, CA 90744
213/549-0840
Prototype installations, kit development

DICO Co., Inc.   (RA)
323 E. Ball Rd.
Anaheim, CA 92805
714/956-2950
Kit for Honda engine in sandbuggy

Don's Werkstatt   (RA)
860 N.E. Cleveland
Gresham, OR 97030
503/665-5252
Fiat X1/9 & Chevette Kits; installations

Far East Trading Co. Ltd.
Makajima Building
Motoazbu 1-Chome Minato-Ku
Tokyo, Japan 106
Tel. 452-0705
Passenger-car kits

Fuel Injection Engineering   (AiR)
25891 Crown Valley Parkway
S. Laguna, CA 92677
714/831-1170
Fuel-injection systems for turbochargers, AiResearch turbos & wastegates
Catalog $2.00

IPD
2762 N. E. Broadway
Portland, OR 97232
Volvo 122 kit. Catalog $2

Joe Haile Engineering   (RA)
4824 Arcola
N. Hollywood, CA 91601
213/763-4514
Motorcycle kits. Catalog $1.00

Janspeed Engineering Ltd.
Southampton Road
Salisbury, Wiltshire SP1 2LN
ENGLAND
Tel. (0722)6955
Automotive kits & installations

Kenne-Bell
212 San Lorenzo
Pomona, CA 91766
714/620-1088
Buick turbo kit for Skyhawk. Catalog $2.00

Kinetics Pty. Ltd.
375 Pacific Hiway (Rear)
Crows Nest, NSW 2065
AUSTRALIA
Tel. (02) 92-8332
Holden 6, Holden 308, Ford
2000cc, Datsun 4 & 6-cyl, VW single- & dual-port conversion kits

Larson Engineering   (AiR)
26121 Van Born Rd.
Taylor, MI 48180
313/292-6643
Custom installations, kits for Corvettes and small-block Chevrolets.

M & W Gear Co.   (RA)
Gibson City, IL 60936
217/784-4261
Gasoline & diesel marine engine kits. Diesel farm tractor kits. Rajay turbos. Write for name of nearest distributor.

Magnum Manufacturing   (RA)
1320 E. St. Andrews Pl. Unit G
Santa Ana, CA 92705
714/540-6888
Motorcycle kits

Mathwall Engineering
Red Lion Garage
Portsmouth Road
Thursley, Surrey GU8 6NJ
ENGLAND
Tel. Elstead (025-122)3191
Automotive kits & installations

Ak Miller Garage   (AiR)
9236 Bermudez St.
Pico Rivera, CA 90660
213/949-2548
AiResearch turbos & wastegates.
Passenger-car, truck and racing kits and installations. Catalog $2.00

Miller & Norburn, Inc.   (RA)
2002 E. Peabody St.
Durham, NC 27703
919/596-9309
BMW turbo kits. Catalog $1.00

Performance First Marine   (RA)
1424 E. St. Gertrude
Santa Ana, CA 92705
714/751-3720
Passenger-car, racing and marine installations. Catalog $1.00

Performance Systems Inc.   (RA)
PO Box 5226
Everett, WA 98206
206/329-2703
Passenger-car kits for Porsche 924, VW Rabbit & Scirocco, Alfa-Romeo and Opel

RV Turbo   (RA)
1656 D Townhurst
Houston, TX 77043
Turbo kits for recreational vehicles and motor homes. Rajay turbo distributor.

Race-Aero   (RA)
3670 Sky Park Dr.
Torrance, CA 90505
213/378-1400
454 Chevrolet marine kit

Doug Roe Engineering
PO Box 26848
Phoenix, AZ 85282
602/969-9958
Prototype development

Roto-Master, Inc.   (R-M)
13402 Wyandotte St.
N. Hollywood, CA 91605
213/875-0634
Turbochargers, kits, wastegates and installation accessories. Catalog $1.00

ROK Stock   (AiR)
9035 S.W. Burnham Rd.
Tigard, OR 97223
Capri turbo kits. Catalog $3.00

Tom Scahill, Inc.
767 Lincoln Ave., No. 10
San Rafael, CA 94901
415/457-9389
Marine engine kits, installations and intercoolers.

**Martin Schneider
Designed Systems**
9063 W. Washington Blvd.
Culver City, CA 90230
213/559-0020
Porsche 914, 924; Datsun 280Z; Honda Civic; Kawasaki, Honda and Suzuki.
Motorcycle kits. Catalog $1

**Shelby-Spearco Distributing Co., Inc.   (RA)
Spearco Performance Products, Inc.**
10936 S. La Cienega Blvd.
Inglewood, CA 90304
213/649-4860
Master automotive distributor for Rajay turbochargers. Auto and truck turbo kits and accessories. Write for name of nearest installation center. Catalog $1.00

Turbocharger, Inc.   (RA)
12215 S. Woodruff
Downey, CA 90241
213/773-1880
Mercedes, Peugeot, Perkins & Cummins diesel kits

Turbo Systems, Inc.   (RA)
1817 N. Medina Line Rd.
Akron, OH 44313
216/666-3503
Passenger-car kits & installations

Weber Turbocharger Co.   (RA)
2228 S. Big Bend Blvd.
St. Louis, MO 63117
314/644-5800
Toyota Celica kit

Z-Car Care   (RA)
11144 Ables Lane
Dallas, TX 75229
Datsun kits

TURBO DISTRIBUTORS & INSTALLERS

ALABAMA

Alabama Diesel Co.   (R-M)
3328 6th Avenue So.
Birmingham, AL 35222
205/324-4406

ARIZONA

R & N Investments   (R-M)
PO Box 1090
Flagstaff, AZ 86001
602/774-2737

Chuck's Speed Center   (RA)
545 W. Mariposa
Phoenix, AZ 85013
602/266-5101
Shelby-Spearco distributor

Scottsdale Automotive Specialists
3428 N. Scottsdale Rd.
Scottsdale, AZ 85251
602/945-1177
Custom auto & marine installations

CALIFORNIA

Corsa Enterprises
14444 Lanark
Van Nuys, CA 91406
213/994-3010
Corvair turbo installations

S/C Performance Warehouse   (RA)
11034 S. La Cienega
Inglewood, CA 90304
213/776-2800
Shelby-Spearco distributor

Turbo Power   (RA)
Box 2585
Oakland, CA 94614
415/562-8397
Passenger-car kits and installations

Wilcap Co.
2930 Sepulveda
Torrance, CA 90510
213/326-9200
Installs turbocharged diesel engines in passenger cars and light trucks

COLORADO

F & M Auto Parts   (R-M)
1729 Federal Blvd.
Denver, CO 80204
303/433-8904

Kenz & Leslie Distributing Co.   (RA)
1965 West 13th Ave.
Denver, CO 80204
303/623-1178
Shelby-Spearco distributor

Sptizer Electrical Co.   (R-M)
43 West 9th Avenue
Denver, CO 80201
303/222-0581

FLORIDA

Interstate Dieselect, Inc. (R-M)
4220 No. Orange Blossom Trail
Orlando, FL 32804
305/293-7971

Stuart Diesel   (R-M)
6515 Alamo Drive
Tampa, FL 33619
813/626-7105

Turbo Tech   (R-M)
870 West 20th St.
Hialeah, FL 33010
305/885-2277

GEORGIA

Turbo Toms
4090 Peachtree Rd. NE
Atlanta, GA 30319
404/261-0373
Custom automotive installations

ILLINOIS

Bellwether Automotive, Inc.   (R-M)
1631 Landmark Rd.
Aurora, IL 60506
312/896-3041

National Auto Supply Co.   (R-M)
1100 Martin Luther King Dr.
East St. Louis, IL 62201
618/271-1285

INDIANA

Bellwether Automotive, Inc.   (R-M)
4520 Secretary Dr.
Ft. Wayne, IN 46808
291/483-8765

Kolb Diesel Service
703A S. Barker Ave.
Evansville, IN
812/464-9141
Tractor-pulling turbo installations

Van Senus Auto Parts   (R-M)
5920 Kennedy Avenue
Hammond, IN 46323
219/844-2902

IOWA

Central States Speed (R-M)
106 East 11th St.
Waterloo, IA 50703
319/233-0711

National Custom Warehouse (R-M)
PO Box 108
Creston, IA 50801
515/782-8485

Reliable Auto Warehouse (R-M)
805 Dace Street
Sioux City, IA 51101
712/252-4633

MARYLAND

Coleman Brothers Speed (R-M)
7443 Washington Blvd.
Baltimore, MD 21227
301/799-1750

G & M High Performance (R-M)
4643 Baltimore Avenue
Hyattsville, MD 21227
301/927-6900

MICHIGAN

Detroit High Performance Whse. (R-M)
31435 Stephenson Hwy.
Madison Heights, MI 48071
313/585-5291

MINNESOTA

Reliable Auto Parts (R-M)
2600 North Cleveland
Roseville, MN 55113
612/636-6200

MISSOURI

Bellwether Automotive, Inc. (R-M)
2269 Grisson Dr.
St. Louis, MO 63141
314/432-2189

NEVADA

Nevada Performance Whsl. Inc. (R-M)
964 Terminal Way
Reno, NV 89502
702/323-1320

Sierra Diesel Injection, Inc. (RA,R-M)
2525 Mill Street
Reno, NV 89502
702/329-4232
Roto-Master & Shelby-Spearco distributor

Turbochargers of Las Vegas (RA)
3580 Polaris Ave.
Las Vegas, NV 89102
702/873-6905
Shelby-Spearco distributor

NEW MEXICO

Miller's Performance Whse. (RA,R-M)
714 South Main St.
Roswell, NM 88201
505/622-7700
Roto-Master & Shelby-Spearco distributor

Tractor Parts & Supplies (R-M)
4000 Osuna Road N.E.
Albuquerque, NM 87125
505/345-8411

NEW YORK

American Speed Equipment Sply. (RA,R-M)
300 Bethpage-Spagnolia Rd.
Melville, L.I., NY 11746
516/420-9595
Roto-Master & Shelby-Spearco distributor

Serra
279 Adams
Bedford Hills, NY 10507
Alfa, BMW, Fiat & Lancia kits.
Catalog $2

OHIO

Paramount Supply Co. (R-M)
13688 York Road
Cleveland, OH 44133
216/237-9164

Paramount Supply Co. (R-M)
1270 Edgehill Road
Columbus, OH 43212
614/294-5631

Paramount Supply Co. (R-M)
3535 Roundbottom Road
Cincinnati, OH 45244
513/271-6810

OKLAHOMA

Thompson's Diesel Fuel Injection (R-M)
2728 N.W. 10th St.
Oklahoma City, OK 73107
405/943-8536

Thompson's Diesel Fuel Injection (R-M)
10388 B East 55th Place
Tulsa, OK 74145
918/663-7666

OREGON

Distributors Warehouse (R-M)
820 S.E. Alder
Portland, OR 97214
503/234-5084

PENNSYLVANIA

TURBOKAR
701 N. Keyser Ave.
Scranton, PA 18508
717/344-7258
48 different turbo kits from various kit makers.
Catalog $1

K & G Speed Associates (R-M)
2136 Darby Road
Havertown, PA 19083
215/789-4421

WSE Warehouse (R-M)
1650 Main Street
Sharpsburg, PA 15215
412/782-4080

TENNESSEE

Diesel Sales & Service (R-M)
928 Main Street
Nashville, TN 37206
615/227-2242

Diesel Sales & Service (R-M)
103 Jubilee Dr.
Chattanooga, TN 37421
615/894-4050

Diesel Sales & Service (R-M)
2236 McCalla Ave.
Knoxville, TN 37915
615/546-7751

Diesel Sales & Service (R-M)
423 West Main St.
Johnson City, TN 37601
615/923-1661

TEXAS

Machinery & Parts (R-M)
1357 N. Walton Walker
Dallas, TX 75211
214/333-6541

Magneto & Diesel Injector Ser. (R-M)
6931 Navigation Blvd.
Houston, TX 77011
713/928-5686

S & S Distributing Co. (RA)
400 E. Vickery
Ft. Worth, TX 76101
817/336-0575
Shelby-Spearco distributor

Sigman-Pittman Distributors (R-M)
9200 Ambassador Row
Dallas, TX 75247
214/630-9200

Tractor Parts & Supplies (R-M)
155 North San Marcial
El Paso, TX 79905
915/544-1576

UTAH

R.M. Distributing Co. (R-M)
2755 So. 300 West, Suite D
Salt Lake City, UT 84115
801/486-3443

VIRGINIA

G & M High Performance (R-M)
5595 Raby Road
Norfolk, VA 23501
804/461-4444

WASHINGTON

Distributors Warehouse (R-M)
1408 12th Avenue
Seattle, WA 98122
206/323-2650

WISCONSIN

Bellwether Automotive, (R-M)
12855-E W. Silver Spring
Butler, WI 53007
414/783-6300

CANADA

ALBERTA

Brake-Drome Co. Ltd. (R-M)
PO Box 1330 Postal Sta. T
Calgary, T2H 2H6
403/253-7501

Pacemaker Automotive (R-M)
8629 126th Avenue
Edmonton
403/474-6446

BRITISH COLUMBIA

Brake-Drome Co. Ltd. (R-M)
4455 Alaska St.
Burnaby V5C 5T3
604/299-6536

Dix Distributors (R-M)
468 Kingsway
Vancouver
604/879-7748

ONTARIO

Canadian Performance Dist. (R-M)
1141 King Road
Burlington
416/634-7741

QUEBEC

Speed'N Sport Center, Inc. (R-M)
3215 Chemin St. Foy
Quebec 10
418/658-3326

AUSTRALIA

Diablo Motors, Pty. Ltd.
212 Haldon St.
Lakemba 2195 N.S.W.
(02) 759-1328
Stocks Gale Banks, Turbonics and Race-Aero marine kits, carries Roto-Master and Shelby-Spearco.

Turbo Motors
212 Haldon St.
Lakemba 2195 N.S.W.
(02) 795-8870
Custom and competition turbocharger installations and repairs.

INDEX

8.9.4445711732